W9-BNO-822

DISCARD

JEFF   COUNTY LIBRARY
         r Avenue
         VA 98339
(36   library.info

DISCARD

JEFFERSON COUNTY LIBRARY
AVENUE
WA 98533

This Is

Running

for Your Life

This Is

Running

for Your Life

Essays

Michelle Orange

Farrar, Straus and Giroux / New York

Farrar, Straus and Giroux
18 West 18th Street, New York 10011

Copyright © 2013 by Michelle Orange
All rights reserved
Printed in the United States of America
First edition, 2013

Some of these essays were originally published, in substantially different form, in the following publications: TheRumpus.net ("The Uses of Nostalgia and Some Thoughts on Ethan Hawke's Face" and "Do I Know You? And Other Impossible Questions"); Rumpus Women ("Have a Beautiful Corpse"); and The Virginia Quarterly Review ("Beirut Rising").

Grateful acknowledgment is made for permission to reprint lyrics from "Gee, Officer Krupke" by Leonard Bernstein and Stephen Sondheim, copyright © 1956, 1957, 1958, 1959 by Amberson Holdings LLC and Stephen Sondheim. Copyright renewed. Leonard Bernstein Music Publishing Company LLC, publisher. Boosey & Hawkes, agent for rental. International copyright secured. Reprinted by permission.

Library of Congress Cataloging-in-Publication Data
Orange, Michelle.
    This is running for your life : essays / Michelle Orange — 1st ed.
        p.   cm.
    ISBN 978-0-374-53332-8 (pbk. : alk. paper)
    1. Title.

PS3615.R28 T47 2013
814'.6—dc23

                                                          2012026978

Designed by Abby Kagan

www.fsgbooks.com
www.twitter.com/fsgbooks • www.facebook.com/fsgbooks

10 9 8 7 6 5 4 3 2 1

The names and identifying characteristics of some individuals in this book have been changed, and some dialogue is reconstructed according to the author's memories.

For my parents, and their parents

Contents

This Is

Running

for Your Life

The Uses of Nostalgia
and Some Thoughts on
Ethan Hawke's Face

Let's call it the theory of receptivity. It's the idea, often cited by young people in their case against the relevance of even marginally older people, that one's taste—in music or film, literature or fine cuisine—petrifies during life's peak of happiness or nadir of misery. Or maybe it's not that simple. Maybe a subtler spike on the charts—upward, downward, anomalous points in between—might qualify, so long as it's formative. Let's say that receptivity, anyway, can be tied to the moments when, for whatever reason, a person opens herself to the things we can all agree make life worth living in a new and definitive way, whether curiosity has her chasing down the world's pleasures, or the world has torn a strip from her, exposing raw surface area to the winds.

During these moments—sleepaway camp right before your bar mitzvah; the year you were captain of the hockey team *and* the baseball team; the time after you got your license and before you totaled the Volvo—you are closely attuned to your culture, reaching out and in to consume it in vast quantities. When this period ends, your senses seal off what they have absorbed and build a sensibility that becomes, for better or worse, definitive: This is the stuff I like. These films/books/

artists tell the story of who I am. There is no better-suited hairstyle. This is as good/bad as it gets for me.

The theory suggests that we only get a couple of these moments in life, a couple of sound tracks, and that timing is paramount. If you came of age in the early eighties, for instance, you may hold a relatively shitty cultural moment to be the last time anything was any good simply because that was the last time you were open and engaged with what was happening around you, the last time you felt anything really—appallingly—deeply.

I worry about this theory. I worry because it suggests that receptivity is tied closely to youth, and firsts, and also because as with many otherwise highly rejectable theories—Reaganomics and communism come to mind—there is that insolent nub of truth in it.

My worry started a couple of years ago, when I felt myself separating, effortlessly and against my better judgment, from what I had unwittingly been a part of for two decades: the Next Generation. It was when I noticed myself taking a step back from the yellow line when the R train blew into the station, rather than a step forward, the way I used to, the way the kids flanking me still did. It was when I began giving more than a passing thought to the age of the people around me—then much more, to the point where I find myself calibrating the age of new acquaintances as a matter of course, ranking a given group in a way that is new and troubling to me, not by interesting eye color or willingness to engage intelligently or suspected willingness to engage carnally or crack comic timing (not actually true; I will always rank by crack comic timing) and not even specifically by age but by age *in relation to me*.

For me it was the subway thing. For others it's a first gray hair, death in the family, weeklong hangover, or the moment an indie sensation's breakthrough single comes to sound like a family of flying squirrels recorded it in a cutlery drawer. I've never done it before so I can't say for sure, but it feels like a peculiar time to greet the first intimations of mortality. Marketing demographics have put us all on a strict schedule, one that ties a person's relevance to the years when he's considered most receptive. It may be that Nielsen-style demos are the clearest terms we've come up with to gauge social standing between the onset of legal adulthood and retirement age. Taste and other less participatory cultural alignments have come to situate individuals in specific eras, dividing generations by band preference or favorite cereal or national disaster, and creating a powerfully unified sense of time's passage that is otherwise pretty hard to come by. We're especially primed, in passing out of that long stretch of peak market desirability, to reexamine our relationship to the culture, which means to examine our relationship with time. But modernity's strange intermeshing of futurism and nostalgia has made time an elusive, sometimes contradictory source of information.

Looking to your peers for a sense of temporal equilibrium can be equally confounding. It seems to me that, between about age twenty-eight and maybe age forty-three, there now exists a gray area, where anyone within that range could be any age within that range. Rather than relaxing into the shared parameters of a condition traditionally known as adulthood, it is this cohort that gets the most freaky and pedantic about how old they are and how old the people within that same cohort might be. Age panic has an earlier onset but more superficial proportions; it's more often tied up in the byways of vanity or status insecurity than given to the headlong realization that we're all going to die die die.

Nothing makes the paradox of the way we now experience time more plain than clock-watching the end of youth. It would appear the clock has come to rule every aspect of who we are and what we do, from daily, micromanaged routines to five-year plans to deciding to marry while you'll still look good in the pictures. And yet we are utterly careless with time, from passing ungodly stretches of it in a state of many-screened distraction to missing that part where you come into a sense of yourself as an adult reconciled with your own mortality and that of the people you love. Entering the prime of adulthood lends a new and dizzying urgency to the polarity of that relationship. Something important is supposed to be happening, but no one can quite say what, or when—only that it had better happen soon, ideally before it happens to that other guy. Unless it's bad, in which case reverse that last part. Until whatever it is that's supposed to happen happens, all we have in the way of orientation to a mean are numbers, and so we look to them.

The generation that felt some pride of ownership over the tech revolution is currently passing through this shadow demographic, eyeballing each other grimly as the teenage natives snicker over our digital accents. By thirty we had gone through four different music formats, which necessitated four different buying cycles, which brought about four different opportunities to revisit the question of where we stand on Alice in Chains. It all feels a little rushed, doesn't it—the crucible of confronting one's own taste and the terms on which it was formed? Somehow the decision to purchase *Siamese*

Dream on iTunes—the old CD too scuffed for a laptop's delicate system—seems fraught with the weight of a larger commitment, like renewing marriage vows, or making some more furtive, less romantic acceptance of the inexorability of the bond. Did I even choose Billy Corgan, or did he choose me?

For all the dorked-out debates about sound quality and texture and ear feel, the music is exactly the same; only time can clarify your relationship to it. But when that happens, we're meant to feel sheepish about aligning ourselves with the past, as though, despite the fairly obvious contiguousness of our bodies and minds and excellent memories for Beastie Boys lyrics, there's no viable, meaningful way to tie it with the present. And, more curiously, despite the pathological pseudo-nostalgic recycling that defines modern popular culture. But then maybe the theory of receptivity has pivoted its allegiances toward a technological sensibility, where content is content and it matters less whether you listen to Dead or Alive or deadmau5 than *how* you listen to the latter's inevitable remix of the former.

In which case the question of taste and cultural alignment recedes, and examining our relationship with time means examining our relationship with technology—which has come to feel cultish, if not cultural—and vice versa. From a certain angle the entire digital shebang has consisted of dreaming up more and more sophisticated ways to contain and control time. Our devices offered themselves as second or even substitute homes, a place where time was both pliable and strictly monitored. We unfastened our watches, which suffered from always and only moving forward, and adopted new and advanced timekeepers that did whatever we wanted with time: tell it, track it, transcend it, save it, spend it, defy it, kill it, record it, recall it, replay it, reorder it, relive it. Very often they do all of those things at once, in the name of simply staying on top of it.

Keeping impossibly current has become the key selling point of smartphone connectivity. In recent ads for one network provider two men are delivered a seemingly fresh piece of news by a third party as they gaze into their devices. "That's so [comically small amount of] seconds ago," the pair smirk each time, to the third party's great humiliation. To really get the jump on time requires dedication, and if that dedication looks like total enslavement to the uninitiated, let them enjoy the view from the pastures.

Moving at a pace that is not just fast—we've *been* fast—but erratic and discontinuous makes defining a self against some shared sense of time untenable. And yet we persist in seeking a binding cultural memory, a common frame of reference—perhaps out of habit, perhaps because it still feels like the best hope for a stable, unified identity. But modern cultural memory is afflicted by a kind of dementia, its fragments ever floating around us—clearly ordered one moment, hopelessly scrambled the next. It's easy to feel as though upholding a meaningful continuum between the present and the past might require leaving the culture you mean to restore.

One result of this would seem to be our habit of leaning on fractional age distinctions and investing meaning in invented microgenerations, if only to get clear of the chaos.

People manifest this kind of thing differently. "Your friend mentioned her age *a lot*," a friend of mine said after a dinner party recently. "It was weird." He had just turned thirty-one and hated admitting it. My other friend had just turned thirty-four and couldn't stop talking about it. "Maybe she's trying to remind herself," I said. The numbers only sound more unlikely as they mount. At a different party a few weeks later, I was sent on an El Caminian emotional journey when someone I barely knew asked me, in front of a roomful of people I didn't know at all, how old I was. Whereas it would have been an ordinarily rude and possibly condescending line of inquiry even, say, five years ago, something about the question and the context had a political, almost passive-aggressive tang. Just what was it he wanted to know, or to tell me? He was thirty-four—older than I was, but only a little, as was everyone else in the room. I know this because most of them were television actresses whose heads swiveled in my direction as the question was being asked, not unkindly but with big, expectant eyes. I want to say—and suspect it could be true—that an actual hush fell upon us.

The dude was history. It was the actresses I looked up the next day. But then I find myself on IMDb fairly regularly lately. I am suddenly in possession of the ages of a number of actors and actresses whom I have been watching for years, in some cases decades. We've been the same age the whole time, as it turns out, it just never occurred to me to check, or to care, until now. Movie stars existed in a distant, ageless realm; even those cast to represent a specific stage of life weren't confined by time in quite the same way. I remember watching *E.T.* and finding Drew Barrymore's charming little-girl-ness exotic, as though she were showing me something I wouldn't otherwise know. But we were almost the same age. I know that now.

One of the great, time-released pleasures of moviegoing is watching the actors of your generation grow older. Maybe *pleasures* isn't precisely the right word—but maybe it is. With time comes the impulse to seek out evidence of accrued wisdom, pain, or contentment—the mark of experience—in their faces. This one had a baby; that one just lost her dad. Along with the R-train moment, for me it was watching Ethan Hawke in *Before Sunset* that left no doubt: this thing was really happening. Life had begun to show itself as more than a series of days, or movies, all in a row, which I might or might not attend.

In *Sunset*, set and shot nine years after *Before Sunrise*'s slacker riff on one enchanted, European evening, the characters played by Hawke and Julie Delpy reunite for a late-afternoon walk through Paris, delicately stepping around the last decade's worth of disappointment and longing. Perhaps the one striking formal difference between the two films is that *Sunset* takes place in real time, where *Sunrise* uses elliptical fades to tell the story of an entire night spent wandering around Vienna. Time had become more present, and the present moment more urgent.

Loping through the Latin Quarter in 2003, Hawke appears gaunt and slightly stooped and basically body-slammed by time. But it was his face—with its rough skin, scored forehead and sunken cheeks, and, especially, the deep, exclamatory furrow wedged between his eyes—that transfixed me. Some said he'd come through a divorce, and it had taken its toll; that's what life does to people. I'd heard about such things but never seen it rendered so plainly, and on the face of someone only a few years older. It was shocking, even a little horrifying. And yet so marvelous to see, so unexpectedly righteous and true. *Testify, Ethan Hawke's Face*, I thought. *Tell it for real.*

If they last long enough and have earned a large enough

share of our hearts, movie stars are often cued to acknowledge time's work on-screen. Traditionally, either a mirror or a younger character reflects the bad news, and we pause to consider it with them. At sixty-one, Katharine Hepburn gave herself a rueful once-over in *The Lion in Winter*. Forty-eight-year-old Marlon Brando was taunted by his teenage lover in *Last Tango in Paris*, "You must have been very handsome, years ago." In *Towering Inferno*, Fred Astaire (then seventy-five) gets the former treatment and Paul Newman (then forty-nine) the latter.

Pauline Kael was galled by this kind of thing. "It's self-exploitation and it's horrible," she wrote about Hepburn's pantomimed requiem for her beauty. But then Kael didn't foresee the coming rarity of actors aging normally on-screen; nor, of course, the futility of an actress fudging her age on IMDb. Neither character acknowledges Hawke's transformation in *Before Sunset*, probably because flashbacks to the previous film, and his previous, almost unrecognizably vernal self, make the point more poignantly than a more direct reference could.

I must admit, I was never much of a fan. I remember finding Hawke too on the nose, somehow, too much the thing he was supposed to be—always an actor first instead of a living, changing, insinuating being, someone who demanded watching. Of the many things I failed to imagine back then, watching *Before Sunrise*, I could not have conceived of a future in which a reprise of his role would feel like an act of generosity. I could not have fathomed feeling so *grateful* to Ethan Hawke for lending his face to a handmade, jewel-cut meditation on what life does to people—a slow-cooked sequel to a film about those too young and smitten to be concerned

11

about what life might do to them. And what was life doing to me? I worry.

I worry, specifically, about 1999.

The year didn't register too broadly on my personal barometers—fairly crap, if nowhere near as crap as 2000. But it was an extraordinary year in film. It was, I am prepared to argue, one of the greatest years for film in movie history, and certainly the best since I had been alive. Possibly the best year in the second half of the twentieth century, but there's a two-drink minimum if you want me to summon the table-rapping righteousness I'd need to go that far. Making this case ten and more years later now, increasingly the rebuttal is written on the impossibly pink and pinker faces of my sparring partners: *But you were really young in 1999. That's the last time you felt anything really—appallingly—deeply. I call the theory of receptivity and now find you slightly sadder than before.*

But it's just not true. I was young, yes, but I was a terrible young person—an embarrassment to my kind, really. And 1999, for me, was a nonstarter; hardly a time, I think, when I found things new and exciting because I was young, or that I now associate with my new and exciting, young world. If anything, I felt old and worn-out and generally skeptical, and it just so happened that the only thing I was good at was spending a lot of time alone, in the dark. I never saw more movies in a single year, it's true, but it was my great good fortune—and I remember thinking at the time, *Can you* believe *this?*

Again *this week?*—that so many important directors of the last generation and the next one seemed to be cramming their best work into the final seconds of the century.

Why the confluence? Hollywood's obsessive chartings account for little beyond box office, and even some critics get their narrow shoulders up about making lists of a year's best and worst films. But perhaps patterns should form the beginning of a story, not an end. Perhaps a run as hugely, almost freakishly accomplished as 1999's holds meaning that we can't get at any other way. If they're anything like Ethan Hawke's face, anyway, the integrity of the patterns formed in our culture can at least remind us of exactly how many miles can be racked up over ten years—what a decade looks and feels like—which is handy information, especially for those who have not yet developed a sense of it for themselves.

Check it out: Leaving aside the big-ticket items that weren't half-bad, like *The Sixth Sense*, *American Beauty* (okay, half-bad), *The Insider*, and, say, horror kitsch like *Sleepy Hollow* and *The Blair Witch Project*, something was up with the year's output of smaller, largely independent, madly inventive films. An era was either peaking or having an intense, pre-expiration paroxysm. It was a culminating moment, in any case, when there was still something like legitimate independent film, and the people with money weren't as frightened about taking risks; perhaps the co-opt had begun, but some fight was still left in the independent system. Even the old pros were stepping up their game, trying something new: Spike Lee brought *Summer of Sam*, David Lynch had *The Straight Story*, Kubrick unleashed the love-it-or-laugh-at-it *Eyes Wide Shut*, Woody Allen offered the underrated *Sweet and Lowdown,* and Pedro Almodóvar broke through with *All About My Mother*.

The reign of 1999 began with the wide release of *Rush-more*, in February. Forebear of all things fresh and wonderful, it set the tone and the bar for the year. Then came *The Matrix* and *Office Space* in March. I snuck out of my own stultifying office job to see Mike Judge's second film over a distended lunch. A multiplex was underneath my office building, and another close by; my coworkers and I all cut out for movies now and then, each pretending we were the only one. Then there was *Go*, *Hideous Kinky* (oh, Kate!), *Open Your Eyes*, and *eXistenZ*, which I zoned out of on a kind of principle.

And then: *Election*. Glorious *Election*. After that came *Last Night*, a scene of which was shot in my apartment building; *Buena Vista Social Club*; then—yes—the first *Austin Powers* sequel; *Run Lola Run*; and the goddamn *South Park* movie. What a great time—a great summer—to be dating, now that I think of it. With *South Park: Bigger, Longer, and Uncut*, I could tell in the first fifteen minutes—as I was cramping up from the laughter gushing from some awesome, astonished wellspring inside me, never before tapped in a movie theater—that Mr. Easter Island beside me would hardly do.

Dick! *Romance*. And then the fall season, where things get ridiculous: *Three Kings* and the one-two crunch of *Boys Don't Cry* and *Fight Club*, both of which spat me into the streets feeling like someone who'd just been kidnapped, injected with adrenaline and heartbreak, and jack-heeled out of a moving car. *American Movie*; *Dogma*; *42 Up*; *Sunshine*; *Girl, Interrupted*; *Holy Smoke* (ohhh, Kate); and *Mansfield Park* are comparatively minor but still pretty fucking good. Then came *Being John Malkovich*, a true-blue circuit-buster, and *The End of the Affair*, which I am prepared to fight about, and finally

The Uses of Nostalgia and Some Thoughts on Ethan Hawke's Face

Magnolia and one of my favorite films of all and ever: *The Talented Mr. Ripley.*

So, about that. About 1999. Then I had just spent four years studying the film and the literature of the past, as though that is indeed where all good and worthwhile things can be found. Then I was recently out of school and unconcerned with continuity, or the connection of inner scheming with the form a life might take in its fullest expression. Then I answered a relative's holiday dinner-table question about what was next for me with the only option that seemed both honest and objectively accurate: Oblivion?

There's a chronic history of that kind of thing, but let's not get into it. Let's just say that even when I wasn't playing the in-house Visigoth at family gatherings, "the future" was a concept that tucked my mind into twilight mode, like a pleasant whiff of ether or the wave of a prestidigitator's hand. In the fog of youth, all of my ambitions were internal and subject to daily renewal, so that each morning I thrashed my way back into the world, having just found my footing when the sun began to set. All of my longings had in some sense to do with time— for time, against time—and the trip wire that kept me from experiencing the world with any kind of reliable, butt-wagging rhythm. At the end of a century defined by its compressions of distance, space seemed more like a cute theory, a dead question. The quest for a modern self is defined not by a map but a schedule; to lack a clear timeline is to be lost. Often I went to the movies to mess with time, to get it off my back or keep it from staring glumly at me from across the room. Just as often I went to get right with it, to tether myself to the present in a way I couldn't otherwise manage.

It worked to that weirdo's advantage, I think, that in 1999, at the movies anyway, so little nostalgia perfumed the air. Through the nineties we dressed like filthy hippies one year and peg-legged mods the next, wearing Goodwill weeds to mourn a time when we didn't exist. For a while, nostalgia was only acceptable in the very young, as though working forward from our parents' generation might show us where we fit into the picture. Back then I figured that the mixed-up, inter-era quality of much of what was going on would make it impossible to reheat on the nostalgia-market stove. But then the eighties returned with the millennium, and the aughts had hardly hobbled out before the nineties came po-going back, and I saw clothes I still had in my closet arranged in store windows for maximum retro cachet. Is it that time already?

Being a practicing nostalgic is no longer a stain on your record; odds are your records will come back into fashion before you begin to miss them. Its prevalence makes it tough to differentiate between meaningful recovery of the past and the perpetuation of a craze. A lot of crap gets unearthed not because it's good but because ours are kitschy times. Often that's the same difference: evoke a moment however you like, as long as it's both past and specific. The yearning behind that impulse has less to do with sensibility than the drive toward a more stable sense of time.

That nostalgia has become an integral part of American culture is odd not least because it was initially considered the exact opposite. In *The Future of Nostalgia*, Russian-American scholar Svetlana Boym connects the beginning of closely measured, delimited time to the birth of what an eighteenth-century doctor called "the hypochondria of the heart." Basically, absent the option of sweating the apocalypse, a pile of closely bordered countries were left in a kind of spiritual pickle. According to Boym, it's no coincidence that, in medieval Europe, the end of the End Times was also the beginning of nostalgia, which is to say of individuals and collectives looking back to sustain a sense of identity; of pooling memory funds from which to draw meaning; and of shrinking time's unwieldy continuum to reflect a specific situation, specific values, and specific ideals. The more objective our measurements for space and time, the stronger our impulse to transcend them with a sense of personalized order. The longing for a sense of confinement—of home—is both personal and communal, its basis purely human, its paradox even more so.

A Swiss doctor put a name to this longing in 1688, while writing a medical dissertation on a pathology he had observed in Europeans displaced from their homelands—students, servants, and soldiers, mostly. Johannes Hofer described the condition in terms of extreme homesickness, using Greek for street cred: *nostos*, meaning "to return home," and *algia*, "longing, or sickness." Over the centuries, treatments for nostalgia included leeches and potions and other earthy voodoos, but the first prescription was the most basic: get back where you belong.

Nostalgists were said to see ghosts, hear voices of loved ones, dream themselves home, mistake the imagined for the real, and confuse their tenses. If they had been able to find vintage candy stores or Ramones 45s on eBay, perhaps they would have, and we'd all roll our eyes and think, *Let it go, man; live in the now.* But in its origins as a mental illness, nostalgia is a fairly pristine metaphor for ambivalence toward modern displacements, the foreboding of the present moment and an untellably gnarly future. Which goes a long way to explaining why the first Americans considered nostalgia to be a weakness of the Old World. They were too far away from all of that, too new and forward-looking for crybaby callbacks to the good old days. Motility was progress, and a national sense of place and pride what they would make it—the future, not the past, was where American dreams were set.

The nostalgia diagnosis had disappeared by the twentieth century (but was revived in Israel, according to Boym), if not before the emergence of suitable heirs like neurasthenia, the diagnosis minted by the American physician George Miller Beard in 1869. Henry James's brother William nicknamed the complaint, which was described as a kind of exhaustion with the new, "Americanitis," and pharmacies began stocking elixirs to restore youth and ward off the anxiety and fatigue Beard blamed on the new world's unwieldy speed and excessive freedoms. Neurasthenic men (including Teddy Roosevelt) were directed to recalibrate themselves against nature's rhythms, while women (including Charlotte Perkins Gilman) were put to bed with orders to quiet their minds. Lengthening life spans only seemed to intensify a focus on the primacy of youth, with F. Scott Fitzgerald bewailing a generation's first wrinkle even while the party staggered on.

I think you know the rest: We now live on a global clock, every standardized minute counted off on the screens we stare at all day. Our world has never been so closely observed and recorded and mediated, yet our lives have never seemed more self-contained. Western societies are increasingly a matter of discrete single, couple, or family plots, private spaces designed to sustain themselves apart from any conception of a whole. That tendency toward a discretionary existence accounts for the familiarity of the floating, customized Xanadu of the Internet, as well as the hunger for community it seemed to satisfy. The clock was restarted, and the challenge to scale one's finite sense of time against an ultimate infinity was compounded by a sense of hair-straightening acceleration—the sudden potential to experience all things, all at once. It became possible—it became progress—to live at a speed and spacelessness that held the present in an exploratory suspension. We could prospect this new world like towheads in Narnia, with the sense that life on the outside was paused where we left it, and that "together" we might invent an end to loneliness.

What nobody told us is that nature may abhor a vacuum, but in its natural state longing is one big sucking sound. Over the last decade, the tightening cycle of nostalgia choking Western culture has proliferated into a kind of fractal loop, and for this we blame each other. But our backward fixations are less a product of the desire to stop the clock or retreat to a more fruitful era than the failure to adjust to a blown-out sense of time. In fact, what we call nostalgia today is too much remembrance of too little. We remember with the totemic shallowness, the emotional stinginess of sentiment. And we experience the present with the same superficial effort. Like overworked busboys gesturally wiping down tables between lunch-rush patrons, we launder the events of the day with the estrangements of irony, the culture's favored detergent—or dead-earnest ideology, its competing brand—just to get on to the next one.

On the one hand, perhaps all of the world's longing has led to this moment. Maybe this is what the poets warned about—Werther and Wordsworth and Whitman, all the wigged-out piners down the ages—maybe it wasn't precisely petunias and print media and high-speed rail they were worried about but *this exact moment*. This, of course, has been said before. It's impossible to know how different our concerns are from those of Hofer's Swiss soldier sulking on the coast of Sweden, or the Dutch student dreaming of her mother's toast with hagelslag at Oxford. It's impossible to know how deeply programmed we are to long for different times, places, tastes—the tinted comforts of memory. It's impossible to know, in a time that is no time and only time and all times, all the time, how that programming might shake out. But one suspects Broadway revivals might be involved.

On the other hand are the human things unchanged by time and technology. Things, perhaps, like the cosmic, wall-eating longing that takes light-years to get to you only to confer—burning past your self and any emotion you have known or might know to your very molecules—the unbearable nothingness from which it came. That stuff's still kicking around. But again, the vessels we fashion to contain and commodify fathomless emotions now often look a lot like *Jersey Boys*, or jelly shoes, or the memes that streak across the Internet, fostering what little cultural intimacy is tenable when we are so many and moving so goddamn fast.

If anything could, recalibrating and redistributing the weight of our shared past might begin to restore a sense of pace to the culture, relieve it from the sleeperhold of easy nostalgias, and reroute the collective longing behind those impulses in some more useful direction. Svetlana Boym says nostalgia outbreaks often follow a revolution, and to the Velvet and the French I suppose we must add the Facebook. Though it seems unfair for a fogyish revival to court its constituents as they move through their thirties, which is to say just as the fog is finally clearing.

I was buying gum and uranium-enriched sunscreen not too long ago when the drugstore clerk was swept into a Proustian vortex by the sight of my gold Motorola RAZR on the counter. "Ohhhh," she sighed, dumping my purchases into a tiny plastic bag. "I know that phone. I wanted one of those *so bad*." She beamed at the memory. "That was *the phone*." It was a rare moment of gadget relevance for me, so much so that I didn't notice her use of the past tense and said something shy about how you don't see many of the gold ones around. My clerk frowned. "Tsssk—not *anymore*," she said. "I'm talkin' like *two years ago*. When I was in *high school*." I punched in my PIN. "I have a BlackBerry now." I covered the phone with my palm and slid it off the counter. "You need to upgrade."

And I did, believe me. Let's call it the theory of receptivity 2.0.

The problem, if you will permit it to be thought a problem, is that I can already feel myself reaching the point my grandmother hit in her eighties. For her it was the airplane, the car, the telephone, the radio, the movies, um, the atom bomb, television, microwaves, space travel, CD, DVD, ADHD—fine. But the cell phone was a gadget too far; my grandma simply topped out. There's a limit to the assimilating one person can do in a lifetime, and she reached it with fifteen years to go. I was the teenager who complained about being made to whip cream by hand in her kitchen, the congenitally late but ultimately enthusiastic adopter of everything wireless, compressed, ephemeral, convenient, and generally knuckle-sparing about the digital revolution. And yet every other week now, when I hear of something like Google glasses—which I guess are goggles that annotate the visible world with information about what can be bought, eaten, or sexually enjoyed therein—my first thought is a grandmotherly *Aaaaand I'm out.*

My knees are still good, my friends! I have perfect eyesight, and you know why? Because I let someone *cut into my eyeballs with a laser.* I don't hold biweekly *Fight Club* vigils in my living room, frost commemorative Tracy Flick cupcakes for friends, or wrap myself around a life-size Ralph Fiennes pillow each night. But the older I get, the more protective I feel of something like 1999, a time that felt interesting even then because it was so firmly allied with the present. The longings I associate with it are longings outside of time, larger than me and the movies both. To experience such a radical burst of cinema in my own time stopped me in my tracks, but hardly permanently. If anything, it kept me seeking that feeling, of being a part of something remarkable, and staying awake enough to know it. If anything, I fear not having it in me to care in that same way about the latest tablet, or to develop strong feelings for what amounts to a delivery system, or to imprint sense memories on a soon-to-be-obsolete aluminum slab. Which is to say I worry less about being left behind than not wanting to board the party bus in the first place.

In a 1968 conversation with Marshall McLuhan, Norman Mailer used the example of plane travel—the latter word, as McLuhan points out, taken from the French verb *to work*—to illustrate his fear of a poorly inhabited present. "I don't want to come on and be everybody's Aunt Sophronia and complain about the good old days, which I never knew either," Mailer said, by way of qualifying his feeling that flying a thousand miles in an hour means moving through "whole areas of existence which we have not necessarily *gained*. It may be confounding, it may finally be destructive of what is best in the human spirit."

McLuhan replied with one of his casually immortal predictions: "If you push that all the way, what it means is that we will increasingly tend to inhabit all of these areas in depth, simultaneously." Mailer took this like a shiv to the spleen. "But we will not inhabit them *well*!" he cried. "We will inhabit them with a *desperately bad fit*!"

I'm not sure I ever knew the good old days either. It's too soon to tell. And believe me, young people, I know the case against me better than you ever could: I rarely go to shows anymore; I don't troll the sites I can't even name for hot new sounds; I never got into Mumblecore; too often I read new books because I'm being paid to; and it's probably a matter of months before I look in the mirror and see Ethan Hawke staring back. I'm right there with you. But tell me, have you seen 1999? I was young then, but it didn't mean that much to me. It seems like a while ago, I know, but it won't be long before you're standing where I am now, trying to sort your personal history from the stuff that stands alone. Time used to do that work for us, but time's a little tired these days. Time needs a minute. For those of us born into pieces—you and me both, pal—the challenge is not *salvaging* a meaningful sense of time but determining how to build one within our current parameters, and then inhabit it well. I guess I can only say you'd be amazed how much the 1999s and the

Ethan Hawkes of the world can help you with that, if you let them.

About two years after moving to New York and not long after the release of *Before Sunset*, I found myself sharing a room with Ethan Hawke. Should you move to New York and stick around long enough, eventually you will too. A group of us were huddled in a penthouse at the Tribeca Ritz for an informal brunch. Whether genuinely felt or a function of decorum, the hostess showed a helpless ambivalence about the space, which she informed me was bought for a song—and here we bow our heads to consider whatever her version of that tune might be—when the building went condo in late 2001. She and I had paused our tour of the apartment to consider the spare bedroom's northern exposure when I felt Ethan Hawke draw up to my side.

I could tell you about the way he ate chicken curry with his hands but parsed a cupcake with a knife and fork, or the loud, actorly register of his voice across the room, or the way, during our brief exchange—the hell-or-high-water piece of him every person in that room was going to claim before he got away—he'd only pause from his uncomfortable flitting to grant eye contact when I paid him a compliment. I remember those things, as well as the view—out of the living room's panoramic, southwesterly window bay—of what seemed to be endless harbor beyond Miss Liberty's straining arm, and the horror I felt when a puzzled author with a blond bowl-cut approached the glass to ask if the lone child on the premises belonged to me. But beyond them is a memory of accrued and connective meaning. Beyond them is simply the sense of being engaged in a new and yet distinctly familiar way with Ethan Hawke's face, and the felicities of time.

As a kid, probably around when I first saw that face, I nursed a secret conviction about how the perfect movie could be made. It would tell the story of a life, start to finish, only instead of makeup and lighting and showy acting, a commitment of decades would capture the effects of time. How had no one thought of imprinting the celluloid version of a story that spanned, say, thirty years with the truth by actually filming it over thirty years? It would be a life's work, and a work shot through with life. If someone just took the time, I felt sure, by at least one measure of default it would be the greatest movie ever made.

I used to refer to myself as a nostalgic child: I mourned our kitchen garbage bin's transition from paper to plastic as though it were the end of the belle epoque; when my father bought a new car, I took it as a personal insult to the past; and as far back as I can remember, I have been drawn to people and art beyond my lifetime's reach. Ten was a tough birthday, as I recall; the ascent to double digits felt so total. How different, anyway, would twelve be from twenty-one, or seventy-two from twenty-seven, or thirty-three from thirty-three? Surely a person had to hit one hundred for time's fullness to register in the same way; the rest is numerical noise.

But it's something like learning of a movie that matches my ten-year-old specifications almost exactly, a film currently listed on IMDb as the *Untitled 12-Year Project*, which began shooting in 2002 and has a scheduled release date of 2015—it is finding out that this movie is being directed by Richard Linklater and counts Ethan Hawke among its cast that gives all of my early, instinctive jockeying with time and its tyrannies a kind of amber—not to say golden—glow. Like that drawing of the old lady whose nose becomes a young woman's chin in another glance, time's sorceries freeze under close scrutiny and flower when permitted a shift of perspective.

Had I known, had time allowed, I would have asked Ethan Hawke about the untitled twelve-year project, if only to game his attentions with another flattering word.

The Dream (Girl) Is Over

A(nother) Theory

True movie stars are born twice. The first birth follows the nativity story that has mineralized into cultural bedrock: centrifugal charm, talent, ambition, luck, and discovery combine to send a mere mortal into the sky, where she is nothing more or less than light to us. The second way is lesser known, which is its point. The second birth is also the seven hundredth, the six billionth: in individual memories and in the collective imagination, a star's energy, once released, is endlessly refracted—orienting us to the archetypal landscape within and forming a kind of cohesive gloaming without. Celestial bodies hang in the sky for billions of years after their death; in theory light travels forever. The same is true of their fleshly namesakes, whom we recognize as uncanny not for their freakishness but their profound and utter familiarity.

What I am saying is that it is my solemn belief that I entered the world with the idea of Marilyn Monroe built into my dreaming mind, like a coiled box spring of memory beneath the mattress of consciousness. So that when I recently watched *Niagara* on the big screen for the first time, I knew a close-up of Marilyn's melting-sundae face the way I know the color of my eyes and the length and shape of my fingers.

Science cannot yet back me up on this. It will come, no doubt, part of the project of reducing our every known and unknown to a matter of mitochondrial DNA. What I have for now is a story, and an attendant question: What if all of life, but especially the part of it that involves consuming art and images, is in some sense a reminder?

I have a suspiciously clear memory of being conned into accompanying my father to a literary event when I was six or seven, thirty years after the last lighting rig and negligee on the *Niagara* shoot was packed up and shipped home to Hollywood. Whether the con was explicit or the result of a misapprehension is in dispute, but in my memory my agreement to the outing was rooted in the promise of an assignation with Marilyn Monroe. Like many born after her death, my awareness of her is not something I can accurately source. Her presence seems innate and my response to it pure but patterned, like the vocal freestyling that precedes the shaping of language. Rather than a clear moment of introduction, my memory ends—which is to say begins—with the certain knowledge of what she represents: everything beautiful and true.

To think of such a creature alighting in London, Ontario! I put on my best dress, smoothed my hair, and hupped into the front seat of my father's oxblood Monte Carlo, ready to be borne to the unthinkably swell part of town where the movie stars hang out.

Where we wound up was between the slanted white teeth of a university-district parking lot. I remember the sunlight pinging off the hood as I gave the car door a two-handed push, and the dawning of one of the biggest letdowns of my short-limbed life as I was piloted into a bookstore and presented at the table where a smiling Alice Munro sat between stacks of her latest story collection. Lovely and gracious despite my dejection, she was hardly the out-of-body encounter I had in mind—the sort I would have when I finally read the book Munro was signing, fifteen years later. It's a memory whose existence suggests the violence of my disappointment.

The Serpent of the Nile

It's probably not a coincidence that chimerical superlatives like *dream girl*, *dreamboat*, *dreamy*, and *man/woman of my dreams* are largely postcinematic. Film's power to build and rebuild romantic ideals penetrated the core of human memory, itself a fluid and highly fungible storytelling concern. Something about the moving image spoke to the phenomenon of dreaming, even felt stolen from it, in a way that written narrative and live performance did not. So that as often as the movies infiltrated our dreams, they seemed to have emerged from some hidden place within us. From the first experiments in film its strange sympathy with the unconscious was harnessed to create archetypes—good guys and bad guys, foxes and fainting ladies—and to enshroud actresses in particular in a reptilian haze.

The effort went beyond the screen. Studio publicity departments often invented an exotic provenance to blur a star's edges with mystique. Press materials for Theda Bara—born Theodosia Goodman in 1885, a Jewish girl from Cincinnati—insisted she was raised in the shadow of the Sphinx. If her blend of Egyptian, Italian, and French blood didn't awe you, her name, it was pointed out, was an anagram for *Arab death*. Claiming otherness freed Bara to play the vamp as nakedly as she pleased. Release from the familiar also freed up viewers to imagine her as a creature who existed only on-screen and in their dreams.

Naturally a more virtuous, ethereal counterpart emerged to both complement and complete Bara's barefoot Hottentot. In 1916, Cecil B. DeMille directed a five-reeler called *The Dream Girl*, launching the film career of silent star Mae Murray. That film has been lost, but recently footage surfaced of the first color screen tests: shot in 1922, they feature a wildly emotive Murray looking for all the world like an archival snippet of déjà vu. Like Bara she is a beauty of her time, with fine features, an imperious, heavy-lidded gaze, soft jaw, and a marcelled bob that undulates in the light. But there is something beyond normative beauty in every bona fide dream girl: you know her, even if you don't.

Their Bodies, Ourselves

Nowadays, when we talk about the shape-shifting of the feminine ideal, the discussion quickly boards the bullet train to "body image," bypassing what's less directly quantifiable for a more straightforward destination. I'm loath to talk about the body. No: I'm loath to *argue* about the body. The yield is sure but limited, and never, ever late. It is, of course, and always has been all about the body. Preferred size and shape, symmetry and ratio, horsepower and shocks, spoiler and chassis—all change in striking and sometimes significant correlation with the times. Yes. But so often this observation is presented as its own argument against the current ideal, and reactionary sound bites stand in for meaningful thought about not just how she should be drawn, but what a woman, at her best, *is*.

The death of a Hollywood paragon like Elizabeth Taylor cues editorial hand-wringing and commentariat blowback about the streamlining of the female movie star. Men queue up to log specious, self-congratulatory elegies, ascribing vague laments for an earlier era's voluptuousness to the bodies of the women who inhabited it. Women, meanwhile, get lost in arguments about the scourge of vanity sizing. But the body's centrality is what sets it beside the point: Marilyn Monroe's measurements were handed out by the same press agents hawking Theda Bara's false passports; I knew Elizabeth Taylor's eighteen-inch waist size before it matched my age. Because they look to our hourglass-starved eyes like more generous, "normal" shapes doesn't make it so, nor does it retro-exempt former standards from their status *as* standards. There is a certain freedom in accepting their lead-fisted rule.

What Is True

More and more we deal in images at the expense of imagination. We ingest them at a pace that promotes instant judgments and insanely regimented standards. We live in viciously scrutinizing times, with the body a site of displaced moral fervor and woman pared down to her parts and posed—an ideal without an animating idea. And yet a reasonably straight line can be drawn from Bara's *Cleopatra* days to the plastic-surgery makeover programs and tabloids inviting us to identify actresses by their bikini bottoms. No one point in the twentieth century—the moving-image century—is disconnected from any other. To mourn for a beauty norm of the past is to forget that we have traversed a spectrum and this is its far side.

The process by which culture-defining dreams are dreamt is unchanged: it requires time, space, and willing energy, in a collective and its individuals. If there is something to bemoan, it may be our confinement in imaginative limbo. The attention of the culture and its consumers is currently too scattered to generate something as massive and dynamic as a new ideal. We have been left to our own tastes and devices, and manage both like small media conglomerates. And they are savvy outfits too—we know too much about the mechanics of the business to fall for the same old star-making routines. Very little that is visual feels new, and this boredom breeds a certain contempt, especially with regard to images of women. A return to the enforced slowness of the serial novel produced the last decade's fully imagined heroines: Bella Swan, Lisbeth Salander, and Katniss Everdeen. Young-adult and fantasy fiction seems to be filling a void in this regard. What began as a seemingly limitless mythmaking tool—the movies—is now one of the toughest arenas for launching an old-school archetype, the kind where it becomes impossible to tell what came first: the dream or the girl.

Just Wanting to Be Wonderful

By her own reckoning, no one dreamed harder of being a movie star than Marilyn Monroe. That longing is manifest in *Niagara*, Henry Hathaway's lusty, Technicolor noir. The first and last director to cast Marilyn as a femme fatale, Hathaway captured some of the most heart-stopping images of the actress committed to film. Before the glittery musicals, bombshell photo shoots, and her diaphanous materialization on a fire escape in *The Seven Year Itch*, *Niagara* ushered Monroe deep into the cultural imagination. Hathaway's canny direction—an almost absurdly long shot of her simply walking away in a pencil skirt and heels is astonishing, as is a ravishing close-up of her sleeping face—and the intensity of the actress's wish to lend herself to our dreams led to the double inception of a movie star.

In one of Monroe's many lingering entrance and exit scenes in *Niagara*, she's wearing a lush, persimmon-colored sundress with sloped shoulders and a peekaboo cutout beneath the bow gathered at her bust. Jean Peters, playing the perfectly lovely earthling to Marilyn's astral projection, and her husband (Max Showalter) are guests at the Niagara Falls motel where Marilyn and her embittered old man (Joseph Cotten) are holed up. During the first evening's festivities the new guests watch her slither by. "Why don't you ever get a dress like that?" Showalter complains. "Listen," Peters replies, "for a dress like that you've got to start laying plans when you're about thirteen."

Even more striking than her wit is Peters's shared appreciation. Marilyn was so fully the dream that it was impossible to begrudge her appeal; she didn't need rivals or homely best friends to temper her threat. In this she is characteristic of the classical Hollywood dream girl: Rita Hayworth, Ava Gardner, Marlene Dietrich, Carole Lombard—all pansexual creations who stood alone. There was no argument about setting unrealistic standards because there was no question: this is pure fantasy. You might dream of looking like Greta Garbo or dancing like Ginger Rogers, but you didn't actually expect to. At their most magical, movie stars sail past that kind of expectation—relieve us from it, really—to delve straight into the muck of our most basic ideas about what is and should be. Brigitte Bardot has spoken of the Marilyn imperative in these terms: "She always was for me what every woman—not only me—must dream to be. She was gorgeous, charming, fragile."

The upshot of generating an ether-penetrating idea of womanhood while bound to corporality was much in Marilyn's mind. Her moment occurred as cinema reached the final peak of its power to create fantasies out of human faces. Modern celebrities deal with different pressures—most a product of the disappearing boundaries between audiences and performers who work hard to seem "relatable," risk-free, *real*. It's tough to imagine one of them complaining, as Marilyn did, about being punished for not fulfilling the superhuman expectations an intimate hitches onto a relationship. "I'm a failure as a woman," she said shortly before her death in 1962. "My men expect so much from me, because of the image they've made of me—and that I made of myself—as a sex symbol. They expect bells to ring and whistles to whistle, but my anatomy is the same as any other woman's, and I can't live up to it."

Of course dreams are not meant to be met, made out with, or married. Dante required distance to dream of Beatrice, and I would no sooner encounter Cary Grant than the star of last night's quasi-nightmare—a giant, feral squirrel that chased an old friend out of a window on her wedding day. Every former infatuee knows that the tendency to invent one's dream lover extends beyond movie stars (or Florentine debutantes). The drive to generate and transfer affections is a basic part of the human profile. Since long before the first woman besotted the first man on the big screen, our desires have followed paths as deathless and unbroken as a blighted star's beams, derived from and carried off to places we can never fully know. If our anointed stars serve any singular purpose, it is as both a source and a safe hub for similarly undefined longing, stored in the same cumulous server as the curious dream blueprints—all those crumbling teeth, public nudities, and dead babies—for our shared anxieties.

La-Di-Dah

The starlight generated during the first sixty years of cinema enjoyed a healthy afterglow, due in large part to classical Hollywood's embrace of archetype and untroubled allegiance to the architecture of dreams. Still, Monroe's popular persona—the giggling sexpot, the dumb blonde, the tragic beauty—does seem like a poor fit for the first postfeminist generation. How is it that Marilyn annexed the part of my mind concerned with what a woman could be?

Certainly by the mid-1970s the erosion of the movies' classic dream girl had begun. The culture's REM needle went berserk for the decade or two I spent growing up, and representations of women veered across the charts accordingly. In between Diane Keaton's patriarchal shutout in *The Godfather* and stuttering redefinition of feminine charm in ironic, oversize menswear, we were slashed, sportified, fetishized, suited up as superheroes, and stripped down to our post–Hays Code glory. What there was little room for during those years was fantasy: the male gaze had been bagged and tagged as part of the feminist project, and to think in terms of a traditional ideal was to earn a lashing with someone's discarded Wonderbra. In the same year that Keaton was anointed as the alpha shiksa in *Annie Hall*, she was martyred to the cause of sexual liberation in *Looking for Mr. Goodbar*. Make of it what you will that both films are set on Manhattan's Upper West Side.

My mother was of the generation of women—Keaton's generation, as it happens—that was educated to the teeth and then sent into an unreconstructed job market. In the late 1970s, she lost interest in the life of raising children and hobby jobs and enrolled in an M.B.A. program. Before I hit the double digits the call of a corner office took her to Toronto, where she has remained ever since. I spent my preadolescence reeducating skeptical friends and neighbors about the arrangement, always careful to stipulate that her removal from our home was not the end of my parents, or my family. They would nod with sober courtesy and I would nod back, until mutual dizziness obscured the original concern. I made the proper noises and decorated the appropriate Mother's Day cards with reassurances that she was doing the right thing for womanity, if not her daughter. My mother donned the chunky power suits, striped the blush up her cheeks, and upgraded a pair of self-gifted diamond studs with every promotion. During visits, I learned to approach her only when she was scrubbed and dressed for bed; the executive armor seemed to transform more than her skin tone. Though I genuinely admired her ambition, echoing it with a near-deranged dedication to whipping the academic ass of every kid in school, about the time that my mother realized her generation's feminist dream, I tucked away all my Wonder Woman costumes and tuned in to a prior frequency.

"I'm not interested in money," begins a Marilyn quote I read at fifteen. "I just want to be wonderful." By the time I was growing up, either/or configurations of womanhood were already completely alien, though liberation came with the hitch of all untested theories: taking full measure of its extremes seemed like the surest way to balance them.

The Mesomorphic Era

Though the dream girl was reduced in stature over the 1980s and early '90s, it seemed unlikely—as long as there were young women and massive screens to project their images upon—that she might actually disappear. Typecasting has always been the two-faced friend of the aspiring movie star, but the roles of the comedienne, the character actress, and the beauty queen settled into smug complacency during those years. As though more naturalistic storytelling and acting styles equaled more naturalistic representations of women. But the categories didn't budge—if anything, they further limited the number of traits that could be ascribed to any one actress. Meg Ryan, Meryl Streep, and Michelle Pfeiffer have tried to exchange places periodically throughout their careers; only the assiduous, almost freakishly gifted middle child met with any success.

On paper, the figure of the beauty queen—and her subset, the man-eater—is the dream girl's closest relative. But a beauty queen's cultural traction was limited: we now had celebrity models for that type of thing; but also, either by virtue of her empty symmetries (Pfeiffer; Kim Basinger) or the remove of reference (Kathleen Turner; Jessica Lange), the beauty queen had the feeling of facsimile. Heavily ironized, cinema-savvy, and tele-lingual, we might appreciate beauty and even use it to enforce a gold standard, but we resisted the creation of out-and-out fantasy women on-screen. *Sex symbol* was understood as a frivolous and possibly destructive term, and the dream girl became either a prop—the "after" reveal of the ubiquitous makeover montage—or a kind of inside joke (see the slow-motion point-of-view shot of Phoebe Cates in *Fast Times at Ridgemont High* and the career of model-turned-actress Kelly LeBrock). Post Princess Leia—one of the last cataclysmic dream girls; it seems significant that she was a pure character from that galaxy far, far away—for the most part we wanted things and people to look *real*, or anyway a movie-fied, maximally attractive version of real.

But in an industry built upon the allegoric potency of its images, the goal of realism—particularly as it relates to the feminine ideal—is pretty unrealistic. For women, this meant a divide between "serious" roles for "serious" actresses on one end and abject eye candy on the other, with a few comediennes and Sigourney Weaver high-stepping in between. In other words, actresses were subjected to all the casting constrictions of Old Hollywood without the potential for something other-worldly to take shape. Conditions were ripe for an unabashed student of iconography like Madonna to claim a spot in the cultural headspace. Music videos were a vital and innovative new form in part because they addressed a postmodern void—the place that opened up when we became too cool to respond to the same old aesthetic tricks and archetypes.

Across this divide, the movies became purveyors of an increasingly specific physical ideal. Anonymous topless babes abounded in mainstream comedies, but well-known actresses were also agreeing to explicit love scenes invariably described as "raw," "real," and "brave." The haggle to disrobe major stars became part of a film's story.

The exposure of Sharon Stone in *Basic Instinct* (1992) was the deceptively cool culmination of this elaborate burlesque. Cast ten years earlier as the quintessential dream girl in Woody Allen's *Stardust Memories*, as *Instinct*'s ciggie-sucking temptress, Stone makes the castration menace of the femme fatale explicit. It's the moment Andy Warhol, shooting a lingerie-clad Edie Sedgwick grappling with one man on-screen, another off, and a third behind the camera, teased out and ultimately denied in *Beauty No. 2* (1965). Both films launched their respective stars: today *Basic Instinct* plays like a sleek but garish genre piece updated with reactionary, late–Second Wave twists, whereas Warhol's shapeless interrogation tape conveys something essential of its time and themes, subject and creator.

Leaving nothing to imagination meant less space *in* our imaginations for the alchemy of archetype to take hold. It turns out that when exposed in 2-D, what lies between a woman's legs amounts to little more than visual information; like a picture of a teacup or acronyms like *2-D*, we'll all process it the exact same way. *Empowerment*, feminism's new watch-word, was used to describe/endorse/defend everything from Stone's playing the V-card (though the actress later claimed she was tricked by director Paul Verhoeven, complicating matters further) to the newly unforgiving, muscle-blistered physiques of performers like Madonna and Linda Hamilton. This, we were told, was *owning* your body: display as decision, sex as a self-marketed commodity. There was a certain de-mocracy in it as well. After all, a measurable ideal is one we might all attain, with enough discipline and a plastic-surgery piggy bank.

Interesting times for the girls just snapping on their first push-up bras and litmus-testing the rumored right to attract attention on their own terms. Why bother with persona or performance in forming an identity when—as long as it was "hot" or "hard"—a body itself might obtain?

Meanwhile, Back in the Cafeteria . . .

Having laid plans at about thirteen, someone like me was still a solid fifteen years from reckoning a dreamed feminine self with an even halfway tenable idea of functionally independent adulthood. This is in fact a pretty sensible timeline. "Being wonderful" is actually an ambition of Einsteinian relativity, and a girl can easily run up a decade's worth of style overhauls, clique-sampling, and guitar lessons sorting out its meaning. The hidden fulcrum of the concern being, wonderful to whom?

Puberty can go off like an IED in the Iraqi desert: one morning you wake up in a German hospital and spend the next six years relearning to walk and talk. All along, the person in search of a personality triages her best interests and directs her energies toward them. A young girl's wish to be seen had a particular backspin in the moment when feminist sex positivity coincided with the STD-phobic early nineties, when even the Catholic schools stopped fronting and rolled out the old condom-on-the-banana routine.

The hockey players at my high school were unbearable, and I dated them all. Their indifference felt like a kind of purgatory; it hardly seemed a worthy arena in which to develop and deploy one's wiles. Ambivalence about subjecting ourselves to seemingly primitive male algorithms ran deeper than the fear of rejection or even disease, into self-reproach. Was it weak to define yourself along a retrograde curve? Can you be wonderful in a vacuum?

I spent four years wrestling at the extreme end of that question, and if my efforts were not successful, they did not go unnoticed. Surely the most decorated nerd at St. George's elementary, I left high school with one distinction: best walk.

Who's That Girl?

Like global bankruptcy and a good orgasm, it happened slowly, then all at once. Around the time that my hair—kept short on my mother's watch—came within kissing distance of my fifth lumbar, the distant outline of a new ideal was spotted riding feminism's third wave. The riot grrrl revolution—a music-based punk movement spearheaded by a group of American, female-based bands—blew through the youth culture with a radical, corrective force. After cramming up against the same old gatekeepers, women who were raised to expect more made a lunge for the mic, and suddenly their smeared faces were everywhere. Much like my awkward phase, the impact was pronounced but brief.

The defiantly wanton postsuffragette flapper—waistless, chestless, bobbed—became a cautionary figure of excess. Eventually the lush, maternal lines of the 1950s bombshell offered a comforting revisal. With the riot grrrl movement, what was launched as a revolution turned into a round of telephone that began with a guttural challenge and ended with a chattering waif in a baby T. The latter was sweet and cute but "edgy," an essentially Victorian vision dressed in street-urchin chic. In her the problem of a new, provocative version of feminine agency was reframed as obviously regressive and a little unhinged. When she was good, she was very, very good. But by the time the words "I think you're my dream girl" were uttered across a telephone line connected to the author's left ear, their meaning had shifted such that instead of merely adding to a mutual burden of romantic illusions, they fell with the force of an indictment.

Who's That Girl? II

In 1993 I moved to the Pacific Northwest, where the tough girls were amassing, with a friend I'll call Aileen. We grew our hair and wore combat boots and baggy cargo pants. Most of our mental energy went to maintaining the certainty that this, finally, was where we belonged. This was independence, maybe. Authenticity—certainly. I had wanted desperately to make the move, but the truth is that from the moment I met her seven years earlier, I would have followed Aileen to the moons of Jupiter. Here was a flesh-and-blood ideal for study, a numinous, red-lipped zaftig with a captivating laugh and confidence so replete that when she first strode into my sixth-grade class in London, Ontario, I felt she had to be American.

For our grade-eight graduation, each member of our class painted a ten-foot mural of our projected occupation. I chose brain surgeon, only because it seemed like the hardest and most impressive thing a boy or girl could be. Aileen went with actress. And if she never made it to the stage or screen, of the two of us she was certainly truer to her mark. As we moved through high school I watched her—everyone did—with acquisitive candor. In being a kind of character she was fully herself. More than OR scrubs and parental validation I longed to manifest the best—which is to say most wonderful, wonderfully elusive—parts of her.

On a summer afternoon shortly before we left, Aileen, her boyfriend, and I convened at our local Chinese joint for tea and fortune cookies. My mother had driven into town earlier in the day to announce my parents' long-delayed divorce. I met the news with supreme detachment: my mother didn't make it to my high school graduation, though I imagined the expiry of her marital pact circled red in her assistant's day-planner. I had resolved not to mention it, but caved between our request for the bill and its arrival, bracketing the news with our customary *check out this bullshit* bravado.

Beneath all that was real urgency: I needed to know how to feel, and how far I was from feeling it. I filled with a private horror as tears like match flares lit in Aileen's eyes.

A few months after our arrival in Vancouver I pushed to the lip of the Commodore Ballroom's stage and watched in fear and awe as Courtney Love unleashed her self-tattered charisma on the crowd. The baby-doll look had reanimated in subversive zombie style, and Love was the queen of the undead coquettes. She spit out cigarettes and screamed at us, between deliriously tight renditions of early Hole songs, for acting like "sullen Canadians" at a punk-rock show. I was alone that night; Aileen wasn't big on the music scene. Or maybe she was working. We both had new jobs and were playing house in an east-end basement apartment, installed below a trio of head-bangers burning out on the finest weed in the land.

It was an unmitigated but highly empowered disaster. Aileen, trailed by pheromone-addled men wherever she went, got mixed up with a seasonal fisherman. After weeks spent pounding the pavement, I landed a job at a Kitsilano coffee shop by simply walking through the door, which might have been my first clue. The owner behaved like a member of the Hawaiian Mafia, squiring me to waterfront power lunches in my secondhand grubs. Turns out I was not criminal front material, though I worked enough customer-free nine-hour shifts to be spraying stale muffins with PAM when I heard that River Phoenix—and my childhood—was dead.

Around that time a midnight grappling session with an odious Frenchman behind the Kitsilano Youth Hostel ripped my earring clean through the lobe. "There goes your modeling career," Aileen said.

A lot of things ended in Vancouver, which I suppose was the idea, though precious little arrived to take their place. Burgled of all of our belongings during the Winnipeg leg of a cross-country lark, we limped home to Ontario. I began shopping in BiWay's little-boys department, preparing for freshman year with five-mile runs, and giving sworn depositions by phone. Aileen went back out West to finish what we started, which is to say she wound up stripping and sunk into heavy drugs.

No Really, Who Is She?

Was it different when we did it because *we* were doing it? Our unextinguished idols, the ones who had lipsticked reputation-searing slurs onto their bodies, began indeed to fade from view. They were raped, as we were; they got older, just like us; their friends died, as ours did; they sold out and so did we. If they were Courtney Love, they suffered terribly, put out a breakthrough album, then settled on an almost touchingly quaint ambition of movie stardom. As though we were not already living through her. As though it were possible to inhabit a higher plane of our dreaming selves than the one haunted by her screwed-up face and napalm howls.

In the years after her Commodore Ballroom show, after her husband's suicide, I watched Love as closely as I did that night. Touring in 1995, she was wild with animal grief, hurling herself offstage and into a pit of young men. There is footage of them tearing the clothes from her body, grabbing at her breasts, and yanking down her underpants, as if rising to a challenge. The issue had moved approximately not at all: Where do a woman's intentions end and the world's indifference to them begin? Is it a statement—subversive or otherwise—if nobody's listening? Or no one can hear you above your breasts?

It was both music and the alternative movement's great loss when Courtney Love regained her composure, invested in a stylist, and began trolling red carpets in bias-cut Versace gowns. It was also a futile exercise. By 1997 the riot grrrl revolution was already being distilled into a highly structured ideal, one too tame for Love's big-shouldered persona.

Dreaming Is Twee

Consider the distance traveled by Winona Ryder between her alterna-girl apotheosis in *Reality Bites* (1994) and her wan incarnation of this new ideal in *Autumn in New York* (2000).

With her slurry, tomboyish diction, marsupial eyes, butter-knife pixie cut, Dickensian slightness, and improbable breasts, Ryder was well known as the muse of 1990s rock stars and movie stars who would be rock stars. For this she was framed as both a throwback groupie and the acceptable face of alternative culture. In the Ben Stiller–directed *Reality Bites*, Ryder plays a recent college graduate and aspiring filmmaker stuck in a stalled job market and trapped between the dubious masculine counterpoints of a wastrel musician (Ethan Hawke) and a media suit (Stiller). Immobility forms a theme for her character, and Ryder's astrophysically complicated allure reaches Hawking-esque heights. And yet, compared to *Autumn in New York*, in which a literally terminally enchanting Ryder alights to show age-inappropriate commitment-phobe Richard Gere the redemptive way of the sprite, *Reality Bites* looks like *Norma Rae*.

Ryder's shivering sad girl underwent a kind of ritual sacrifice in 1999, when newcomer Angelina Jolie devoured her in every frame of *Girl, Interrupted* and licked the screen. But Jolie was quickly isolated and quarantined as an anomaly; she eventually shed the force of her personality and slipped behind the imperial mask of her beauty. As the new millennium began, for a host of young actresses and the young women watching them, there was Angelina and there was the rest of us. The leftover ingenues—including our Winona—were increasingly cast as pint-size oracles, elusive handmaidens, and afflicted, psychosexual fabulists partial to non sequitur and orange hoodies.

After years of manifesting mainly in referential fragments and glistening body parts, the dream girl had finally been wholly reinvented. Aggression, autonomy, sexual agency, and several varieties of stature had been bred out of her prototype in the screenwriting lab. Fully realized, she transmutes the rebellious energy of third-wave feminism into a set of soothing eccentricities to be applied directly to the culture's cowering manhood. Throughout the 1980s and early '90s, a prurient focus on the body stood in for a more fully imagined ideal. By the turn of the century, ingenues were still beholden to the warped terms of this kind of realism, but the focus had shifted from purely physical objectification to the tyranny of "personality."

If you really wanted to, you could find modest overlap between this new type and every innocuous female character to cross the screen with a few marbles either missing or swirling around upstairs. What sets the modern dream girl apart from vaguely similar creations of decades past—like Shirley MacLaine's lovelorn gamine in *The Apartment*, for instance, Liza Minnelli's divinely brazen Sally Bowles, and a host of early Goldie Hawn roles—is the extent to which she's presented as both wildly original and straight out of the coffee shop. She lives in your world, somewhere between sex and safety. Not just believable, she's so well within reach you may already have met her.

(A question: If the true dream girl seems to have emerged from our imaginations, does the fact that this version feels familiar qualify her as the real thing? To me it doesn't matter whether she was inspired by "real" women—something her creators often claim—or triggered an avalanche of jejune posturing. Some have called her a pure projection; with its suggestion of overlay, superimposition gets closer to the trouble. All two-dimensional tics and self-conscious dysfunction, she is more formula than fantasy, more personality than persona.

Rather than distinguishing themselves, a wide array of actresses have been swallowed by the mantle of her mannerisms. The character is so stuffed with this fatuous, hipster fairy-tale idea of personality that she jams the imagination instead of colonizing it.)

More insidiously a male creation than anything as obvious as Sharon Stone's cervical cynosure or the newly mainstream porn stars, this was an exclusive, divisive ideal. Though she set off a kind of daisy chain of mimetic desire, real-life girls were not invited to share in her invention.

It took real-life girls—many of whom wondered whether they were supposed to try on this new costume of quirks or congratulate filmmakers for finally getting them right—a while to figure this out. On the set of *Garden State* in 2003, actress Natalie Portman described her character, a literal spastic who draws the lead, Zach Braff, out of his world-phobic catatonia, this way: "Sam's just a really . . . she's a funny girl. Most parts written for women, especially romantic parts written by guys, are like some weird ideal of what a guy would want a girl to be. Like, she's hot, she takes off her clothes a lot—she also *really* likes sports. And this is a real person who's got problems, and she's funny and she's just as interesting and complex as the male character, and I appreciated that."

Having problems and being "funny" became leading dream-girl qualities. For those of us out in the field, the new girl appeared as both a watered-down affront to iconoclasm (or sadness, for that matter) and a willful force to be reckoned with.

And Then There's This

There was a period, when the Internet was still a largely written medium, where it became frighteningly possible—even necessary—to cultivate not just a new persona but a new *type* of persona. Of the options available for poaching, few were as dependent on voice as the dithering new dream chick. E-mail was the perfect contagion for an ideal defined by her physical and metaphysical absence. For the cohort coming of age just as intranets spread through college campuses, e-mail offered a new forum for an old romantic exercise. Inventing both one's self and one's ideal reader is the epistolary prerogative, and in e-mail's first, great epistolary era, I was not alone in playing Edison at the keyboard.

Especially in the early, sweaty stages of acquaintance, e-mail opened up a kind of perpetual empty stage, an endless call for encores. Though courtly protocols lingered into the age of digital woo, the distancing, disposable aspect of e-mail was also a kind of equalizer. In the unregulated realm of online communication, women didn't worry in the same way about appearing too forward, too interested, too available. What was this back-and-forth anyway but a pixilated game? Private correspondence was soon confined to screens that homogenized the idiosyncrasies of text, temperament, and time into the rigid uniform of font, format, and instantaneousness. We learned to work around these deficits—explaining our moods, drafts, and deletions, and using space, ellipses, and emoticons to develop a grammar that might somehow mimic the intimacies of longhand.

What remained—and will remain, as long as there is language between us—is the extent to which one could glean, between and beyond a lover's words, a sense of what is being sought. It didn't take long for young women still conducting intersex experiments to notice that the combination of constant availability and spectral absence had a kind of incentivizing effect. Long-distance relationships cropped up at awkward and often insurmountable coordinates, *emotional infidelity* was midwifed into the lexicon, and all around the world, certain girls were discovering that what uncertain young men often responded to—off-line too, but somehow more palpably on— was the perpetration of a dream girl whose allure was based in her being not quite there.

This is not the elusive, untouchable quality—the *presence*— that writ the dream girls of old so large. This is the banal absence—of stability, of ambition, of selfhood, of sexual threat, of skirts that pass midthigh—now associated with the approachably edgy, adorably frantic, real-person-who's-got-problems. Maybe it was a class-action-size case of co-dependency: though she reached the status of dream girl, she feels more like a fun-house reflection of millennial masculinity in crisis. Her widespread attraction suggests the extent to which she reflects a young man's fears about finding a place in the world, much less figuring out the opposite sex. Like a girly mini-me, she follows in the proverbial hipster dude's shadow, filling his ear with life-coaching tips or just adorable chatter, skipping behind him on the path to mutually assured regression. In the movies, the new version of a happy ending for these stunted young men is not marriage or more than a provisional suggestion of romance. Instead the stories revel in the bittersweetness of edging a reluctant boy into manhood, whether his twittery comrade merely disappears at the end or indeed dies trying to get him there.

Often, as with Portman in *Garden State*, Charlize Theron in *Sweet November* (2001, RIP), and Kirsten Dunst in *Elizabethtown* (2005), avatars of this ideal attach themselves to the mixed-up young man with blithe aggression. They forge rehabilitation programs, scatter aphorisms ("Men see things in a box, and women see them in a round room" and "I'm impossible to forget but hard to remember" are two from the latter), and declare faux-obscure cultural allegiances that feel written in a particular way: they reek of the self-conscious blather of wee-hour e-mails, the personality-as-taxonomy rubric of online profiles, the ideal as an unending feedback loop of references mucked into a vaguely female form.

I'm a Substitute Person, I Like It That Way

It was in fact *Elizabethtown*, Cameron Crowe's unintentionally self-reflexive meditation on a man's first, headlong failure, that inspired the critic Nathan Rabin to finally put a name to this trend in 2007. Christening her the Manic Pixie Dream Girl, Rabin riffed out a few salient qualities: "[She is] that bubbly, shallow cinematic creature that exists solely in the fevered imaginations of sensitive writer-directors to teach broodingly soulful young men to embrace life and its infinite mysteries and adventures." She's also divisive: "The Manic Pixie Dream Girl is an all-or-nothing-proposition. Audiences either want to marry her instantly (despite The Manic Pixie Dream Girl being, you know, a fictional character) or they want to commit grievous bodily harm against them and their immediate family."

The name, of course, is perfect. And in his first pass at wrangling the phenomenon Rabin struck upon its paradox: the MPDG seems to be both someone else's one-dimensional idea of a dream girl and a general rejection of the dream girl tradition. Since 2007, Rabin and others have worked backward to legitimate the coinage, drawing up a lineage that includes actresses like Claudette Colbert and both Katharine and Audrey Hepburn. Contradictions and inconsistencies in the search for forebears (Jeanne Moreau in *Jules et Jim*? Seventy-five-year-old Ruth Gordon in *Harold and Maude*?) have cheerfully been cited as part of an ongoing, trial-and-error effort to establish her as a player across film history. But to deny the ephemerid nowness of the MPDG is to deny her of her full, fluttery due, and to deprive the genesis story of a uniquely flimsy nonpareil of its telling modernity.

How Happy Is the Blameless Vessel's Lot

Rabin is not alone in struggling to pushpin the iridescent wings of the MPDG to the page. Two of our best screenwriters have taken a crack: one result is sneakily self-aware, the other a dismal satire. Charlie Kaufman's *Eternal Sunshine of the Spotless Mind* (2004) puts Clementine, the pushy, damaged dream girl played by Kate Winslet, where she belongs—in Jim Carrey's besieged memory. Kaufman absolves Clementine of patented MPDG behavior by making her wise to the jig, as it exists in both the film and Carrey's imagination: "Too many guys think that I'm a concept, or I complete them, or I'm gonna make them alive," Winslet says. "I'm just a fucked-up girl who's looking for my own peace of mind. Don't assign me yours."

Often cited as evidence that Kaufman has the inside track on the phenomenon of sassy savior girls, the line is set off by Carrey's wistful reply: "I remember that speech really well." In fact Winslet's edict is an advanced MPDG-ism—articulating the illusory crux of the attraction is part of maintaining one's aura of beguiling insight. "I had you pegged, didn't I?" Winslet gloats. "I still thought you were going to save my life, even after that," Carrey admits.

"I'm just a fucked-up girl who's looking for my own peace of mind" is not a disclaimer, but Clementine's statement of allegiance to her kind. It's believable because neither of them really believe it.

In *Anything Else* (2003), Woody Allen broadened the pathologies of the MPDG into morbid unwatchability. Earnest, young every-schlub Jason Biggs falls in love with Christina Ricci's tiny emotional grifter on sight, and why not: she couldn't be more pixieish if she coughed stardust. But Allen, attempting to ingratiate himself with a new generation, seized upon this new type with startling contempt. He also puts a little old-school Woodman backspin on her: Ricci is a diabolical litany of narcissistic tics and tortured neuroses; the worse she behaves, the more gravely Biggs is bound to her. This despite Allen's own warnings (he plays Biggs's misanthropic mentor), which fairly gong with rue for a time when it was the seventeen-year-old bird who wound up blowing your mind with her philosophical backhand. "She's a hormonal jitterbug," Allen cries, "who'll have you holding up filling stations to keep her on mood elevators!"

The Hud Principle

If explaining this crash-helmeted Kewpie doll's sudden ubiquity or even throwing fences around the matter seems like too massive an undertaking, there is something simpler to consider, and that is whether calling her any kind of dream girl is bogus chiefly because she wasn't properly dreamed up in the first place.

In referring to the early era of cinema as "the golden age," in part we refer to a time when movies were experienced in a state of aesthetic innocence. Our first impulse was to build palaces around them: opulent wombs lit up with new life, they encouraged us to dream together. Theaters of war, literature, religion, myth, nationalism, and technology have all served the same purpose: they open a forum for the telling of stories about who we are and might be. Inevitably those stories shape our sense of what is best and worst in us. The movies were a new way to extend the gestation of human ideals into our dreaming lives.

As a culture and its conduits fragment, the dreams we dream together become fewer and farther in between. The ideals we produce reflect this fragmentation: they work harder for less return; their influence is broad but transitory and superficial, or concentrated but esoteric. Thinking of the MPDG's persistence, I am reminded of Melvyn Douglas in *Hud*, warning the teenager making pie eyes at Paul Newman's tumbleweed hustler, "Little by little, the look of a country changes because of the men we admire."

That the new millennium's first beacon of femininity is a gnomic grown woman in ankle socks and neon jelly shoes feels less like an organic outcome than a perversion of the process. I think of this much-admired *her* the way I think of natal wards and nurseries filling up with children whose fathers and mothers were selected from three-ring-binder profiles, without the assistance of those known and unknown bits of magic that ever drew us to our mates.

I can't imagine that I was alone, as the aughts wore on, in feeling a gorge of dread and mortification rise every time one of these painfully constricted specimens motormouthed across the screen. Her rate of replication seemed to suggest something dire about us. The idea that enough versions of the same type should add up to archetype seemed to bode poorly for the movies as well. As any woman who ever flirted with the trappings of frailty, flaunted her spectacular oddity, or advertised the depth of her knowledge of early Small Faces LPs knows, frailty, flaunting, and advertising are the dispiriting sum total of this ideal. For those still wrestling with the Monroe Doctrine—wonderful to whom?—she offers too sparse and specific an answer and adds too particular a melancholy to the perennial dream girl demurral—*But you don't even know me!*—and its breathless protest: *But I do.*

It's Jess. That Girl Is Jess

We live in a have-not era of feminine identity. I don't know what else but an acute case of Stockholm syndrome could explain the fact that instead of formulating a meaningful response, or even just drafting a letter of apology to the next generation of girls, young female artists have internalized the MPDG and begun breeding her independently.

The most conspicuous example of this is Zooey Deschanel and her wide, periwinkle eyes. A favorite on the independent circuit, Deschanel found mainstream success by specializing in mildly varied flavors of the MPDG, most notably Summer in 2009's *(500) Days of Summer*. At thirty-one, she launched a single-camera sitcom called *New Girl*, the first major network series built around the charm ballistics of the dream girl du jour. Conceived and written by another young woman, playwright Elizabeth Meriwether, the show's tagline is "Simply adorable." Deschanel, also a part-time chanteuse, sings the oopsy-daisy theme song: "Who's that girl? *It's Jess!*"

Deschanel, who wears butt-skimming rompers, ballet flats, a springer-spaniel *perruque* of hair, and baby-doll stamps of rouge in and out of character, capitalized on her epitome with a girly service Web magazine, also launched in 2011, called *Hello Giggles*. Aimed at Manic Pixie Dream Girl Scouts, the site's contents fall under headings like "Treats," "Social Studies," "Home," and "Beauty," and its exercises in cooking and craft tutorial suggest the collecting of merit badges.

In *New Girl*, recent dumpee Jess moves in with three young men. By pretending these men find Jess to be a huge and highly aggravating drip, the show activates an ultimate MPDG premise: it takes a special man to recognize this girl's sui generis appeal. In the first few episodes, Jess often slides from speech into song and back; an early subplot involves her inability to say the word *penis* without atomizing in a sparkly puff. "I just got out of a long relationship" goes a typical declaration of self-insufficiency, "and I don't know what I'm doing emotionally, or—let's be honest—sexually."

That such a self-conscious, ghettoized romantic ideal is now the center of a network television show has been hailed as a kind of breakthrough. The traditional, live-audience sitcom has been dead for a decade. To revive the half-hour format, shows like *The Office* and *Modern Family* adopted a meta-documentary style, as though constantly seeking the camera for a slow burn or pausing to debrief what just happened in a talking-head interview captures something essential about both modern life and modern entertainment. With channels proliferating to accommodate the endless niches and crannies of our viewing desires, and manifold delivery systems for the latest episode of *30 Rock*, television is not the audience mobilizer it once was. The viewership for today's most popular series is nowhere close to that of a top show over the last decades of the twentieth century.

Which is why *New Girl*'s arrival only highlights how everything about this character has been forced upon us. It's a case of a bush-league ideal finding its fractured level. To attract even a niche audience, Deschanel has to stretch the MPDG personality to a painful extreme, performing the desperate bricolage of her weirdness to the point of exhaustion. It makes the issue plain, which is that whether you are trying to create an archetype or hoping to pull at the bar, calculation will always work to a certain extent, but the things we seek and cherish most in life and in each other are beyond measure. The only surprising thing is how well television's smaller stakes suit this big-screen creation. The context of a sitcom is just artificial enough to can and preserve her meager illuminative powers, like a firefly in a mason jar.

A General Call for Submission

Often when we talk about the way movie and television landscapes are peopled today, we are talking about equal representation. Seeing one's self reflected in the culture has become a moral imperative. A white woman complaining about the way (overwhelmingly) white women are represented might seem a little rich when other ethnicities are rarely seen—much less promoted as ideals—at all. And yet I think what has happened within the relative majority tends to enforce the point. It is not enough to be represented for representation's sake; there is a larger, more elusive morality to consider. Because although we are born into the world with some sense of everything that is beautiful and true, like our palettes and our retinas it needs to be switched on—by storytelling, illuminations, ideals that remind us of what it means to be alive and how it feels to dream.

We seek the big stories and examples instinctively; the question is what we are leaving to be found. Without a rich cultural serial to follow, we become vulnerable to the persuasion of extremes. Today we measure our worth against impossible beauty standards and the nebulous metrics of personal branding. We police public "role models," as though it were preferable—or possible—for any one of us to see any other exactly as she is. As though a perfect example is the only one worth following. Or we worry about unrealistic expectations, the flawless body that gets more distant even as it crowds us further into a corner. Well-conceived ideals require space to take hold, but they leave space too, for the determination of some ultimate self, and for self-respect.

My call, more general: we must find a way to continue dreaming of each other. If it seems simple, it should. If we could just rest our minds for a minute, it might even be easy. The more difficult it gets to clear the necessary space, the more necessary that space becomes. Our ideals will occupy some other theater, perhaps, as yet unimagined; embody some other truth, still to be conceived. It need not—it must not—be designed in the image of any one thing, past or future, heightened or hyperreal. It just has to be a dream, and it has to not be this.

Have a Beautiful Corpse

1

At fifteen I knew I had a lot of living to do, especially if all went according to plan and I was dead by twenty-four.

That kind of timeline doesn't really allow for things like grade-ten English class, yet there I was every Tuesday and Thursday, chafing under the rule of a new recruit named Mrs. Klapstein. Looking back, I would put her around twenty-five, fresh out of teachers college. At the time she registered only as someone of teaching age, an indeterminate bracket that had nothing to do with me. Mrs. Klapstein didn't see it that way; I suspect she had ideas about playing the pupil-friendly radical at a regimented Catholic school. It was 1990—*Dead Poets* and all that. This shook down in various ways for me during our semester together. She once stoked a class discussion about unreliable narration by wondering aloud whether I had the hots for Holden Caulfield. A few weeks later, after I busted some fresh moves to "Let Your Backbone Slide" for a school assembly, she casually noted my "very sexual presence onstage." I waited for the right opportunity to retaliate.

Several years earlier I had begun cultivating my completely unoriginal fixation on James Dean. As soon as I was old enough to make excursions to the used-book store in downtown London, Ontario, I culled every two-bit, second-hand Hollywood bio from the premises. I scoured the television listings for his films; I begged my dad to add *East of Eden* to that week's rental pull. He was beautiful, of course, the thoroughbred combination of virile and vulnerable that drives the girls wild. Perhaps more important, Dean easily dominated a category I had been populating with candidates since I was a child: narratives of tragic greatness.

It's a taste I picked up honestly, being raised Catholic, but also in a family whose stories could be considered classics of the genre: my father's mother, an English Ph.D., dead at thirty-four of tuberculosis; his older brother, a brilliant doctor, dead at thirty-six of a heart attack; his younger sister, an accomplished opera singer, dead at thirty-three of an auto-immune disorder; his luminous twin, a mother and social worker, would die in her mid-fifties of cancer.

I was eventually confirmed under my deceased aunt's name, but on the whole, enshrining the departed and transforming our sad stories into house scripture was not my family's style. In fact the dead were rarely mentioned. Instead of saints I made them movie stars—a feat aided, no doubt, by the dazzling uniformity of their beauty. I would spend hours in front of the black-and-white portraits arranged in my grandfather's den in Sudbury, Ontario, and never really shook the feeling that their fates formed a bloodlined tradition: we are amazing, and we die young.

It was certainly ever thus with James Dean; he was practically family. As a pocket cineaste I transposed my sideline in Orange mythology and began to connect most privately and emotionally to the lives of big-livin', big-dyin' movie stars. I swapped old photos and my grandfather's 16mm home movies for *Giant* and *Rebel Without a Cause*, but the gist of the experience was the same. What I couldn't get over, what slayed me continually, was the irreconcilable trick of looking at someone so vital, so immutably present and exquisitely responsive, and yet so indelibly, utterly gone.

The transfixing survival of the images of stars like Montgomery Clift, Marilyn Monroe, and Natalie Wood made a pupil of me, and immersing myself in narrative study felt like a natural and necessary extension of that education. I consumed their life stories as though they were holy texts. I read the entire Shelley Winters oeuvre at fifteen, and it was worth it for the one or two Dean anecdotes alone. I picked her second volume for a book report in one of the post-Klapstein years.

But back in 1990, in the coldest (and alternately hottest) classroom in the west portables, Mrs. Klapstein was trying to feather up the curriculum, get us kids *engaged*. One of her Holden-inspired assignments about voice and identity had us devising a sort of personal crest—a motto accompanied by a representative sketch of ourselves and our legacies.

All right, cool stuff, I remember thinking. *Engage this.*

I drew a gothic tableau of myself laid out in a coffin—candelabra, weeping cherubs, the works—and beneath it I inscribed the Dean mantra: *Live fast, die young, have a beautiful corpse.* When the assignment came due, I set mine on her desk with a smile.

Cry for help is a phrase that makes my dad groan on a good day. Applied to his daughter—as it was during the phone call Mrs. Klapstein made to my home that evening to gently suggest

I be put on a suicide watch—it was insupportable. Asked to explain myself, I made a shameless appeal to rank: I had had enough of her Montessori horseshit, I said, and was merely calling her bluff. And perhaps she was calling mine. Certainly the fastest living I'd done by grade ten was on the Himalaya at the Western Fair.

"She was just playing with her," I heard my dad tell my mother over the phone, with the barest glint of pride. And while it's true that I had contempt for Klapstein—if only because she seemed to want my respect and insisted on a kind of proximal, kindred status—and I wouldn't be within squinting distance of suicidal for another six years, what's truer is that the Dean blueprint for both living and dying was the most powerfully suggestive of any I had come across up to and including that point.

What I didn't understand then, and for more of the following years than I care to admit, was that my response to Dean—and to the numerous doomed performers I was drawn to during that time—stemmed less from morbid anomie than its direct inversion. For a subaltern little squeaker still forming ideas about the adult world—and how to avoid, or fool, or conquer it—the movies and a certain caliber of their stars felt like the world's most captivating private tutor. They could teach you how to dress and behave and seduce and show strength, but the best of them transcended the lessons of persona and posing to suggest something essential about how to live, while you're living. In the same way that the myth of his life was swiftly conflated with the transporting quality of his performances, watching James Dean it was only too easy to confuse the notion of living and dying like him with a keener longing, that is, to *die* like him.

"It seems like the big distinction between good art and so-so art," David Foster Wallace once said, "lies . . . in be[ing] willing to sort of *die* in order to move the reader, somehow . . . And the effort to actually do it—not just talk about it— requires a kind of courage I don't seem to have yet."

Whether that effort is a product of courage or compulsion is a question those who revere and then grieve artists like Wallace struggle with. What is the fallout—personal, moral, cultural—of seeking and then gratefully accepting such a death? In a talk titled "Nurturing Creativity," the writer Elizabeth Gilbert quoted Norman Mailer ("Every one of my books has killed me a little more") before lobbying for a reformed definition of genius, one that rejects the self-directed language of death and suffering. About the burden on artists to maintain sole custody of their talent she says, "It's like asking somebody to swallow the sun." Gilbert favors a more passive, classical notion of creativity, where artistry flows not from but through the artist.

The extra-individual theory does seem preferable to dying a thousand deaths a day in the name of better than so-so art. But Gilbert removes the causal connection between hard spiritual labor (call it *suffering* if you must) and what we instinctively recognize as its product: deeply committed, transcendent, *necessary* art. And yet her fundamental question persists: Why does there seem to be a high correlation between those willing to *die* and those, whether driven by some devouringly personal or insidiously public imperative, who actually perish?

The idea of the artist as exemplary sufferer, as Susan

Sontag pointed out, was a modern creation, one derived from an essentially Christian sensibility, where suffering puts the pilgrim in touch with his true self. If a suffering soul is considered more authentic, and we look to artists to seek out the truth, on some level the more an artist suffers the more truthful we believe her to be. That attitude permeated a newly psychologically and self-aware culture so quickly and so deeply that it became impossible to say what came first, the ideal or the artists who exemplify it. Aspiring artists began to seek out opportunities to suffer, sacrifice, live ascetically. Or they felt themselves unfit for the task if they embodied too many otherwise valued attributes: health and well-being, affluence and easy living. Those things the rest of a secular culture could enjoy knowing the artists were out there suffering for them, assuaging what religious guilt remained.

Beyond all that, I want to say, good art is good art, and good art is timeless. I also believe that no work of art can or should be entirely separated from its time. But the degree to which a creative pursuit and its context are shackled together only intensifies; too often the story we attach to it seems in danger of subsuming even good art altogether.

Often we have a sense of resignation when those who move us profoundly—who *die* for us—die in an unnatural or untimely way. They were too pure or just too fucked-up to live, we agree. "Oh, what's the use?" critic David Edelstein wrote in his review of *This Is It*, the film compiled from Michael Jackson's final concert rehearsals. "He was a mess and destined to self-destruct." Even a friend of Judy Garland's admitted that his first thought upon hearing of her death was, "Yes, why not? It was inevitable, wasn't it?" Arthur Miller used that same word—*inevitable*—about his former wife Marilyn Monroe.

America is not a country otherwise known for its fatalism. Fatal optimism, maybe. And yet when it comes to our most celebrated artists, we speak easily of destiny and determinism, free will and inevitable fate. We slip into the language of myth and prophecy.

A few things seem to be going on there. When rationality and the promotion of "realness" rule a culture, conditions become ripe for a sort of lizard-brain backlash. Nietzsche believed Greek tragedy to be a perfect art form because it balances Apollonian idealization and individualism with the darkness of Dionysian reality, where human beings are bound by a sense of "primordial unity." A play like *Oedipus Rex* is a masterpiece in part because it is *useful* to the public; by catalyzing and imploding our most basic fears, suffering is set into its proper balance and tragedy becomes a source of affirmation.

We discount our own participation in popular culture, as though great tragedies can only play out in repertory theaters or come clothed in togas. But in the same way that these artists show us ourselves the way we'd like to be, their dissolution gives us a way to enter a discussion about death that has otherwise been all but silenced. These modern tragedies don't yield a similar balance in part because both sides of the Nietzschean equation—science versus art; the self-sacred *one* versus the animal *all*—are currently out of control, having metastasized to the point that they effectively snapped the thing balancing them. Now they roll around the cultural landscape freely, occasionally knocking into each other and thus conceiving the terms of our shared stories, which in the case of our fallen cult heroes has come to feel less like the rebirth of tragedy and more like tragedy stillborn. If the last century of American popular culture has taught us anything, it's that that stuff's gotta come out somewhere.

Europe did it all first, of course. Their shift toward cult heroism began a century earlier, around the time in which John Keats lived and—perhaps more important—died. In one of the several portly bios of the young bard, author Andrew Motion describes the particular period in English history that allowed for Keats—a poet who felt himself unknown at the time of his tubercular death in Rome at age twenty-five—to become wildly, posthumously famous.

Motion writes of England's old feudal order being reorganized, after the end of the Napoleonic Wars in 1815 and in the wake of a trade and manufacturing boom, into a social structure vested in "money, property, talent, secular belief, parliament, the middle class, and an industrial class of laborers." England was reborn as "a self-conscious nation. They encouraged a cult of heroes (ranging from Spenser and Shakespeare to Nelson and Wellington) and cultivated a sense of shared values." The English, in short, "fell in love with themselves . . . smothering differences and difficulties in order to create the image of a united nation."

This was the world in which Keats wrote his best poems, and it subtracts nothing from his genius to note that this was the England eager to inscribe his work and his myth into the pantheon only after his early death in 1821.

If World War I had a reanimating effect on America's sociocultural infrastructure, with World War II the transformation was manifest. The New Deal, the rise of the middle and labor classes, and a focus on talent, fortune, and property created the conditions for Americans to truly—and then at their considerable leisure—fall in love with themselves. Our cult heroes, in the new era of the moving image, were more often movie stars and athletes than writers, although politicians with great hair and star quality could still contend. Initially the value placed on the celebrated had some correlation to their ability. Stars were expected to sing and dance as well as act and be beautiful. Politicians had to demonstrate their talent for perfecting the union, for getting shit done.

Slowly, perhaps inevitably, self-consciousness slid into self-obsession. By midcentury, the bones of Theodore Dreiser's *American Tragedy* (published in 1925, a psychic twin to Fitzgerald's boom-as-bust *Gatsby*) were being reassembled to tell the stories of our cult heroes. We thrilled most when they could commit to its full trajectory: humble beginnings, uncommon gifts, bridling ambition, discovery, stardom, hubris, excess, downfall, death. Monroe, Dean, and Elvis Presley are the holy trinity of this particular denomination. In the postglamour 1960s and early '70s, rock musicians—Jim Morrison, Janis Joplin, Jimi Hendrix, Brian Jones—were more often martyrs to the faith.

Even as the cornerstones of the cult of tragic greatness were being set and our lives grew more sheltered and domesticated, the public's appetite for realism was sharpening. The "Method" hit Hollywood in the early 1950s, and its explosion of what was false or mimetic in performance reflected and fueled this hunger. Actors following Russian pioneer Constantin Stanislavski's sense-memory method were encouraged to infuse their characters with past experiences and personal psychology, and audiences internalized the idea of acting as a form of self-dramatization. The strengthening pop machine brought us that much further into actors' lives. We began following an artist's life at least as closely as her career; eventually the two were married in a public narrative bound by the need for a strong dramatic arc. Andy Warhol made the earliest and most indelible comment on the permeability of this popular mythology with his coterie of invented "superstars"—damaged socialites and hard-luck drifters whom he packaged in the look and story that sold. You no longer had to *die* for your audience, although often and one way or another, you wound up dead.

In the pre- and postmillennial decades the growing preoccupation with the private lives of public figures converged with and was quickly overtaken by a parallel obsession with fame itself. As tabloids and tabloid TV evolved, inventing an audience and its appetite for the "real" story behind the star, we sought to reveal our heroes to be more like us than unlike us. By closing the gap between stars and their audience, it was permissible—even logical—to declare open season on the fame they enjoyed.

3

Socialism is . . . above all an atheistic phenomenon, the modern manifestation of atheism, one more tower of Babel built without God, not in order to reach out toward heaven from earth, but to bring heaven down to earth.
　　　　—Fyodor Dostoyevsky, *The Brothers Karamazov*

When I was growing up, the centripetal fascination with old-fashioned stardom was about to give way to the entitlements of the famous age. We became more concerned with the things we *deserved* to know about public figures and what we were *meant* to be ourselves. Talent was no longer the main thing you needed to get over; if you could master a couple of the star narrative's bullet points and look good in your underwear, the public would take you on as a boarder and barely hold a grudge. We moved toward an age of celebrity simulacra like Paris "This Is Just a Character I Play" Hilton, and the word *icon* became so widely and ill-used that *The New York Times* banned it from its pages. The new celebrity economy seemed unstoppably bound for a kind of nirvana: an inelasticity of demand for this kind of synthetic entertainment meant we could eventually all wind up "entertaining" each other, generating our own subnarratives of stardom and feeding the parts of ourselves instantly gratified by recognition, "followers," our own names in little pixelated lights.

A mean patch of briar lies between our parallel cravings for stories that are "real" and those with mythic dimensions, and some of our best artists have found themselves tangled up in it. Anyone who has posted a picture of herself toasting champagne with the VIPs from a pit of self-loathing or tweeted the day's workout stats while weeping into a quart of raspberry sorbet has felt a tiny measure of this particular sting for themselves. The Internet is the ultimate realist medium—real people, real time, real messy—yet everything about the way we use it to perform our lives (and to a certain extent our culture) for one another confirms the manufactured terms of our beloved reality entertainment. It's all about the edit.

That we seem intent on forgetting this suggests the extent to which we are drifting from a shared sense of reality. The line between performer and performance is long gone. The line between performer and audience continues its slow fade. In a time when all of the information we consume in a day—whether it's a news report out of Libya or a YouTube search for a Billie Holiday song or a long-forgotten friend's post on your Facebook wall—falls under the rubric of "content," the line between performers is blurring as well. After national self-consciousness comes a nation of self-conscious individuals, and after that a homogenization of the nation's central precepts: money, property, and public recognition shift from shared values to rights. Which is how they are fed back to us, until suddenly the health of an entire country depends on the constant retail of fiction: stories about homes we might own, stocks that might soar, how we might look, the lives we might lead and more crucially advertise in a kind of panicked, perpetual present haze of—and I would urge you to consider the term—*status updates*.

The new American dream is to build a really bitching personal brand, and the result of all that tap dancing on all those individual platforms is a pervasive kind of narrative decadence. We race to consume and regurgitate the hour's large and small events for each other like patricians in a postmodern vomitorium—to know them first, translate them into bitter capsule form fastest, and be shocked or stirred or perceived as in any way less than totally savvy about these things the least. Even within our self-contained realities we become dulled to what's real and what's not, and further desensitized to what lies behind our fellow performers' virtual scrims. From the vantage of the individual platform, even the narrative of tragic greatness seems less a product of secular anxiety—a sort of surrogate Christian allegory—than one more of the stories we devour out of self-interest. We take heart instead of horror in the idea that anyone can be famous, but we are performers with no interest in dying for each other. It seems related that actual death is by far the most awkward thing for the Internet to handle. Because it's so real.

4

When I was nine, I saved up for my first biography, a pulpy, mass-market life of Michael Jackson, the kind with scratchy paper and those cold, thick-paged pictures in the middle. I didn't own *Thriller*. I didn't need to own *Thriller*—*Thriller* was circulating in the water supply—but I wanted that book.

For a while it became a part of my body. I carried it around, slept with it, and spent afternoons cradling it on the couch. I studied Michael's modest upbringing, homing in on the first appearance and acknowledgment of his talent. I thrilled to the timeline of its development—from the moment it was discovered, then discovered again, then once again, until it made its way to me. I sought out the story, hoping in some sense to organize the energy irradiating my television screen.

Because despite being an enormously gifted and dexterous vocalist, Michael was first and then foremost a visual phenomenon: See how young he is! Look at those little feet go! And with his brothers, the way talent separates itself! And now see how handsome! How lithe and graceful and *literally sparkling*!

Michael was a dancer, sure, but more than that a *mover*. For what would become the biggest performance of his life, the 1983 Motown 25th Anniversary concert, Jackson chose to lip-synch to "Billie Jean." I became a student of his charisma that night, convinced there might be some kind of proof for the exchange of energy between his body and mine. For me the charge of his performances always carried a postscript to self—not to get myself famous or become rich enough to keep a baby chimp, but to learn, literally and otherwise, how to *move*.

Movie is the shorthand that preceded *talkie*. But it's the latter term that faded away. It's the movement that sets the form apart (*Action!*), and the beauty of bright, moving bodies that transfixes. In that sense, Michael was a movie star in the same way Elvis was a movie star even before he shook his business in *Blue Hawaii*. They were basically made for motion pictures. If anything, Elvis's acting career, in neutering and homogenizing him, subtracted from his movie-star-ness. Eventually he reclaimed it with a musical TV special, during the taping of which he famously ejaculated in his pants; even little Elvis died for us. Michael insisted on calling his videos "short films," and the producers of the Academy Awards, who included him in their 2010 "In Memoriam" montage, apparently agreed.

On a Saturday morning a year or so after reading the Michael Jackson biography, I settled in front of the TV, fast-forwarding through the commercials with my remote arm raised up high. Devoted to keeping my moves current, every Friday I set the VCR to tape *Friday Night Videos*, which aired well past my bedtime. The show often had guest hosts; on the weekend in question it was a tiny woman in welding shades, Yoko Ono, and her sweet-faced son.

They were there to mark the fifth anniversary of the death of her husband, John. His story, sketched out in brief, evocative strokes, shook me to the bottom of my pink flannel jam-jams. I watched the "Imagine" video over and over, contrasting it with the footage of a younger John in pageboy caps and Pierre Cardin suits, the black-and-white Beatles taking over the world. And that was pretty much it. From that moment in 1985 until the year punk broke, I rode out an especially barren period in popular music on a strict diet of John Lennon's Beatles, supplemented—sometimes even surpassed—by every band bio, memoir, and history I could get my hands on. And I did have to lay actual hands on them, back when mining data was a more physical ordeal.

What John Lennon introduced me to, together with the great pleasure of his music, was the culturally engraved narrative of tragic greatness. Where Michael Jackson was at an apex, still walking on the moon, Lennon's death had completed his story. That particular combination of greatness and tragedy punched out a ten-thousand-piece puzzle inside me. His life seemed to me thrillingly, ineluctably merged with his art, and his murder an act against that art so total and devastating it could hardly be fathomed, and never at length.

5

My only clear and openly publicized objective for the future, from the time I began to consider it, was to get myself to New York. At sixteen I rode a Greyhound into Manhattan with the rest of my drama class, where the objective crystallized into a many-pointed ache. We visited the Actors Studio and bought fake IDs in Times Square; I finagled permission to stake out the Letterman show. It was as I thought—the city where you made yourself happen—and I swore I'd be back. A dedicated drama geek, I quelled private ambitions to act with a steady course of magical thinking, frustrating my teacher more than once by auditioning and then ditching on the callback. I thought I was battling the Canadian impulse against distinction, the mortification of wanting something too much.

It took me several years and one disastrous monologue from *Come Back to the Five and Dime, Jimmy Dean, Jimmy Dean* to understand that being temperamentally unsuited to acting didn't mean I couldn't find a way to *perform*. Though all of my daydreams were about standing in front of people and holding their attention somehow—emoting, dancing, yodeling—I lacked the wiring to connect a growing shyness in the world with my inner showbiz slave. If every fantasy musical sequence in every teen movie ever is correct, the specific quality of that longing is a condition of being a modern teenager. In many ways high school is just Hollywood without money: we make stars and audiences of each other. We watch each other all day and, if it can be arranged, all night too. We learn how to behave and what we're drawn to, the people with presence. I made studies of the kids around me, drawn almost gravitationally toward those who held my attention. I longed to observe my classmates undetected but refused to wear my glasses. With their faces softened I couldn't tell who was looking back.

When I think of this I think of Luke, the enigmatic power forward I followed around until he gave in. If Luke felt like a flesh-and-blood star, I had chosen better than I knew. Older, a diffident hockey player with a brother in the NHL, he was the first one to put me on his knee and get me onto both of mine. The last time I saw him he was naked and rampaging through a party-ruined backyard—the way all of those nights ended. But there was something new and unpleasant in the slant of the evening, something precipitous. The outdoor lights were blinding, whiting out the faces that weren't cast into shadow. We crashed into each other helplessly, as though the years of studying and negotiating these same bodies had finally driven us mad. As though suddenly aware of having stayed too long and clutched too many red plastic cups at the carnival. His antics were getting darker and more dangerous; there was a new viciousness in the way Luke hurled his body around. I can see his Vitruvian silhouette cut out by the floodlights. I hadn't yet graduated but high school was clearly over. He was shaking both fists above his head and roaring when I turned to a friend, chilled, and said I didn't think he'd make it to twenty-one.

In fact he got to twenty-eight. From what I understand, he had fallen into the traps set by his beauty, which was extreme. Modeling, bodybuilding, and the attendant obsessions and excesses. He always told people he'd go young, we all remember that now. I saw him in a dream the night I heard, clearer than I had in a decade. He pulled me into the center of a party to slow dance, but his phone kept interrupting with text messages written in coded gibberish. Soon he slipped out of my arms and walked out the door, the exact walk I didn't know I remembered so well. I followed him one more time and found him running toward a pier. I'd just started to make up some ground when I saw him skitter off the platform and hit the water with a smack. A few days later I was told it was suicide, but no one knows for sure, or wants to say.

6

Jack Warner, the head of Warner Bros. studio, did not take the news of James Dean's death well. He had placed a sizable bet on *Rebel Without a Cause*, which was weeks away from its release, and the star had made a sucker of him. "Nobody will come to see a corpse!" Warner scoffed. Well, isn't it pretty to think so.

Times were changing; even the experts were still figuring out this new medium's special dispensations. It had not yet become as clear as it would in the wake of Dean's death that part of the pull of the movies was the way that they intertwined heavenly visions of human life with the suggestion of death and resurrection. Quentin Tarantino makes indelible use of this interplay in *Inglourious Basterds*, when a woman is revived moments after her death—on a disintegrating screen and then an undulating veil of smoke—to deliver a vow of vengeance. Although the movies would seem to provide a modern platform for the work of Greek tragedy, it's probably not a coincidence that we began to lose touch with the conditions of death and loss just as a potent medium and its proofs of immortality came into view.

We don't really favor body viewings in this country. There seems to be some class snobbery in it, as if only religious peasants could be into something so earthy. Our leaders no longer lie in state in the traditional sense; their caskets are covered in flags or smothered in lilies and laurel. (Ironically, the ever-present photographic threat may have much to do with that; it seems telling that most of us still agree that recorded pictures of a corpse are disrespectful, if not sacrilegious.) Call me a Catholic peasant, but I think there is something to the viewing ritual: in our private lives it reminds us of the limits of our bodies and confirms a loss that can otherwise seem unfathomable; with public figures it provides essential evidence that even the great and powerful must die. Today we watch the big funerals on television or online as spectacles, performing our responses to performed death in real time. Perhaps the closest we get to a culturally bound reckoning with mortality is the way we study the final scenes of a star's life, as though they might yield the abiding secret—again, a secret embedded inside the moving image—of how a human being can be here one second and gone the next.

Needless to say, the kids went a little crazy for *Rebel Without a Cause*, and Jack Warner was obliged to eat his stubby tie. Since Dean and *Rebel* it has become something of a tradition that a posthumous artifact be delivered as part of the celebrity mourning ritual. As news carries ever quicker and video clips stream ever faster, that ritual begins in the seconds after a death announcement hits the Internet. Instead of waiting six weeks to watch a final film (although we still do that too), a kind of impromptu farewell performance is cobbled from 911 recordings, often pathetic final public appearances, B-roll of a body being wheeled from a building (the footage of Marilyn Monroe blanketed over on a stretcher and the peeks into the room where she died is a point of origin for this kind of thing), surreptitious morgue snaps, autopsy reports, and bleary security clips (Diana on a haunting loop, forever passing through that revolving door).

With someone like Whitney Houston, a pop superstar who slipped away in the bathtub of a Beverly Hills hotel in February of 2012, there is a sudden rush to return the artist to her prime. Alongside the tawdry police-blotter gawking, people share YouTube clips of old performances and iTunes explodes with sales. Within a day of Houston's death publicists were circulating bulletins about the cash crop already being planted on her grave. "She died young, tragically, and mysteriously," one blared, "the three hallmarks of a value investment."

At the time of her death, Houston had a film awaiting release—a value investment, no doubt, but also an opportunity for her fans to mourn together. In the meantime, final images of her were made public even before she died—frantic paparazzi shots of Whitney Houston leaving last night's party. Most felt like fragments: she appears disheveled, even a little wild, in a short black dress ruched to her body. Hair hangs in her face, and as always her gleaming skin appears to be a single high note away from breaking into one of her famous flop sweats. She is partially hidden by others or seems to be twisting away from the camera with bared teeth, yelling or having just yelled. Together the photos give the feeling of a predatory altercation in progress; this is a woman who couldn't walk to her car without producing images out of a Picasso detail. Some were helpfully cropped to direct your attention to points of interest and together cataloged the scratches on her wrist, the liquid—blood? wine?—running down her leg, the distended belly in profile.

They called her bloated, but we've all been watching Whitney Houston's body for long enough to know that what little extra weight she has on her she carries up front. It's kind of lovely, actually, and the most mortal hint of her most of us ever got. But in the same way that nothing illuminates the body's divinity the way talent does, rarely does a body appear more wretched to us, more useless and husklike, than when that kind of talent is destroyed or disappears too soon. And so the sadistic theme of the past decade's coverage of her life was fulfilled in the hours after those pictures were published: habeas Whitney.

7

It's the television programs that drive home how we have come to crave these stories. *Behind the Music*, *A&E Biography*, and *E! True Hollywood Story* have broken the formula into beats and commercial breaks. Because the narrative arc is now paramount, *A&E* can get away with a one-hour "biography" of Amy Winehouse that contains fewer than six seconds of her actual music. These kinds of shows air with a persistence that would make a North Korean broadcaster proud. They also share a ruthless structural genius: unless its subject is already dead, each episode is understood to be an unresolved, changeable document—downfall, decay, and sudden or premature death are just a few edits and a rebroadcast away. Within days of Heath Ledger's 2008 death we could watch his whole story play out, now new and improved with its "tragic" and, let's face it, more satisfying final act.

Because they are cheap and there are many hours to fill, you don't have to be a lodestar of tragic greatness—a Whitney or a Michael—to get the treatment or have anything much to do with Hollywood to fuel a *True Hollywood Story*. Our appetite has grown deep and indiscriminate; the demand is too great to be met by the few brontosauric talents still roaming the landscape. It takes too long to invest in the real thing anyway: we lack the attention span required to sustain an artist's forty-year career, and the market is no longer built for that kind of longevity. We rely on corporations to mass-farm artists seasonally and look to the story of Elvis wandering into Sun Records, Madonna at the Danceteria, or Michael Jackson being shepherded into the presence of Berry Gordy as relics of an almost adorably organic past.

Instead faded teen idols, troubled B-listers, and reality stars like Anna Nicole Smith have become the tragic-star narrative's bread and butter. On a twenty-four-hour news cycle, squeezing tragic ecstasy from these stories is a tall order even when our most cherished artists are the subjects. The substitutes get the same forensic treatment, but the results are that much grimmer. Within hours of child star Corey Haim's death in early 2010, a popular entertainment site carried the banner headline "VIDEO: First look at home where Corey Haim died." As though we had all been waiting for it. Another gossip site released the 911 call documenting the sudden death of Brittany Murphy in late 2009. For ten minutes, listeners are invited to imagine the actress's lifeless body on the floor as her husband counts off chest compressions and her mother falls to animal keening. Many of the comments on the Murphy 911 call expressed bewilderment and self-disgust, as if those who clicked through had expected to hear something other than an audio recording of a young woman dying in her mother's arms.

Every few weeks now, it seems, this kind of thing hits a fresh apex. All along the collision of cravings for the "real" and its inverse—escape from reality—is breeding spiritual confusion, especially when it comes to the stories we tell about things that used to matter to us, that we used to do well. Instead of drawing collective succor from supernaturally gifted individuals, we're left with sucking the private lives of lesser and no-talents dry, drifting that much further from a meaningful idea of what it means to *die*.

8

In October 2009, a young woman thrust a flyer into my midsection as I entered the midtown Manhattan theater where Michael Jackson's *This Is It* was making its world premiere. I folded it into my bag and found a seat. In his live-from–Los Angeles introduction of the documentary, cobbled together after Jackson's death from rehearsal footage, choreographer Kenny Ortega called it "the last, sacred documentation of our leader and our friend." When it was over, the dead man having danced and sung and issued dazed protestations of L-O-V-E for his long-suffering crew, I pulled out the densely printed piece of paper. It was an urgently worded warning about all of the things we weren't going to see that night, things hidden "by those who are making a profit from the screening of this movie." Michael was not well, the flyer said. Two color photos were offered as proof: 1997 Michael—athletic, vital, and sheathed in tailored lamé —and 2009 Michael, with his sunken chest and two red licorice strips for legs. His management was working him to death; it was Colonel Tom Parker all over again.

The flyer only spelled out what we were all thinking; some of us were there specifically because of those thoughts. The hope, running beneath the surface of the average viewer's mixture of conflicted penitence and morbid curiosity, was that this "sacred documentation" would retrofit some evidence of suffering, of ultimate sacrifice, to Michael Jackson's story. Traditionally, the posthumous artifact completes the story of tragic greatness by allowing a star's public to implicate and then exonerate themselves from responsibility for his or her death.

"So far as we feel sympathy," Susan Sontag wrote in *Regarding the Pain of Others*, her examination of the moral complexities engaged by images of human suffering, "we feel we are not accomplices to what caused suffering. Our sympathy proclaims our innocence as well as our impotence." When it comes to our most blighted stars, the generation of this sympathy is both an indulgence and a relief. In Jackson's case, anything short of drooling catatonia would do. He was transformed from an industry joke and fifty-cent freak show back into an exalted deity, and all it took was a glimmer of the old magic and a few well-executed dance steps.

In the same book, Sontag refers to a gruesome photo that Georges Bataille kept on his desk. Of the 1910 picture of a Chinese prisoner being subjected to death by a thousand cuts, Bataille wrote, "This photograph had a decisive role in my life. I have never stopped being obsessed by this image of pain, at the same time ecstatic and intolerable." Sontag explores this response, comparing the subject to Saint Sebastian: "[Bataille] is saying that he can imagine extreme suffering as something more than just suffering, as a kind of transfiguration. It is a view of suffering, of the pain of others, that is rooted in religious thinking, which links pain to sacrifice, sacrifice to exaltation—a view that could not be more alien to a modern sensibility, which regards suffering as something that is a mistake or an accident or a crime."

If Sontag's assertion is true in a personal sense—and I

am not convinced it is—when applied to the pain of others, it is refuted by almost every facet of modern celebrity culture. Still uncertain is whether our attraction to publicly staged suffering is as deeply rooted in religious thinking as it has long seemed. In the case of widely acknowledged talents like Kurt Cobain and Michael Jackson, pain was linked to sacrifice, and sacrifice eventually to exaltation. That is how that story goes. And yet more and more that telling is the exception to the rule. For the Greek tragedians suffering was a key to knowledge—less for the sufferer than for those looking on. That the exploitation of washed-up models, sex-tape curios, former child stars, and anonymous tormented civilians is currently paying for half of the advertising on television suggests that the hunger we are sloppily trying to satisfy is less for holy transfiguration than tragic catharsis. But finding meaning in popular mythology is less and less possible when we consume these cut-rate knockoffs of a master narrative while eating cucumber sushi alone at our desks. What that produces is the opposite of ecstasy.

"People don't become inured to what they are shown—if that's the right way to describe what happens," Sontag wrote, "because of the *quantity* of images dumped on them. It is passivity that dulls feeling. The states described as apathy, moral or emotional anesthesia, are full of feelings; the feelings are rage and frustration."

9

Catholics are taught not to use the word *worship* with regard to anyone but God Himself. And although the extreme adulation of any one of us would seem inherently dangerous, the need to single each other out seems as equally an intrinsic part of our nature. The fight against that nature, some say, has led to everything worth anything in Western civilization. It has also led to a degree of self-consciousness that precludes the outlet of tragedy or even traditional cults of personality; whatever role each played in facilitating a kind of cultural health has been ceded. Yet our appetite for myth persists, like an embarrassing growl from within.

The great twentieth-century tragedies bordered on Grecian in their balance of the enlightenment of individualism and the darkness of its dissolution. We followed these stories in real time, sometimes over decades, and found meaning in their full expression. But the terms of realism began to interfere with the stories themselves, and their mythology became a marketable commodity—something to be broken down and sold off for parts. The institution now requires little more than willing bodies to run smoothly, mass-producing a form of popular tragedy that doesn't leave room for more than a quick revel in the misfortune of others. Apollo has left the building, and it behooves us to wonder what becomes of a culture left to its own undirected desires and devices. Without gods, in other words, is everything permitted?

It's hard for me to feel anything other than lucky that I caught the wave just before it crashed. That I got a taste not only for death but *dying*. The stories were too powerful to resist, and because I wore the T-shirts and bought the books and slid a little too passively along the vector of celebrity intrigue, I am implicated in the current state of affairs. I am part of the reason that the *National Enquirer* is now eligible for a Pulitzer Prize. I am responsible for the irreversible mutation in the narrative of tragic greatness: I've been here this whole time, clicking confusedly away, reshaping the stories that matter and the way they get told.

And yet I can't regret it. I don't. Because I saw Michael Jackson move and in a single, seismic heartbeat I wanted to know everything, about everything. Funny that it seemed less possible to be like him than to *be* him. I longed to become that sublimity, to meld with it somehow. I still do.

FOURTH GRADE

NEW FRIENDS   Jillian Denise M.

ACTIVITIES   Public speaking course

ACHIEVEMENTS   Acedemic

AWARDS   acedemic

WHEN I GROW UP I WANT TO BE—

☐ Fireman   ☐ Astronaut   ☐ Mother   ☐ Airline Hostess
☐ Policeman   ☐ Soldier   ☐ Nurse   ☐ Model
☐ Cowboy   ☐ Baseball Player   ☐ School Teacher   ☐ Secretary
☑ Michael   ☐ _____
  Jackson

SIGNATURE   Michelle E Oranger

One Senior, Please

GOD: *A man down on Earth needs our help.*
CLARENCE: *Splendid. Is he sick?*
GOD: *No, worse. He's discouraged.*
                    —It's a Wonderful Life

What a dramatic animal a plane is—always racing against
some evil spirit!
                    —E. B. White, 1935

Only recently, in one of those dubiously fine moments where a dried mess of twigs accidentally ignites a perturbed little flame of observation, I noticed that the American relationship to mortality and the American relationship to flying share certain pathologies. Though routine in practice, both death and flight remain pretty outrageous in theory, which means a liberal application of denial is required to keep things running smoothly. How else could it be that despite a morbid aversion to reminders of our mortality we have normalized a form of travel that was at first quite logically regarded as the Death Wish Express and remains by any standard but the statistical one the most dangerous thing you can do while reading a Patricia Cornwell paperback. It seems significant that much of the flying experience—the personal entertainment centers, the pilfered Xanax and bihourly running of the snack cart, the contrived casualness of phrases like *cruising altitude*—is designed to obscure what's actually going on.

And yet by placing it in our hands the miracle of flight has only made us more impatient with the physical world. Specifically with the persistence of our bodies, and the ordeal of carting them across oceans or continents or just to Pittsburgh when our minds are already there and our senses tell us it's a matter of stepping up one gangplank, closing our eyes and breathing burnt, carbon monoxidic air for some amorphous duration, and stepping down another. Adding to the fastest-available mode of human transport's endemic frustrations is the recent, subtle reconception of the passenger as an anomalous piece of luggage—subject to scanning and probing, too heavy to be checked and too unwieldy for the overhead cabin. In more ways than one, modern air travel promotes a state of self-suspension. *You* were in Marrakech yesterday morning; *you* got in to Melbourne last night. But who knows what to call the thing that writhed in coach for the time gained or lost in between, except a body that cannot yet be shipped separately. Even the fearless resort to a form of Zen denial—the old zone-out—to get through. Decades—whole lives—can be bound by similar terms of distraction: a feeling of disassociation from what's really going on, how we're getting where we're going and what we have to forget to get there; the sensation of finding ourselves in strange places and not entirely understanding how it happened; our stupid bodies' finally insisting on their own limits and the limits of time. Both shaky fliers and thanatophobes are best advised to try not to think about it, which probably says it all.

———

I was flying to Halifax and contemplating my own death when I was given reason to actually confront it. Poor weather the previous evening meant Newark Liberty was jammed with hollow-eyed, white-lipped travelers at seven thirty on an April Sunday morning. A faulty check-in kiosk had buggered my first of the roughly two dozen transactions it takes to transition from person to plane passenger in 2011. I was waving to an obviously doomed agent beyond the scrum of shuffling, ticketless zombies closing in on her when the magical one-hour mark passed, then striding toward a second agent at the moment my seat was given away. Approximately two minutes later I was advised to stake out my original flight on standby; they would only print me a ticket for the next one, four hours out.

At the gate I watch the standby vultures—two women with their teenaged daughters—hover by the check-in desk, knowing they feel as entitled to my spot as I do. A middle-aged man in puffy sneakers and expertly brindled jeans is desperately trying to lose his temper with the agent on the other end of his cell phone. "This is *your guys'* fault," he insists. "It's *your* fault I'm in this position now." His voice is high and catches on the long vowels. "*You* guaran*teed* I would get on this *flight*, and now it's *not going to happen*." He's in a customer service free fall and he knows it. It's like begging someone who's stopped loving you to look you in the eye, and as painful a scene to watch. The flight is boarding now, but that doesn't stop him. "*Something needs to happen*," the man pleads, convincing no one.

Then the vultures, last in line, are flagged at the gate. There are only three seats left and four of them. The man finally dismounts from his BlackBerry, lobbing a parting curse in mid-click. You could see what it cost him, but by that point he had an audience in need of closure. For the next twenty minutes the two of us watch the women pinball between stages of acute aviation grief—denial and rage—before agreeing to a different itinerary. Then up goes puffy sneakers, like the last faithful kid in church. Ten minutes later up I go as well, making pointed, exculpatory eye contact with my fellow passengers as I find my place.

I've always enjoyed the pomp and semaphore of the seat-filling pageant—the mental blowing on the dice as the wheel spins, the scanning of faces for a signal, the hopes and dreams crushed by the last-minute arrival, the barely squelched mutual disappointment when the inevitable comes to pass, the enigmatic pointings and phrasings of the moment of reckoning: *Is that you?* Yes, it is. *Are you here?* I am.

So it was that I devastated an overgrown young man by claiming what by that point in the game any rational flier would have assimilated as an empty seat, recalibrating his mood and sense of an ultimately just world accordingly. But what followed shunted the controversial boarding of two apparent stragglers into distant memory. We waited another hour as the aggrieved foursome's luggage was rooted from the hold; a second hour piddled by after that. Halifax headwinds required extra fuel, and random bags were eventually hauled out to make room for it. It's not safe for five-ounce shampoo bottles and crumpled underpants to fly, is what I heard, but the human cargo stays. In a tone that grew more defiantly nonchalant with every update, the pilot advised us that some of our bags would arrive on a future flight. Even with routine debacles such as this it's rare to be promised future bullshit while the current bullshit is still very much in progress. *Sorry 'bout that, folks.*

The quiet of animal endurance settles over 120 tightly packed humans resigned to their fate. Not even the acquainted speak. Loathing seeps into what breathable air is circulating, and one by one people begin to drop off just to escape it. I can feel the consciousness leeching from my seatmate, whose broad shoulders and bulbous knees have a straining quality despite reasonably well-fitting street clothes. As his weight deadens, his big, bran-colored head lolls into my sight line and rears up violently, dipping back into view a beat later. I consider fixing him to my lap just to kill the suspense. I can't sleep in anything but circadian darkness and full horizontality, and after the usual bout of grotesquely Darwinian sexual fantasizing, I begin herding omens for lack of anything better or less obvious to do. The mechanical groans and sudden lurches, the inscrutable red print on the wing engine, the irresistible misfortune of narrowly avoiding my own death—and is that a ripple of worry passing over the flight attendant's face? I've never been a *bad flier*—funny how that admonishing term took hold—but I spend the remaining tarmac time waving every signal of advancing doom into the hold with little neon batons.

During our half-hour descent into Halifax, a thunderstorm grips the plane like a one-year-old conducting a wooden-spoon symphony on the kitchen floor. After about four minutes of that you start to reckon with a new reality. The density of the fog beyond the oval cutout has an absolute, anywhere quality, and though we are suddenly, miserably aware of hurtling through the sky at hundreds of miles an hour, there is no measurable progress. Only a forever kind of throttling and the disembodied, just barely unclutched arm beside mine. I am working to accept either imminent death or sustained, nauseous stasis as my future when the blacktop leaps up and a fine, exhaustlike spray shoots out from below. I tip my forehead against the window, trying to settle the gorge in my throat, and watch the wheels spinning madly, smoking like the feet of a cartoon bird with the force of our arrival.

I am heading straight to Melville Heights, a Halifax retirement home, to spend some time with my only living grandparent. The visit was prompted by a recent call from her caretakers; my mother, traveling from Toronto with her husband, Frank, is scheduled to arrive later in the evening. The cab ride from Stanfield International is long and only slightly less emetic than landing a 727 in the middle of a Maritime typhoon. The seat-belt light flashes in tiny, red protest throughout, and not for me: Esmail is the driver's name, and a little water never hurt him. We maintain the velocity at which rain droplets squiggle across the glass in great, spermatozoic patterns, converging to spawn fatter droplets in the far corners of the windshield. Esmail gestures casually to a six-car pileup in the opposite lane. "I hear about this," he says, noting detour plans to himself for the way back.

A demolished hatchback sits at the nucleus, surrounded by five vehicles at frozen angles. Beyond them a ring of fire trucks, ambulances, and police cars form a cellular wall. Certainly life had divided within it. Esmail asks me what I'm doing in Halifax, and I tell him I am visiting my grandmother. "Ahh," he says with the approving warmth such plans generally yield. "How old?" I tell him, and he nods, smiling into the mirror. "My father was ninety-five." We contemplate the silent second half of that sentence by the light of the flashing seat-belt man—ever stalwart, ever strapped in.

I had claimed Purcell's Cove as my destination, but upon arrival Esmail, already fond of correcting me, says that we are *near* Purcell's Cove, not *in* it, and cuts my fare accordingly. He hands me his card and asks after my return plans. If you need me, he says, I'll make myself available. We are talking about a taxi ride, but those words wash up on some farther shore and begin to build a hutch, where my regard for Esmail might live.

As I sign myself into the building, the smiling older woman behind Melville's front desk asks me, by way of greeting, if I am Rita's daughter.

I stop writing and look at her. "Granddaughter."

"Oh, I see," she replies brightly. "How nice."

I pen in the time and pause. "She's ninety-five you know."

"Is she!"

Yes, she is. Her age had been a source of familial pride for the past two decades: Rita Boyle, eighty-two and off to India; Rita Boyle, eighty-five and taking furloughs with her garrulous Greek boyfriend; Rita Boyle, eighty-eight and dominating at the Highland Golf Club. My grandma the movie lover, ninety years old and still driving her little red Sunfire to "the show" twice a week, often collecting less mobile—and younger, she always noted—old ladies on the way. This is the story we liked to tell.

At her eighty-fifth birthday party, an event she agreed to despite her innate reluctance to cede any ground to time, my mother toasted my grandmother's "will to win," a phrase I did not soon forget. I stood up and said a few words as well, "hero" being one that I remember. This is how we all want to wind up, we said. This was someone who seemed to be cheating expectation, nature, biology, and defining for herself what a long life could be. What I did not grasp then was the extent to which my grandmother's late-life iconoclasm was not an extension of her adult life but a complete inversion of it, as if she had earned an autonomous self, paid in decades at the mercy of expectation, nature, perhaps even biology.

Clinical depression is one of the growing tally of mental illnesses made up solely of self-reported symptoms. Medically defined it is a set of emotional, psychological, somatic, and behavioral symptoms occurring over time. Lack of appetite and sleeplessness, for instance, combined with feelings of worthlessness, despondence, and suicidal ideation, if experienced for more than two consecutive weeks, would meet the diagnostic criteria for a major depressive disorder. These were the symptoms that had brought my grandmother to Halifax—where my mother's younger sister Jeannette, a psychologist, is based—in 2007, about a year after she woke up in her London, Ontario, apartment feeling "bummed."

In retrospect, it was a poignantly casual choice of adjective. She used it for several weeks, as if to curb her condition by force of descriptive will. *Bummed* is not part of the *DSM* checklist; *bummed* is the common cold of mental illness. Oh, you're bummed? *Too bad; feel better!*

Then, just as summer and her beloved golf season were about to begin, Rita ended a call with my mother with an expression of love—pretty much a first for them. It was as if, my mother told me years later, Rita knew she was about to go "down the rabbit hole." As if to say goodbye.

Before her reinvention, in her late seventies, as a silverbacked picara, I had not formed any defining ideas about my grandmother. Not particularly loving, or present, she wasn't cold, or absent either. Although we lived in the same city while I was growing up, I didn't see much more of her than birthdays and holidays obliged. She is a figurative outline in my early memory; whereas my paternal grandmother, Margaret, comes to me with a sensory fullness and emotional freight—the reward, perhaps, of the inscriptive force of her personality: everything she said and did seemed to tell the story of our family. Weeklong babysitting stints yielded forty-page novellas crafted for my parents, with highlights including my five-year-old self's acquisition and subsequent overuse of the word *attractive*, and abridged transcripts of the phone calls she took from each of her five other children. It never occurred to me to wonder why one grandmother would travel seven hours to look after us when another lived a short drive away.

Rooted in the same northern-Ontario home where my father was raised, Margaret Orange embraced the role of matriarch, bearing three children with my grandfather Robert, a widower who already had three toddlers (including my father) when they married in 1948. She was a powerfully social woman and became socially powerful in turn. Impeccably mannered and a little imposing, she was the kind of antiquated lady who might advocate for women's education but never learn to drive. If you were a well-behaved child, her warmth was infinite.

She was my first pen pal. I wear the University of Toronto ring she never took off and graduated from the same school—where my parents met—sixty years after she did. Three generations in a sentence, on a finger. Tough to compete with that even if you wanted to, and Rita was disinclined to play family narrator. A champion gabber, talking with her was like watching someone unpack a rummage closet: you were less a partner than an implied observer, waiting for the last pack of mummified golf tees to be placed at your feet.

I never knew much about my mother's family, who seemed

half-composed compared to the epic sprawl of the Sudbury Oranges. Watching Rita endure her eighty-fifth birthday party, I realized that her story had eluded me in part because it was under constant and private revision. It was told only in the present tense, and then under great editorial restraint.

Marie Antoinette Rita Meunier was born in 1915 in Montreal, Quebec, the second of five children born to a redoubtable French Canadian woman and a proportionally degenerate gambling man. The family moved to Toronto, Ontario, when she was a girl; financial burdens forced Rita to drop out of school at fourteen to work as a full-time secretary. In 1939, Rita and Latham Boyle—a red-cheeked Irish Protestant with a big laugh and a bigger temper—huddled into the sacristy of Toronto's Sacré Coeur church. His parents had threatened not to attend the wedding; her Roman Catholic parish insisted on protecting the Eucharist from heathen cooties. Latham played hockey for the Toronto Maple Leafs' farm team—the Marlboros—as a young man and was deployed to the Queen Charlotte Islands, off the coast of British Columbia, during World War II. He returned home months after my mother, Jacqueline Claire, was born and paid the hospital bill—a grand total of $54.50 in pre-health-care Canada—from afar. The check was accompanied by a note:

Dear Rita,   RBY June 14
Jackie has sort of taken care of my membership at
Cedarbrae [golf course] for the year 1944 for which
believe it or not I am most happy.

                                        Latham
P.S. Save this + we will show it to her when she is twenty.

When she was just shy of that age, my mother and her sister were the subject of a Hamilton, Ontario, newspaper article titled "Moving Didn't Hurt Jackie, Jeannette." The sales job Latham took upon returning to Toronto was itinerant, which resulted, among other things, in my mother's enrollment in seven different schools before her high school graduation. Written in the blithe, can-do style of the days when the local paper would publish your address along with your name, the op-ed seeks to reassure a generation taught to equate a thriving family with a stable community and home equity that even those who must follow the work can have it all. The Boyle girls' story, which ends with scholarships and my mother's placement at a good university, "should prove to many families who get transferred now and then, it is possible to live a rich, full life and do well in spite of these small annoyances."

It's a neat little bite of 1962, that clipping—pert, narrow, and yet deeply insinuating. That it has a place of honor in my grandmother's scrapbooks—which I hauled out, to her dismay, whenever I visited—seems inevitable. Being named in the paper without having committed a felony or otherwise disgraced your family was (and, to a lesser extent, still is) a major event. But beyond that—say, fifty years beyond it—the clipping suggests the way the stories we are told about ourselves develop an agency outside our control, whether one is a public figure languishing in a tide of bad press or a private citizen pulled into the cultural narrative. In this case, a family of neo-gypsies is held up as an example of what it means to persist in a restless new world.

In my memory the article was hard evidence of my mother's triumph, which felt often enough like evidence of my lack. For us, the usual patterns of "in my day" parent-child coercions had a particular design: I was attached, in the most physical way, to the comforts of family and community; my mother believed change put hair on your chest and prepared you for a world that favors the adaptable. Our crucible in this regard was my refusal, at age eleven, to move from London to Toronto, where she lived, to attend a fancier middle school. For me it was never a consideration; if my attachment to home was a weakness, I had no interest in the alternative. The one-bedroom apartment of my mother's disappointment had many mansions.

Only in recent years have I learned that my grandparents never owned a home, that the constant displacements were a strain on Rita's mental stability, that my mother was still sharing a bed with her sister when she graduated from that good university. Only recently has it occurred to me that chagrin scans as an unspecified emotion to a child, and chagrined is precisely how my mother felt about that article—a complex scenario and its consequences overwritten in the authoritative abstract. I hardly suspected that she had been dazzled by my father's family—with their open-house chaos and habit of lingering at the table for heated, postmeal debates—in the exact way that I was. There was little sense that I would ricochet between the same competing ideas of what it means to be a woman: independent and agile versus rooted and stable. If the article left no hint that the noted scholar Jacqueline Boyle would eventually leap from cosleeping with her sister to a marriage bed and deferred career at twenty-two, certainly it was effective in keeping me off the scent of what those moves meant for my grandmother.

The second of the family's transplants, from the outer Toronto suburb of Scarborough to the eastern-Ontario city of

Kingston, triggered Rita's descent into the earliest of the depressions that carved an alpine pattern across her life. Separated from her family and friends for the first time and alone with two young children, she kept the house and organized the schooling, taking her daughters to see *Bambi*, *The Wizard of Oz*, and Gene Autry oaters, the entertainment of choice in Latham's frequent absences. But neither domestic routine nor the movable oasis of moviegoing could prevent the abyss from pulling open. Within the year she grew shrunken and opaque, functioning basically and saying little. On bad days, the kind of chiding mothers sometimes use as a scare tactic—maybe I'll just drop you home and get myself some ice cream; I'll put you out of this car if you don't cut it out—acquired the tone of a soothing mantra. In her most wretched moods she would threaten to take my barely school-aged mother and her little sister to the movie theater and leave them there. Then one day she did.

My mother doesn't remember how she got herself and her sister home, except that it was a long, bewildered trudge, her child's mind punctured by the sense that something was terribly wrong. Their afternoon's affliction suggests a rough scheme of depression itself, extreme versions of which have been described in terms of obscurity: black veils lowering; black dogs blotting out the sun; blackness indeed visible, the palette of consciousness run to an unyielding monochrome. But what cornering violence is done behind this cover? By what cunning is the formidable mechanism of a human being suspended, inverted?

Though inclined toward the idea of depression as a complex but fundamentally responsive phenomenon, when I have looked at my grandmother's face these last few years, translucent and ravened of its flesh, her eyes trained and expectant and her mouth parted on the cusp of speech, I think of it in not just clinical but conquering terms. I envision the tunneling of better angels, pursued to the ends of a quiet mind by a bouldering force, a cancer without cause, a morbid, ungoverned appetite whose ultimate, consuming will for release confuses the sufferer and then elicits her collusion. I imagine the sufferer knowing, within a last, windowed attic of consciousness, that she is in trouble; and that the tunnel, sensing a remaining source of light, will eventually seek and swallow this place too.

Loss of interest in once-pleasurable activities is a fast track to a depression diagnosis. No one had to tell Rita that the demon had returned; her daughters recognized it quickly as well. But if hope and disbelief mingled in my initial response to her sudden withdrawal, when I learned that she had stopped going to the movies, my understanding of her suffering shifted.

Many Catholics Rita's age, including my father's parents, developed a lifelong aversion to moviegoing in the 1930s—a measure of the success of the Legion of Decency, which at the back of Catholic churches posted lists of the films whose contents would condemn one's soul to hell. Save the apparently infallible *South Pacific*, my father never knew Margaret to see a film. "I think she thought movie theaters were filled with rubby-dubs," he told me, "or filthy midgets." But if Rita ever paid any heed, she was long through abnegating by the time I came along.

My first memories of both my grandmother and moviegoing are combined. She loved a matinee, though for Latham, who wore a hearing aid all his life, movie theaters were dens of frustration and extortionately priced snacks. For a year or so in the early 1980s I became her movie buddy, a sidekick invariably as excited about the chocolate-filled bulk baggies tucked into the far reaches of her purse as I was about the show. What we saw was always her choice, after all, and I'm less concerned now that I was taken to see *Arthur* and *Night Shift* as a six- and seven-year-old than saddened that I was the most viable candidate for the job.

I made my first plane trip during that period, a flight to Rita and Latham's mobile home in Tampa, Florida, on a Wardair 747 airbus. My brother and I were dressed to fly in pressed blazers and shiny shoes. Photos show us nestled into middle-row seats, heads clapped by giant headphones, his and hers comic books propped in our laps. My main memory of the flight, aside from the seizure and mastery of one more in life's long series of opportunities to prove my mettle, is the appearance before me of a shrink-wrapped cornucopia that contained, among its personalized treasures, thimble-size plastic shakers of salt and pepper. *This*, I thought, scanning the individually wrapped items for things to season, *is the life for me.*

Another photo from that trip: the moviegoers are posed in a golf cart: me on the left, properly pleased to be riding shotgun in a tiny car, Rita at the wheel, browned and shrunken, baring a few teeth in lieu of a smile. I hadn't noticed the details of her expression or posture until she pointed them out to me, two decades later, when I gifted her with a calendar featuring pictures of our family where, say, Chippendales or rare English roses might be.

"Oh," she said, recoiling at the old back-nine snap. "I can't look at that. Look at me—you can see how sick I was."

What might a child understand about that kind of illness? Death, with its absolute terms and dramatic scope, might engage a porous imagination more readily. Choosing that photo as an emblem of our bond was a clearer expression of it than I could have known. Shortly after it was taken, Rita was hospitalized for the second time, a six-week stay. During her first hospitalization, in 1969, she received electroconvulsive shock therapy that temporarily redacted her long-term memory. She was released in time for her youngest daughter's wedding.

In the moment, I let her reaction to the photo pass without comment. A reflex, maybe, and one honed with good reason. Soon after that, an outside conversation was begun, and for the first time I learned about her suffering over decades when mental illness was treated variously with indifference, quackery, barbarism, and mercenary cant. I plied family members reluctant to discuss the bad times, especially when she was doing so well. "Look at me," she'd said. It's the only reference I had ever heard her make to her depressions, or would hear.

Those years—after learning of her illness and before the relapse—formed a peak in our relations. The pattern indicated a bout of depression every ten to fifteen years, but instead of triggering an earlier onset, my grandfather's sudden death in 1987 seemed to head it off, and her renaissance commenced. She wanted to go to the show again. And she wanted to talk.

Over the years I have been told stories about her neighbors and golf buddies and grocery clerks many times over, three generations back and several marriages across, but I never heard her say her father's name. As a teenager I avoided her calls if I didn't have at least ninety minutes to spend counting the words I wedged in on one hand. During my university and early working years in Toronto, the odd letter would arrive (Rita's prodigiousness on the horn had a proportional aversion to long-distance fees), filled with news of her meals, her neighborly adventures, and her next transcontinental tour (only Antarctica went unseen).

But not until my 2003 move to New York City did our correspondence develop a meaningful rhythm. Within a couple weeks of my arrival her first letter was slipped into my mailbox, a familiar balm during those early, disorienting days. Leaving Canada for the United States was a controversial move in my family; historically the departed were rarely heard from again. Unlike Bulgarians, say, or Sri Lankans or Ugandans or even the Dutch, Canadians cannot pine openly for the land of freedom and opportunity. Because we have plenty of both, dreams of America bring the question of ego close to the surface, and Canadians find very little more unfortunate than ill-fitting britches. Pursuing a move to the States is regarded as unseemly but somewhat inevitable, like an admission to peeing in the shower, or applying to a reality show. Still, many Canadians harbor a detailed defection scenario. Mine involved being trauma-wrapped in Old Glory at the border and swept into a block-long limo bound for the land of relevance, where unlimited credit cards and an abrasive spouse await.

My parents accepted my decision to enter the film studies program at New York University, but like everyone else they had doubts. Rita, meanwhile, began slipping me provisional missives—always with a freshly pressed "greenback" folded in—every other week. It seemed the farther I went, the more interest I held for her. The encouragement was oblique, as was her way, with the exception of an early curveball sent right over home plate: "Well, you weren't going to be happy until you did it," she wrote. "Now it's done."

If proximity blurs perspective and intimacy distorts reason, perhaps the gift of the distance my grandmother has maintained throughout my life is that she's had me in focus all along.

The Melville complex, conceived in the recent tradition of elder care, gives a graduated structure to inexorable human decline. For the freshman they offer "independent living," a proto-dorm with dollhouse attractions including an on-site hair salon (shampoo and set for fifteen bucks; updo for twenty-five), a game room, and nurses roaming the halls with the day's meds nested in little plastic cups, like Mother Pharma's eggs. On another floor of the same building is the next level of care, for those who need assistance with the business of living. Across the road and down the way is Melville's nursing home, which makes no bones about its form or function and is therefore little mentioned.

My mother and my aunt settled on Melville in early 2007, when Rita's depression was proliferating beyond the means of their phone calls, meals deliveries, and biweekly visits. Toronto, though closer to her home and most of her family, was beyond consideration financially, with a five-year waiting list and starting rates in the vicinity of five thousand dollars a month for some five hundred square feet. The market is growing as steadily as the population is aging, and people like my parents are already planning for an independent dotage, refusing to be nursed into death in a curtain-lined cot, and never considering that their children might take up the cause.

Almost four years after that move, Rita is on the verge of being kicked out of independent living for various bodily insubordinations. The terms have an existential vagueness: if you can't take care of yourself, you can't stay. My own independent lifestyle couldn't stand the scrutiny.

On this, Palm Sunday, the lobby is trimmed with secular displays of psycho bunnies, mutant eggs, and an insinuating pink plastic moss. The elevators, papered with cheery reminders about the weekly meetings of the bridge club, the cribbage club, the "news and views" club, the men's club, the knitting circle, egg painting, and something called Red Fridays, tend to make me melancholy. Your every theoretical desire anticipated and presented back to you in bubbly script.

The elevator doors, also tailored to the slow-moving residents, are programmed to hang open an extra ten seconds. The halls are wide and have bars along the sides for unsteady walkers, whose ranks my grandmother has recently joined. After a knock at number 407, I open the door and peer in. Inside I see the top of Rita's head at the other end of the apartment, beyond the galley kitchen. She is sitting in a favorite chair, one of a long-lived, velveteen husband-and-wife pair. It's just the one now, the second chair having recently succumbed to an accident. Last year she was moved from a one-bedroom into a studio, her surroundings seeming to whittle in ruthless sympathy with her flesh.

"*Ohhh,*" she says, a light, wobbly sound of agreement. Rita repaints her new favorite word every time, not with new colors but a whole new palette. She watches with interest as I hump my luggage through the door. *"Hello."*

Even more frail than I remember, Rita's body is reduced to the joints beneath her black slacks and gray cotton top. Only the toes of her purple, embroidered velvet slippers touch the ground, a dainty effect that reminds me of the pride she was known to take in her appearance. Raised up tough and superthrifty in every other respect, Rita has no memory of ever washing her own hair; after her mother stopped doing it, she began a lifetime routine of weekly visits to the salon. French to her core, she ate and dressed simply but very, very well. An accomplished chef whose kitchen turned out well-distributed pots of soup and pans of muffins, her modest parcel of extra weight in later years was a constant source of resolve.

I used to puzzle over her letters, typically a newsy log of minor complaints and small but potent comforts. She would spend a paragraph describing the baking and eating of a single pineapple-coconut muffin, split and topped with cut strawberries ($1.47 a pound at Price Chopper) and cream whipped by hand, then savored with a cup of peppermint tea as rain sluiced down her balcony doors after her return from a matinee. Though I was often warmed by these private contentments, the greener, more impatient part of me—the part that was more confused all the time about how to please myself—would think, *Why is she telling me this?*

Hailing the arrival of Vidalia onions from the south in a 2004 letter, she laid out her dinner plans—calf's liver with piles of fried Vidalias and finger slices of green pepper. "It doesn't take much to please me these days," she wrote. "And I take great pleasure in all the good produce we are able to get from all over in the winter." How strange that these kitchen dispatches should read as almost radical to me now.

Today her uneaten lunch is draped with a napkin on the kitchen table. Days of upright dozing in the copper-colored chair have pressed her white-blond hair into a tufted corona. The rain is marine, soaping the windows in tidal, car-washing whorls. I first saw her like this in early 2007, during a trip to London to help clean out her apartment. I remember her drifting through the rooms, already twenty pounds lighter in her cotton nightie, as we apportioned her life's belongings. I can see Rita hovering in the kitchen doorway as my mother succumbed to the desperate mood and began shouting about uneaten pizza in the fridge, a misunderstanding that left us all spent. Beyond the shock and heartbreak of that day, what I have felt in the face of my grandmother's suffering is humility. Only a fearsome and disarming force could account for that kind of transformation, and perhaps as often as I begged it to leave her be, I prayed that it would spare me on its way.

I fill the candy dish and place it by her with a fresh glass of water. Rita leans over, ever cordial, and lifts a single chocolate-covered raisin to her mouth. I take a seat across from her, on the hard-cushioned couch she'd had re-covered in royal-purple twill a few years back, and watch her chew. We haven't really been alone since her move to Halifax. My letters are neatly filed on a nearby shelf, their envelope tops lightly frayed in the old style, back when correspondence was an art with its own set of tools. Her expression remains dazed but attentive, and I realize I had hoped for too much.

I had told myself I'd be happy just talking about the movies and would settle for the weather. But the hope that Rita would relent—the belief that she *could* relent—lingered. Part of me still believed I could make her feel the play of time working against us—that it would become unavoidable, and it was a kind of sin not to acknowledge it. It's a weakness of mine, and not only with ailing ninety-five-year-olds.

When I was twelve years old, while saying goodbye to my perfectly lively paternal grandmother under perfectly normal circumstances, I became certain, in a ghastly instant, that I would never see her again. The scene has slow-motion clarity: my dad behind the wheel, Margaret riding shotgun, and me in the back. She was heading to the train station after my drop-off at school. I thought I might draw one last hug, but Margaret remained in her seat, twisting over her left shoulder as we idled in the staff parking lot. I never lost the toddler's impulse to plank out with grief when a loved one leaves the room, or the city; like most of us I just learned to hide it better. But the awful twinge bracketing the bright, brow-lifting smile and *Goodbye, dear* she gave me—the shutter release of memory quietly engaging—was different. Six weeks later, Margaret succumbed to the gallbladder cancer that was at its steady work that morning, and throughout the days she had spent babysitting my brother and me.

That week I had taken to recording her secretly, with the Dictaphone I had requested, after coveting the one in my mother's briefcase, as a Christmas present. It felt a little sordid, but I couldn't seem to stop. During our early breakfasts, before my brother woke up, I would slip it out of my housecoat pocket—one always dressed for toast with Margaret—under the kitchen table, easing down the record button as she launched into one of her soothingly discursive stories. I didn't mention these recordings until after she had died, when everyone was too distracted to think much of it.

From then on, interrogating parting moments for signs of the inevitable became a kind of personal safety issue, like buckling up or checking the stove before you leave the house. I was always turning back to rinse a last glimpse of a loved (or, frankly, barely liked) one in developing fluid—just in case. I wanted to be on top of every story, a step ahead, and fancied I had the gift. I have a digital voice recorder now, my job requires it, and I brought it with me to Halifax.

Life at Melville is meal oriented. Once a week, a sheet of printed foolscap is slipped under each resident's door: seven days, seven dinners, five components (appetizer, entrée, starch, vegetable, dessert) per dinner, at least three options per component. A morning could be parceled to settling the forthcoming week's menu. The idea that we revert to a childlike state in old age feels condescending, too simple to be human. Illness and infirmity are unwilled dependencies, after all, and even infants, I reminded my mother when she characterized Rita's latest decline as a regression, will cry when their diaper is full.

Yet structure—particularly feeding structure—takes on a devotional strictness in the elderly that most plainly suggests the cherished routines of childhood. If life is bookended at all, it may be by the assertions of the body, and the demands that we push into dormancy as adults, believing they can be mastered, subjugated, or separated from a nimble, developed psychology. Even in depression, even when she refused much of what was on her plate, mealtime called to something basic in Rita. A two-inch stack of menus from weeks past sits on her ottoman. Unwilling to throw them out, she turns to the pile often, as if for comfort. That page of foolscap is the last evidence of preference or appetite in Rita's life; her visitors tend to examine it like an illuminated text. I was to join her that night in the dining room, a culinary battleground I had visited before. If I had any remaining innocence I left it there: it's been fifteen months since my last Melville meal, and the words *vegetable medley* still make me flinch.

Rita's stunned but pleasant look has been turned my way for fifteen minutes when she asks about my flight. I make it brief; it seems perverse to bring news of worldly monotonies into that room. This is my first mistake. A disappointed flicker in her expression confirms that a solid air-travel epic calls to that same something basic in even the semicatatonic among us. I think it's because these stories reinforce a common and yet still mildly exotic experience, making folklore of a particularly Western concern: this is what happens when you relinquish control.

During our vigil at the gate, my standby comrade had turned to me as soon as his phone call ended and repeated, in perfected narrative form, what I had just heard. This is standard introductory behavior in airports, and elsewhere, should the topic arise. Language is no barrier: the story of stranded passengers, refused vouchers, and fat-ass seatmates will be pantomimed, if it must be. Witnesses to these oaths repair to a boredom-proofed place inside themselves, politely waiting out each unexpurgated detail, then seizing the moment to reciprocate with a butt-numbing misadventure of their own.

So I go back to the beginning and give it to Rita in chapters, with character arcs and a strong moral finish. Her thin, chugging coughs signal appreciation along the way. Then the quiet returns. It's the dead air I find toughest, despite being a longtime proponent and regular practitioner of comfortable silences. Rita, on the other hand, was the most Italian French Canadian I had ever known: for her silence was death. If something about her smoke-bombing monologues was disconcerting, beyond the lack of interest in or mercy for the person trapped in their blast radius, it was the sense that they formed an offensive line against some unseen pursuant. To see Rita mute was like looking at a woman just robbed and still standing in the street, stripped of everything that identified her as an actor in the world.

My last trip to Halifax was a heartbreaker, a winter voyage marked by every available impediment, yielding only a sense of its own uselessness. Rita's surpassing indifference had been painful—usually she rallied a little—but the larger frustration was more abstract. Her company *did* have a new, childlike quality, but she was not the source of it. The point at which the elderly and the infirm slip from protagonists in their own story to players—or even pawns—in the stories of others had arrived. There but not there, she was cognizant but more withdrawn than ever. It seemed we had only our bodies and their proximity to offer, yet I felt myself malignant somehow, as though every syllable of the talk that went on without her endorsed her living disappearance. My mother had come to think of the trips as support for my aunt—there was no return on any other kind of investment—and suggested I do the same. But who was this phantom sitting among us as we chattered with forcible gaiety, supporting each other until our gums ached?

I was defeated by that trip. Though I kept up the occasional letter and phone call, when the next year's visit came around, I passed.

With two and a half hours to go to dinner service—garden salad, roasted chicken with rice and broccoli, and lemon meringue pie—I begin recording. After twenty minutes of silence and the production of a sour feeling—the deceit of experiencing a personal moment with one eye on posterity—I press stop. The rain is a CGI sea creature thrashing against the apartment's picture windows. I owe the rain money and slept with its best friend. The wind, a wingman, judders the glass in its frame. There's an electric-blue bunny in my lap, a stuffed animal mistaken for an infant by the nurse who sweeps in with the afternoon's dosage of I don't know what.

Shortly before the nurse's appearance Rita had made the effortful series of facial expressions that signal she is about to speak. We had been contemplating each other openly for a stretched-out moment. "You look like the Madonna, sitting there," she said.

A few weeks into my first semester at NYU, in the fall of 2003, a letter arrived with a trio of ticket stubs enclosed. Rita had been saving them from her weekly matinees and filling each one out with longhand impressions of the according film. They ranged from a few salient words to a sentence or three, with circling, capitalization, and underlines used for emphasis, a schema that took on a precise and—to me—thrilling grammar over what turned out to be a two-and-a-half-year project.

The saving of ticket stubs like memory chips in an external drive I understood and endorsed—as a teenager, I began tucking every one of mine into a wooden box I had painted for that purpose—but the reviews struck me as inspired. I saved her stubs together with mine and asked for more. Soon I was receiving regular shipments, telegraphic bulletins from the Rainbow Cinemas—the only functioning business left in London's failing downtown Galleria—where she could catch a show for $2.50 just as she pleased. Two-fifty is what I remember movies costing when I first ventured to the same Galleria as a kid. She didn't mind going alone anymore. When she mentioned a companion on the stub, it was usually to note how gravely the dead weight or drippy attitude next door had compromised her viewing experience.

That fall I watched films all day as part of an academic regimen, with no tickets to show for them. At night I went to the movies with a man I was seeing, and indeed it was mostly him I saw. My moviegoing equilibrium was off, and the ticket stubs were a reminder of the basic mechanism of pleasure and response—movies as they are ideally watched.

The format did not confine Rita's multitudes. Her take on *Brokeback Mountain*—"Excellent portrayal of Homosexuality in the 60's. Now let the Gays + L. live in peace (over) + marry each other + not spoil other lives. Great scenery"—was the first I knew of her thoughts on the subject. She saw everything— more than me, in those days—and as often as she applauded stories of gay liberation (*A Touch of Pink*: "Amusing. My companion didn't laugh"), the afternoon's selection ran afoul of her conservative streak. "Didn't know they were Divorce Lawyers + I am not comfortable with that Subject," she wrote about Pierce Brosnan and Julianne Moore on the ticket stub for *Laws of Attraction*. "Worth $3 though." Just six months earlier, however, in November 2003, she had been delighted by *Intolerable Cruelty*, the Coen brothers farce: "*Fun* picture about Divorce + Pre-Nuptual Agreements. Good." (The $2.50 ticket price is circled.) She was similarly ambivalent about representations of violence and shady behavior. Though she was plain about the former on her *Million Dollar Baby* ticket stub ("Good Movie. I don't like Boxing or any Violence"), *Kiss Kiss Bang Bang* found her in a more suggestive mood ("Black Comedy—hard for a 90 yr old to follow but interesting. I liked it").

Rita on *Once Upon a Time in Mexico*: "Love Johnny Depp. ⅓ Good, ⅔ Guns Guns Guns." She added my favorite aside of the bunch in the left corner of the stub: "?Comedy?" She radiated contempt for *Match Point*, which she found "Dreadful. Bad Person in this Woody Allen Movie—I left before the ending. British," and seemed wearied by *Closer*, "A tale of unfaithfulness (Don't go!) + hurting each other."

But here she is on *The Woodsman*, a film I found bleak to the point of being unbearable: "Excellent. Study of Pedophilia." And then at the bottom: "In good taste." Sometimes sex is all in good fun: "Made a special trip alone to see this," she wrote on her *Sideways* stub, "Hilarious sex scenes"; "Good Research," she wrote about *Kinsey*, "Enjoyed it!"; "Plenty of sex," she advised, writing about *The Door in the Floor*. And sometimes, as with an ill-fated trip to *Where the Truth Lies* on a restless afternoon, it's horrifying: "I was appalled at the (over) amount of raw SEX in the movie, every which way—ménage à trois—etc—everybody left in a hurry when it was over. Don't go."

I didn't go. But I did wonder how the movies help us know one another. We didn't talk much about them in person (in person there were always matinees to see), and she seemed more prepared to send the ticket stubs than discuss them. I was aware that a minor treasure was forming, one whose value would only accrue with time. During my second year at NYU I was accepted into a film-criticism seminar with Jim Hoberman, then the presiding eminence at *The Village Voice*. He challenged us to bring imagination, critical fortitude, and good writing into a fairly strict format. I made copies of a Rita Boyle ticket-stub collage one week and passed them out in class.

They were a marvel of critical economy to me then. As I lay them out now—seventy-nine in all, the last one received in April 2006—I see a puzzle made of puzzles. In trying to unlock it I have arranged and rearranged them according to chronology, enjoyment level, genre. I saw many of the films alongside her; some, such as *My Summer of Love* ("No one told me it was about two girls pushing the envelope—experimenting (over) drinking etc. I think you would enjoy it"), I still haven't seen. I wonder if she thought of me while she watched *Garden State* ("Good re: <u>30 year olds</u>") and try to accept that she probably did. Movies are where the less overtly emotional among us spend a fair amount of time trying to figure other people out, and it's not mine to say whatever conclusions she came to about me vis à vis Zach Braff are wrong. I contemplate the times she cried watching a film I found banal (*House of Sand and Fog*), her knowing enthusiasm for unmitigated fluff (*Under the Tuscan Sun*), her openness to the "weird but clever" (*Eternal Sunshine of the Spotless Mind*), the movies that slid through her mind pleasantly but without making a single impression (*Prime*), the memories stirred by stories involving what she called "my era," like *Ray* ("<u>Best Picture of 2004 for me</u>," she wrote, and I smile now at the authority and humility combined in those last two words, the mark of a natural critic), *Vera Drake*, and *Good Night, and Good Luck*. The shrugging off she gives to Hollywood blockbusters is hard for someone who watches them for a living to resist: *The Longest Yard*? "The longest football game—<u>boring</u>." *Spider-Man 2* had a good story line but a "Weird Opponent. Saw it by <u>mistake</u> but <u>glad I did</u>." Though she enjoyed the special effects in *Harry Potter and the Prisoner of Azkaban*, it was "Too long. ~~Who was the~~ Dozed off for 2 seconds." And the behemoth *Lord of the Rings* elicited her shortest shrift: "1 hour too long." Ninety-year-olds have even less time to waste on computer-bay bombast than the rest of us.

The ticket that keeps filtering to the top is for *Charlie and the Chocolate Factory*, which she found terrifically whimsical, another winner for her beloved "J. Depp." Beyond testifying to that love (which surmounted any sin, by the way, including *The Libertine*), the tickets are most simply and consistently a record of hours spent and things felt. Together they form an impenetrable mosaic of life lived in real time; individually their concision forms a portal onto the figure of a woman alone in the dark, gazing up at the big screen's moving bodies with their illuminated skin, communing with a story to create something separate and new. An afterthought floats at the bottom of the ticket: "Wish I had a 7 yr old along."

I've been telling the tale of the ticket stubs to willing listeners since it began. "What a great story," they always say, and I agree. "You should write about it," they add, at which point I feel compelled to fill in the rest.

Illness has a concentrating effect on memory, whether it sets a life into sudden relief or slides the better part of that life to a far side of the scale. "I want to remember him at his best," we say. "Don't think of me this way," they say. As if we might choose. And perhaps we can, to an extent; perhaps we should. But memory has its own mind. Like a soothsayer it reveals and explains our true experience of the world to us as we age, shuffling and redealing the moments of our lives into strangely proportioned patterns. The things we thought mattered—even made us who we are—recede into the background. The things we didn't even know we knew—or have denied knowing or refused to know—stubbornly present themselves for scrutiny. Memory doesn't recognize our received ideas of what's memorable—the performed or grandiose; the picture-friendly—or of whom we are at our best. It might reflect the distortions of ego, but has no ego of its own. It's one of the more startling rewards of both being human and human being.

Is it possible to defy or control—or, in the modern argot of self-maintenance, *manage*—such a process? Is it advisable? Every day we seek signs of death by another name. We call it a failure to be beautiful, to be successful, to be relevant, to be remembered, to be our best. In an anti–memento mori culture, illness is the penultimate failure, and we forget its pain of death on a kind of principle. But something would seem to be missing from an idea of what it means to live a full life that refuses to acknowledge the necessary conditions. It erodes the larger sense of what it means not just to be fulfilled but to be human, so that illness is always a source of shame, and death a complete surprise. The cult of longevity is building a paradox made of protein shakes and hormone patches: we obsess over our bodies even as we fail to imagine their decay; we extend an idea of ourselves into an ideal future without fully accepting that our bodies have to follow us there, or acknowledging the inhospitable terrain that awaits those who "win" and make it to old age. The value of the elderly extends beyond their testimony to the world as it was. We need them perhaps even more to remind us of what it is to get old, and to show us how to die. It has gone unspoken between us that, although it is painful on both sides, for many reasons the only thing worse than my seeing Rita in her deteriorated condition is not seeing her at all.

About a year before Rita fell ill, a reporting errand led me to Weill Cornell medical school. On a damp January evening I attended one of the recruiting sessions students are invited to throughout their first year, as they decide on a specialty. I was told they tend to be informal and involve student-oriented incentives like pizza and pop, which makes a pretty competitive lobbying process sound more cool and casual than it actually is. I imagined the dentistry department holding a screening of *Marathon Man* with complimentary hits of nitrous, or the surgery team unveiling a booby-trapped corpse in lieu of postmeeting snacks. But how might you sell a bunch of twenty-two-year-olds on adult-diaper duty and managing dementia?

The geriatrics department was well aware that they rank only slightly above psychiatry on the sex-appeal scale. In a bold move, the recruiting committee focused its pitch on basic human decency. Only the truly compassionate choose to be geriatricians, a sun-starved young woman informed a group of about two dozen students, which means a higher level of care and fewer assholes on the job. Yes, the pace is slower and the stakes smaller, she went on, but a rapidly aging population makes a compelling (and also compassionate) business case, with geriatrics poised at the top of a supply-and-demand cycle. What she didn't tell them is that geriatricians are currently the worst paid of all doctors, and those who opt to treat the elderly get none of the debt and tuition incentives offered to other specialties.

Most of the students were tractor-beamed directly back to their textbooks as the meeting broke up. One who lingered told me that the social element of these meetings has as much to do with specialty crunching as anything else. Geriatrics, he had decided, was good people. I looked him up recently; he went with oncology.

The elder-care boom described that night did not arrive in time for Rita. Six years later, there is one geriatrician for every two thousand Americans over the age of seventy-five. Her early appointments with a geriatric psychiatrist were months in coming, unsatisfying when they arrived, and of little consequence to her condition. She was put on antide-pressants that exacerbated her somatic symptoms; an eventual medication switch only put a new name to the status quo. If it was sometimes difficult even for those of us who knew better to keep in mind that she was ill—that a lack of cognitive impairment didn't mean she was *choosing* not to care—for her doctors the source of her despair made little difference. Her condition was normal enough for a ninety-one-year-old with fewer friends by the week.

She had talked of suicide before the transplant to Hali-fax. The move seemed to stabilize her. In the ensuing three and a half years, the terror of those months mellowed into consuming anxiety, a restlessness that cut her phone calls short and eventually confined her to Melville. She didn't feel safe, she said, outside of her chair. Early on she had asked for help—she was desperate for relief and continued to hope we might find it for her. Over time her pleas were fewer and less forthcoming, though she was most open with my aunt. Shortly before I arrived, Rita had confessed to be-ing a bad person. Despite doing less and less to keep herself alive, she told her youngest daughter that she was afraid to die.

Join your hands out in front of your chest with your arms rounded and your elbows high and you'll have the rough shape and size of the clock hanging way up on Rita's living-room wall. An hour passes broken only by one practiced soliloquy, delivered in response to a question about my love life. She listens with the same astonished expression as I tell her that New York is a place where the men either can't stop competing with you or refuse to start.

Both of her daughters divorced—a double blow to Rita, although she didn't discuss it outside of wounded asides and coded messages on ticket stubs. Nor did she finagle me with spells or curses or other inductions to marry. My grandfather might have felt differently. On his first visit with my parents after their engagement, Latham fell to his knees and crawled to my father's feet, thanking him for making his twenty-one-year-old daughter's university career worthwhile. "I thought it was a scream," my mother recalled later that evening, as she settled into my aunt's Halifax apartment and my eyebrows explored the upper reaches of my forehead.

Throughout my disquisition on dating in New York City, Rita stole urgent glances at the clock, which is white with huge black numbers in a kind of treble-clef font. In the absence of follow-up questions we return to silence, her head swiveling back to the clock a few times a minute. She raises an index finger to her mouth and bites the tip gently, adopting an almost comical posture of contemplative worry. When I ask her what she's thinking about, she lifts her eyes and says,

"Nothing in particular." A few beats pass, then Rita slowly pivots her chair toward the wall, a silent forfeiture, and fixes her eyes on the clock for the remaining half hour.

The Melville dining room's massive solarium windows join the sky to a thickly wooded reservoir. As we shuffle into the seating area, a woman calls out to Rita. Outside, the sky is sullen, stung by the storm and looming close to the glass like an accusation, like an aquarium whale. Her hearing has declined somewhat, but I wonder if Rita means to dust this insuperable woman, who is already dining with two others. Seating arrangements are cliquish and hotly contested.

"Oh, Rita! *Ree-tah!*" After the third call I touch my grandma's shoulder and point in the woman's direction.

"Oh," Rita says. *"Hello."*

"I went to visit Marge Lowe yesterday," the woman announces as we putter up tableside. "No one's heard from her since she left, you know, but her spirits are good." The other women murmur. "She's in *good spirits.*"

I want us to make it through this interaction but I can feel my smile tacking, and Rita can't pretend to give a shit when there's a chair nearby that needs sitting in.

"I just thought you'd want to know," the woman concludes, with a bathetic moue that takes the remaining wind out of my goodwill. "She said to send her regards."

"Oh, good," Rita says.

The crash of a cutlery dump carries over the dining room.

"Is that your daughter?"

———

Dinner is served every evening to fifty double-tableclothed tables, and at 5:30 the room is humming with news and reviews of the night's menu. At precisely 5:25, Rita had reached to clip on the gold earrings she keeps in a dish by her chair and insisted we not be late. The waitstaff is a mix of scurrying high schoolers and brisk middle-aged women. They greet residents formally, meeting their cranky demands with Teflon manners. Mrs. Boyle's requests (no ice, dressing on the side, no dessert) are made in a low, querulous voice that startles me. I wonder what they think of her here.

As we're seated, the cafeteria crier repeats her news about Marge Lowe exactly (spirits good; sends her regards; *thought you'd want to know*) to a second arrival. I hear it twice more before the meal is over. Rita tells me she and Marge shared a table before Marge's recent transfer to the nursing home. After drizzling a perfect orange loop of dressing over a finger bowl full of salad, Rita raises her fork like someone with nasty but necessary work to do, and I decide to let the meal pass in silence. I'm supposed to make her eat but I learned a long time ago that I can't make anyone do anything.

One of the few men at Melville—tall, cardiganed, aquiline nose; prime men's-club material—sits down to dine directly in my sight line. He adjusts his place setting, folds his newspaper, and fans out his napkin with transfixing deliberation before requesting a glass of beer—a Sunday treat—to go with his steak and baked potato. When all three arrive, I watch him crop dust the steak with salt so intently that he turns his heavy lids on me with a look that would freeze the warts off a witch's nose. I settle on him again, like a fly, after a desultory flitting about. I tell the waitress to bring Rita's pie anyway, and she tucks in like she was expecting it all along.

Melville residents run from retirement age to mobile no-nagenarians; walkers fender-bend between the dining-room tables and line the far wall. The building is clean and modern, collegial and dignified—hardly the moaning void often associated with old-age facilities. Yet it is distinctly a world apart, a place where things begin to move so quickly it seems there's no movement at all; where there's a new Marge Lowe every hour, and you rocket from your midthirties to your midsixties in the blink of an old woman's eye.

As if to contain the secret of this sudden acceleration, a sort of narrative vacuum forms around the residents; though not the space designated for dying, it would seem to be where the story ends. Melville is for living and convening, eating and exercising, but not for the outside world, or "independence" as it's otherwise defined. It's an elegant resort with no return and no postcards. I clung to Mr. Sunday Times, whose life's attitude seemed preserved in his posture and placid self-containment, so contented with himself and his surroundings, yet so apart from them. Nearer to my right a white-haired woman sat alone, reckoning with her bacon-wrapped scallops, a human shipwreck arranged into her dinner-hour best.

Rita refuses to use the walker her daughters bought for her, and she's not interested in my arm either. She skims close to the wall on the walk back. Even a late interception by my mother and Frank, just arrived from Toronto, doesn't dissuade her. She shuffles on to her door, hunches over the lock for an extended struggle, moves into the living room, and lowers herself back into her chair. Only then and there can she mobilize the energy necessary for anything else. I get the sense that her entire day is built around pulling off that walk, a contest of weakness and will that's difficult to watch in part because it feels too familiar.

My mother responds to her mother's Prairie-flat affect by winding herself into a type A tornado. Laundry is triaged for washing or replacement (more than once I've seen Rita stripped of days-old clothes where she stood), rations are cited for replenishing (Rita has dubbed her, not incorrectly, "the food police"), and, most relentlessly, the family silver is polished before she will consider sitting down. I'm pretty sure the ideal visit would involve no sitting at all. I have watched my mother bent over the Boyle tea set, elbows wagging, for the better part of every previous visit, a scene completed by Rita's staring into space and my watching askance with a prickling neck, prepared to fire up some old coping protocol.

But we all react to the eighty-pound elephant in the room with a form of extremity. Frank, a congenial whistler whose own mother passed away in 2009, at age one hundred—still sharp as a mongoose and prone to the odd, unreconstructed racial slur—tends to glower over Rita's apparent rudeness before long, making his oppression known with passive-aggressive asides. My mother is calmer this trip. After noting, prethreshold, that the wreath hanging on Rita's door is out of season (door hangings are the Melville residents' version of a profile photo), she casts off her parka and collapses on the couch.

We don't stay long; this is a pickup mission, with a proper visit to follow. Their flight had been almost as harrowing as mine, and after trading stories—surely we had all faced death to reach this room—and condoling our mutual nausea, we leave Rita to her giant TV, deliverer of what she told me earlier, on prodding, was her one remaining pleasure: televised golf tournaments.

I ask if we can stop by Deadman's Island on the way to my aunt's apartment. Only a few blocks from Melville Heights, it's the burial site of nearly two hundred American soldiers who died in British captivity during the War of 1812. A poor excuse for an island at high tide, when the water's low it's more of a thinly treed mound attached to the mainland by a muddy isthmus. As we park and climb down the hundred-some stairs leading to the shore, Frank tells me that a few years ago a developer had petitioned to build luxury condos on the grounds. The men buried there had been all but forgotten, and the prison that held over eight thousand prisoners of war on Melville Island, just across Halifax Harbour, was converted into a yacht club a decade back. But committees were formed and the dead got their due; their sinking graves were declared a heritage site in 2005.

As we pick our way along the shoe-sucking shore and onto a brown hump the size of a softball diamond, the telltale plaques come into view. They describe the smallpox epidemic that ran through the prison and how its victims were quickly scraped into the earth, where their bones might mingle with those of Spanish and French prisoners from wars past. The names of the latter are long gone, but those of all 195 Americans, rescued from archival oblivion, are listed along with their rank, unit, and date of death. Seaman, soldier; private, prize master; boatswain, militiaman; Chesapeake, Rattlesnake; Eliza, Polly Ann; Vixen, Lizard; Friendship, Hope. I can't tell their ages but imagine them to be a small fraction of my grandmother's, whose life span already accommodates two world wars, the ascent of the airplane, women's much-rumored liberation, the birth and death of Rita Hayworth, and the seemingly immortal inception of the digital age. I know it's supposed to be funny, the image of an old person grappling with new technology, but whenever I watch my grandmother lift a cell phone to the vicinity of her ear as though it were an old shoe, I am filled with the queerest sadness.

My elders are anxious to leave. The sun is setting and the tide, my mother the oceanographer insists, is coming in. In three weeks, upon touching down in Honolulu for a conference, I will receive an e-mail notifying me that, after continued decline, Rita was taken to the ER and diagnosed with metastatic cancer of the liver. They don't bother to trace its source, admitting her directly to palliative care. I will snap the message off when I hit the word *cancer*; it seems impossible to receive such news while checking my BlackBerry in a moving taxi on a tropical island.

"Well," Rita will say in the doctor's office, "that's that."

Later I will listen to her breathing through that same device while facing into the Pacific. I will tell her that I love her, that I'm going to try to tell her story, and she'll say, "Okay."

It's a futile phone call, exactly like the rest. And yet, as the days go on, I will hear of a bedside transformation. Rita will say the things we wish the dying to say, and to say I suppose when we die ourselves: she is at peace; she is going home. I will wonder if the doctor, aware of the power of diagnosis as a personal storytelling device, had decided to play editorial God. Rita had cleared several complete physicals since her depression's onset, showed no definitive symptoms, and in addition to her sudden spiritual calm reported no physical pain. Perhaps it's a more viable ending than dying of sadness; perhaps it's the first time cancer did anyone a favor. There is a script to follow now, and it is taken up with relief.

Shortly after my return from Hawaii I will meet with a friend whose grandmother, also ninety-five, had died the previous week. My friend is more shaken than she had imagined she would be, as far as she had imagined this death at all. The funeral was a shock: her father wept—unthinkable—and her grandmother's body was laid out in an open casket. My friend thought the practice macabre. "I don't want to remember her that way," she'll say. By any standard it was an ideal death: sudden, and on the heels of a birthday celebrated by an entire community, the last pages of a small-town pastoral. But there is gothic history there—incest, abuse, suicide—and though my friend felt ascendant compassion for her grandmother, she never knew the woman well. Her peers have responded with a sympathetic shrug: *What did you expect?*

"But I find myself devastated," my friend will tell me, her eyes focused and growing full over our gin and tonics. "Just that idea, that life can be imperfect and . . . *over.*"

After two weeks, her daughters at her side much of the time, Rita will receive what the nurses allege to be the lowest morphine dosage they've ever used to treat a terminal cancer patient. This is the last stage, when we begin to talk about a dying person's pain with authority. In recent years I have wondered about the nature of depression, specifically Rita's depression, turning it about as a biochemical event, then as part of her biography, her response to the world and her role in it, an expression of some intimate and mysterious grief. But is there, for once, more comfort in the meaningless option? Certainly there is comfort in morphine, a drug, at last, of consequence. When I hear it named I know that she will die, and in the opiated coma that will carry most of us away.

As the days pass, I will be told that this is the most peaceful time in Rita's life. Her Melville apartment will swiftly be emptied and her furniture off-loaded to charity; even her wrinkles fall away. Some days she will eat, some she won't. Another pattern will form and we'll start to settle into it, despite everything.

And then, on a Saturday afternoon in early June, Rita Boyle dies on the ninth floor of the Queen Elizabeth II hospital in Halifax, Nova Scotia. I will be in the act of writing this essay when it happens, her letters and ticket stubs spread across my desk, my digital recorder cued to the twenty minutes of her audible breathing. My mother will leave the message as I am finishing for the day. I will pass the several hours I wait to return her call immobile at my desk, watching the longhand words around me transfigure, the false ink on the screen a blurred and hopeless rival. Had I lied to her when I said I would tell her story? Does even trying amount to a sort of lie? Perhaps all I can offer is the setting down of a space, one whose highest aim is that you might roam, however elusively, within its borders.

Soon after Rita's letters stopped in 2006, I was paid to watch and respond to a film for the first time. Two months later I was voted into a critics' group and could gorge myself in hermetic studio screening rooms. This, I was told frequently, was the dream. This was progress. In the last five years, on the rare occasion when I venture out to a theater, the ticket stub bypasses the groaning stash, slipping instead into the large manila envelope where I keep the rest of my tax receipts.

Later that evening, when I return her call, my mom, ruminant and a little tipsy at the resort hotel where she has reunited with Frank after a long stay in Halifax, will tell me about the last time she saw her mother. Their days together had grown full: the lower the tide, the safer the passage onto the island. A smile was still too much to ask, however, which is probably why my mother tried it as a command. I will feel my ribs fuse together as this story begins and think of Rita's laugh, which was more of a private chuckle. My mother will describe how, when other persuasions failed—it had been so long; *just one smile*—she offered to help, using a fingertip to push the corner of her mother's mouth up over her gums. She will recall the way Rita strained to hold the expression on her own, how she almost got there.

My time on Deadman's Island has drawn past what patience allowed. My mother and Frank grow smaller, trudging inland along the shore, tiny yet familiar figures beneath their flapping hair and coats. Still bent over the plaque when they step onto the mainland, I turn to leave at the sound of a wind-strangled call. *Surely*, I think, stopping for a last look at the humble crest of sod, its beard of striplings, and the shattered light of the water beyond them, *I will not see this place again*.

Beirut Rising

In my opinion, Lebanon is the scene of a historic test that will determine the future of humanity.
                              —President Mahmoud Ahmadinejad, Iran,
                                                          July 25, 2006

Beirut's hopelessness relies upon its resilience. There are those who praise the courage of its people, their valor amid despair, but it is this very capacity for survival, for eternal renewal, that is Beirut's tragedy. If the city were allowed to die—if its airport closed forever, if its imports and exports were frozen, its currency destroyed, if its people gave up—then its war could end.
                              —Robert Fisk, *Pity the Nation*

A joke went around Beirut during the summer of 2006, as the taunting and touchbacks between Israel and Lebanon finally set off the spark of war, involving a notoriously swish section of the city called Achrafieh, a neighborhood whose idle doyennes are known for their opulent dress and fondness for face-lifts. When Israeli general Dan Halutz, freestyling over an escalating duel of war drums, threatened to "turn Lebanon's clock back twenty years," so the joke goes, it was the best news the women of Achrafieh had heard in decades. Tack on a few more and we'll talk.

Today the Lebanese appear poised to turn back that clock all on their own. Eighteen months have passed since the final cease-fire with Israel was brokered in the Levant, and although the bombing stopped and the bodies were returned, Lebanon's latest in a bullet-pocked history of violent conflicts left the country in limbo. That's the optimistic take: many fear this latest war to be the beginning of a backward slide.

But then the country's current spiritual, economic, and political crisis was already in progress when the Israeli tanks rolled in. Its most obvious source is the cataclysmic blast that killed the country's former prime minister, Rafic Hariri, on Valentine's Day 2005. Three years later, evidence of the explosion, which killed twenty-two others and gouged a fifteen-foot crater into the ground, still blights Beirut's Mediterranean promenade. The stretch of the seaside corniche where Hariri's assassination took place looks only recently repaved; the water mains still erupt regularly, dousing the decimated buildings on either side of the street with Beirut's version of a fire hydrant's jubilant summer spray. The site is one of the more spectacular markers in a city liberally engraved with its history of suffering.

That most useful breed of dreamer—the kind with resources—Hariri symbolized a hope for peace in Lebanon, the seat of his most extravagant dream yet. Having chosen the mountainous, coastal country of his birth as a pseudo-retirement destination in the mid-1980s—despite the minor buzzkill of a raging civil war—in the ensuing decades Hariri threw his sizable financial lot and professional acumen into restoring Lebanon. Derided for the ruthlessness that made him a billionaire and accused of seeking little more than glory—a political parvenu coasting on his fat bankroll and steamrolling charisma—Hariri was a Sunni Muslim, a nouveau Saudi who had left Lebanon to make it big in construction. His tenacity eventually earned him a loyal electoral base, however; he was elected prime minister twice, first in 1992 and again in 2000.

In 2004, Hariri resigned in protest over a Syrian power play to extend then-president Émile Lahoud's term beyond its legal limit, a move that soured Hariri's previously tolerant relations with Syria, Lebanon's neighbor and occupier. At the time of his death it appears he was pushing, with the aggression that won the hearts of his people and assured his death, for the withdrawal of Syrian troops. Syria entered Lebanon in 1976, shortly after the onset of the civil war, which erupted in 1975 in the wake of a civilian shooting in Beirut's Christian neighborhood of Ain al Rouamanah. Yet another in months of clashes between the Christian Maronite Phalangists, Palestinians, and Druze, Sunni, and Shia militias, the drive-by shooting killed two Christians and two others and led to the retaliatory slaughter of thirty Palestinians. Sixty eyes for eight, and suddenly it was war. In the dark cascade of violence that followed, Druze Socialist leader Kamal Jumblatt formed a ramshackle alliance with Yasser Arafat's PLO, the Christians made frenemies with the Israelis, and Syria, doing its best big-brother impersonation, moved into Lebanon under the auspices of keeping the peace. The Syrian occupation lasted, on and off, for almost thirty years. They finally succumbed to global pressure and left in 2005—two and a half months after Hariri's blood ran through Ain-Mreisse.

Though the effects of the civil war can be seen on every corner and felt in every other face, citizens of Beirut rarely refer to it directly. Talk of war—if not politics—is scrupulously avoided or effaced with dry humor. The Achrafieh joke was one of several offered to me, during a 2008 trip to Lebanon's capital, as a proud representative of the native mordant, melancholy wit—as Lebanese as the dishes of olives, parsley, and radishes that set their tables. "You have to laugh," I was told, "or else . . ."

The ellipsis may in fact get closer than a hundred thousand words to capturing the terrible potentiality paralyzing Lebanon, which recently went six freighted months without a president and is sinking into the worst economic depression since the civil war. "As if they were the result of some natural calamity rather than a man-made catastrophe," journalist Robert Fisk wrote, the Lebanese refer to the fifteen years of civil war as *al-hawadess*, or "the events." The postwar attempt to rebuild the country's infrastructure was ardent but somewhat cosmetic. Recovery has further been waylaid by the inexorable rise of the Shia faction who call themselves Hezbollah—"the party of God," the former militia now recognized as a political party.

Hezbollah is the latest in the country's long line of party crashers. Having filled its dance card with some of civilization's greatest empires—Phoenician, Persian, Roman, Byzantine, Arab—Lebanon was under near-consistent Ottoman rule from the sixteenth century until 1920, when the French, one of the Allied countries divvying up the Middle East after World War I, assumed control. The French conceived of a "confessionalist" democracy for Lebanon, a system that attempted to represent the country's major religious groups (eighteen are recognized) by population and mandated a Maronite Christian president, Sunni prime minister, Shia speaker of parliament, and Orthodox Christian deputy prime minister. This outrageously utopian conception of power sharing was confirmed by a National Pact when the Lebanese gained independence in 1943, and it actually worked fairly well, until it didn't. Not everyone was happy with the pact, and the largest divide fell between the Muslims, who wanted closer Arab relations, and the Christians, who wanted to develop ties with the West. Beyond geopolitics there is simple geography: Lebanon, despite its French-drawn borders, will never be entirely self-contained and could only stave off the region's veritable staph infection of national and sectarian conflict for so long. Until April 13, 1975, to be exact.

There has not been an official Lebanese census in over seventy-five years. The underlying fear is that the increase in the country's Muslim (and particularly Shia) population and dwindling number of Christians will set a power shift in motion, essentially handing the country to Hezbollah. There is a pattern to the way Lebanon's fissures blew into fault lines, and that pattern is repeating now. The process has consequences most of Beirut's citizens—who refer to Hariri's assassination as "the earthquake"—can't bear to contemplate, much less name.

I met Carlo amid the jumble of the Amman airport in early January of 2008. I remembered him from the tortuous check-in line back in New York: short and compact, he was dressed for a trendy wine bar rather than a transatlantic flight. Carlo introduced himself a continent and several crushing cinematic offerings later, having noticed my cortisone spike when the ticket agent collected all of our passports and disappeared behind a red curtain with a magisterial flourish. An agent at JFK had nearly relieved me of my visa, plucking it out of my passport and tossing it onto a pile of scraps as though it were a receipt for Toblerone and duty-free tequila; I was as on my guard as a person filled with vegan plane food can be. One of the handful from our enormous flight transferring to Beirut, Carlo expressed an expatriate's qualified pride to this first-time visitor: "Everything in Lebanon is beautiful—except the politics."

We were following a strutting airline clerk through the brightly lit duty-free bazaar when Carlo inquired about my intentions. Was I not being guided or hosted or otherwise sponsored? Did I not speak Arabic? Initially I found the negative formulation of many of the questions one is asked in Lebanon charming; in this case, for instance, it seems to leave room for the affirmative option. It didn't take long to imagine its darker applications: *Did you not meet the man in question? Are you not involved in a major multinational conspiracy? Were you not traveling to the Middle East alone and for no apparent reason?*

I had to admit, to Carlo's complete lack of surprise, that I do not speak Arabic, though I can make do in French. More than fifty years after the end of France's brief but penetrative mandate, the language still gilds Lebanese vernacular. Unluckily for me, most are loath to use it for more than "hello," "goodbye," and "thank you very much indeed."

Carlo moved to New York when the war broke out in 2006; his wife couldn't make this trip on account of being seven months pregnant. I asked him how often he returned to Beirut, and for the first time his friendly voice turned flat: "I don't." His dad was ill, he explained, and if he didn't come home now . . .

I turned to look at him. We were seated in a long, narrow lounge crammed with baggage to the point of immobility. An entire day had passed without us, and it was night again. The young woman beside me had ended a phone call just before takeoff and wept pitifully into the window for most of the eleven-hour flight.

Carlo asked me a question that, though it became quite familiar, I was never able to answer to anyone's satisfaction, including mine: "Why Beirut?" I told him I had come to explore, that I had a standing interest in the city and a couple of weeks free, which was true enough. His open face flickered, unsold. He asked where I was staying and I mentioned the hotel I'd picked because it looked clean and was close to the sea. Still skeptical, he had a final and ultimate question: "Is no one waiting for you?" I told him no, or rather yes; Carlo's expression of confusion and dismay proved infectious. It's not Beirut's fault, I wanted to add. No one is waiting for me *in general.*

The arrivals deck at Rafic Hariri International Airport on a random Tuesday night has the caricatured charm of a Norman Rockwell frieze. Lebanese are stacked five and six deep against the barrier, dangling cheap bouquets and hot-pink teddy bears, scanning each new face with gleaming eyes. I kept my head down, remembering Carlo's stricken look; he saw this moment coming. He blew past me at customs as I was puzzling over the entry form's request for my father's first name, like a password. Carlo had people waiting and was three checkpoints ahead of me when I lost sight of him for good.

The scene at the gate shouldn't have surprised me. Though it's smaller than Connecticut, with a population of fewer than four million, the scattering of the Lebanese across the globe is second only to the Jewish diaspora. Some estimate it at over fifteen million; almost three times as many Lebanese live in

Brazil as in Lebanon. The civil and 2006 wars account for a significant portion of the outflux, but roaming is something of a national pastime. Leaving Lebanon may be the only pan-Lebanese tradition.

On stepping outside the building I was marked by a group of men idling around a taxi stand. The tallest one led the charge, his hand outstretched for my suitcase. The first practical bit of advice one gets about traveling to Beirut is not to pay more than twenty thousand lira (about $14 U.S.) for the ride from the airport, and to settle up front. I and the huddle of disgruntled drivers that formed around me were making a time-lapsed orbit toward Tall Guy's cab when he answered my calls for a number: thirty-five. I shook my head and reached in to cover his grip on my suitcase. Tall Guy whirled around in disgust, tossing his head and snorting like a pro.

I was preparing for the second act when a small, sharp-eyed dude in a red bomber jacket made a lunge for my suitcase and carved an expert little doughnut with its wheels. Suddenly a soldier was in the mix, roughing Red Bomber Jacket away; hot-faced arguments ensued, everywhere scorn and smoky breath. When it seemed I would not extract a ride—or myself—from the scrimmage, a sleepy type on the perimeter stepped in to mutter, "Twenty dollars," real low. I nodded and he swung my bag away from the curbside vehicles, back into the building. Inside we boarded an escalator and blazed a circuitous path in silence. At length I was handed off to a second man, who led me out onto an upper ramp, where a single, unmarked Hyundai was waiting with a driver already inside.

Two weeks after this scene played out, Beirut's taxidrivers staged another in a series of strikes over rising fuel prices in Lebanon, a one-day protest that sparked rioting in the streets.

Lebanese soldiers began firing on the protesters, leaving seven dead and more wounded. Electricity shortages and rising food prices have been particularly acute in south Beirut and the southern region of Lebanon, large sections of which are controlled by Hezbollah. The Shia and Christian opposition, backed by Syria and Iran, have accused the American-backed government of punishing southern Beirut with the blackouts that have grown common in Shia villages in the south and the eastern Bekáa Valley. With no president, parliament, or functioning cabinet to address these concerns or even officially meet the accusations, violent protests and road blockades—a clear path to attention—grow more frequent.

Beirut's airport is blissfully central; fifteen minutes after the cloak-and-driver routine on the arrivals deck I was contemplating the metal detector at the entrance of the Palm Beach Hotel, an elegant, proud, exceptionally creepy facility whose "luxe," seafoam-green parlor broke my heart on first sight, and every day after that. The decorating scheme appears to have involved Zsa Zsa Gabor's swallowing a flatbed full of crown moldings, chasing it with the contents of a dolphin tank, and then vomiting all over the lounge. About one hundred feet out the front door and off to the right is the site where Hariri was blown to pieces by two thousand pounds of TNT. The sign marking the area is in Arabic, and for the first couple of days I assumed the gutted buildings and ragged streetscape were a more anonymous addition to the city's general disarticulation.

Say the name to someone of my generation and their eyes still widen: Beirut means bad. Lebanon's war dominated the world stage during the 1980s—along with Iran-Iraq and the Russians in Afghanistan—as Vietnam, Cambodia, and North Korea had in previous decades. I recall Beirut most vividly; it's the center of a country and its tragedy. It was a name I knew at eight years old, scanning the cover of *Time* on our kitchen table—probably hoping for the painted glare of Prince or Madonna—and finding yet more images of Beirut's carnage and rubble, its seemingly endless issue of grief, ruin, dust-etched tears.

Beirut meant "the Paris of the Middle East" back in its midcentury heyday, back when my twenty-four-year-old father was offered a teaching position at the city's American University in 1966. It was a young man's gambit—a few years to burn on a kind of French playground—but he turned it down, opting for a stint in Rochester, New York. A year or so into that move a letter arrived informing him of a change in his draft status, and it was so long Rochester. By the late 1960s resident aliens and teachers—previously protected by a shifting set of conditions—were being conscripted to fight in Vietnam. A few years after returning to Canada my father accepted a professorship in the London of southwestern Ontario—the thriving, many-treed, oppressively well-adjusted town where I was eventually born and raised.

Founded in 1866 as the Syrian Protestant College by an American missionary named Daniel Bliss, the American University flourished in the first half of the twentieth century, then had a fairly steady decline throughout the second. Walking along the street named for Bliss on the AUB campus, I wondered what the twenty-first century might have in store for Lebanon's jewel of higher education. Many of the graduate programs shut down during the civil war, and today a

Lebanese student with the means to attend university will most likely enroll abroad. Even the staunchest foreign students eventually evacuated in 2006; relatively few have opted to return. The bombings and high-profile assassinations rose in number and severity across 2007—a Christian legislator was killed in September and an army general in December; Hezbollah was blamed in both cases—and the election for a new president has been delayed eleven times since Émile Lahoud left office in November. The entire country seems suspended with dread, wondering if the next shot fired or explosion detonated in Beirut's streets will be the one that sends Lebanon tumbling. The twelfth attempt at a presidential election was scheduled for January 12, 2008, several days after my arrival in the capital. In retrospect, it would have been a good thing to know.

Beirut is not a walking city. Neither is it a driving city, nor particularly a public-transportation city. When I ask the meticulously coiffed hotel concierge for the best way to get to the famously rebuilt downtown area, also the site of the National Parliament, she tells me to walk along the shore for a while. "Eventually . . . ," she advised, "you'll want to turn right." A pause followed and our eyes met over the glossy front desktop, each of us awaiting very different things. "Ask someone on the street," she added finally, above the peals of a suspiciously well-timed phone call. "You can't get lost."

Indeed, I could. The problem with getting lost in Beirut is that looking lost is tantamount to looking suspicious. Few people are in the streets, fewer still who are alone; within seconds of setting out I knew that neither strolling nor stopping were viable options in a walking tour of the city. The idea, securitywise, is to slow down the cars—with zigzagging barricades that prevent vehicles from tossing a bomb and zooming away—and speed up the people. Private guards patrol the front of nearly every building, and the Lebanese army is out in force on most corners. There is only hustling with your head down, grateful for the cover of the January chill.

When I finally found the downtown—a peanut-butter-colored, art deco suburb built up around crumbling mosques and churches—only soldiers roamed the area. A maze of barricades and riotous spirals of razor wire made accessing a building that seemed mere steps away a triumph of will and logistics. Turning down a new block meant another search of your bag and your person by another young man with a long, elegantly snouted automatic rifle strapped across his back. The high-fashion shops lining the radial streets off Nijmeh Square are shuttered on a given afternoon. A mean wind was whipping in off the Mediterranean; over an hour I saw fewer than a dozen civilians. I wound up on a wide, wildly trafficked avenue, where I was finally granted a full vantage of the imperious Al-Amin Mosque. Hariri was building the Al-Amin at the time of his death; he's buried there now, along with his seven bodyguards. The mosque appears blown from blue and gold glass, as though it were set down among a ragged sandbox city and could as easily topple or be taken away. I pulled out my camera to take a picture and felt the nearby soldiers resettling their focus. It was my first, fuzzy twinge of what became a full-blown case of paranoia.

Nowhere is Beirut's resilience more apparent than in its reconstructed city center, read a tourist guide I picked up later that afternoon. *In 1990, Downtown was in shambles, a deserted no-*

man's-land, a ghost town. I had stopped at the Virgin Mega-store—found on all tourist maps of Beirut—because it was adjacent to Martyrs' Square, the memorial I had hopelessly been stalking, fended off by an intimidating show of barri-cades and wire. The Virgin Megastore, a four-floor behemoth, was open despite all appearances. I know there are four floors because I traveled—in escalator slo-mo—to each one, trying to find someone who would take my ten dollars for *Lebanon 2006: Official General Tourism Guide*.

After that I ate a pound of almonds, tore my pants on an errant coil of wire, and declared Round One for Beirut. I had been searching throughout the afternoon for an outlet adapter for my computer, continuing a saga begun the night before, when a timorous young woman made five separate trips to my room, each time bearing a new contraption that fit neither my machine nor the hotel's outlets. The power was sort of fluid anyway, coming and going throughout the day. That morning I had been using the hotel's desktop when the whole place went dark. I hadn't yet moved past the page where the last guest, a built young man of indeterminate ethnicity, left off: iCasualties.org, a real-time database of coalition forces killed in the Iraq and Afghan wars.

Adapt, adapter, adaptive; I was sure I had packed the fucking thing. I made one last try, ducking into a tiny cell-phone shack on the way home. The skinny teenager man-ning the gadgets was just about to tell me he was sorry when I saw exactly what I needed sitting between his phone and his lighter on a shelf behind the counter. "That?" He tossed it to me. "You can have that, I don't even know what it is."

The young sir at the front desk gave me the usual directions: "Go this way, then go that way, then ask somebody—you can't get lost." He was just a kid, all soft and facially unsorted and yet so assured. "Let's assume I'm lost *right now*," I wanted to reply. "What would you say then?" After a night spent vomiting fattoush and hummus, I was on my way to meet Felicia—a stranger, a friend of a friend—at a café in Jamia. She had suggested a taxi but I wanted to walk.

The Prague Café is on the AUB campus, close to Hamra Street, where I was relieved to find a healthy stream of civilian life. On this Friday afternoon the place was filthy with smoke and great-looking people. A small chalkboard hanging behind the bar appeared freshly erased and reinscribed: *When a woman has a nervous breakdown, she goes shopping. When a man has a nervous breakdown, he invades a country.*

Felicia's friend Rafael was the first person in Beirut to accuse me of being a spy. "People are going to think you're a spy," he said as we arranged our knees and elbows around a low-slung coffee table. "Are you not a spy?"

I told them I had come to Beirut to research a short story; to his credit, Rafael didn't blink. I tried not to seem too desperate for the company, and Felicia—home visiting from Dubai, where she reluctantly took a reporting position a few months previously—attempted to ignore her BlackBerry's violent seizures between our cups. Journalism jobs are hard to come by in Beirut; the city tends to attract the best. Like most of her friends, she's gunning for Cairo. Rafael works for an environmental group and mentioned being recently escorted away from the U.S. embassy, where he had gone to take pictures of the waterbirds—unheard of in the city—drawn in by the large pools that collected in front of the building after a heavy rain. He only got off a few snaps before the guards closed in.

The presidential election was scheduled for the next day, and I may as well have fired a starter pistol into the café's smoke-stained ceiling when I asked if it would actually happen. I was thrown clear of the ensuing debate, with its unfamiliar names, dates, and technicalities, regaining purchase only when Rafael equated Lebanon's political détente with the other dark force currently occupying his life: a punishing divorce. What he had realized, he said, was that the nature of the split with his wife and the nature of Lebanon's disintegration shared certain patterns. The breakdown in communication, the antipathy born of long-term alienation, the petty marshaling of protocol—it was all there.

"Ultimately, it's all about power," he said, his eyes rounding with epiphany, or caffeine. "It's not about who's right or what's best or some deep belief. You lose sight of all that, and it becomes about who has more control, who comes out on top—who did what years and years ago and who has to pay." Felicia and I sipped and fiddled at our drinks as Rafael slumped back into his leather armchair: *"Power."*

It's hard to talk about anything else when you're breaking up. Try, and be amazed at the tunneling your brain does to get back where it wants to be. Everyone in Beirut talks politics, all the time. It's like history's longest breakup between the world's most promising couple, argued by the Middle East's greediest lawyers, and contingent on the custody of several million traumatized children, who will grow into needy adults with trust issues and a tendency to freak out other countries in bed.

Gathering himself from his chair and another of divorce's

palpable aftershocks, Rafael wrapped up with the two things I needed to know for my stay in Beirut: "Everyone thinks everyone is a spy. And they might as well line the whole city with razor wire."

Hezbollah emerged in 1982, a pet militia of the Ayatollah Khomeini. They trained under Iran's Islamic Revolutionary Guard to fight the Israeli invasion of southern Lebanon, which had left between twelve and nineteen thousand Lebanese dead, many of them Shiites. Led by Beirut-born secretary-general Sheikh Hassan Nasrallah since 1992, Hezbollah—the only militia not forced to disarm after the end of Lebanon's civil war—is cited as a terrorist organization by both Canada and the United States, whereas most of Europe and the Arab world recognizes them as a legitimate resistance movement. Prior to September 11, 2001, Hezbollah was responsible for the deaths of more American citizens than any other Islamic group, most notoriously the 1983 truck bombing that killed 241 marines in their West Beirut barracks, out by the airport. Court documents called it "the largest nonnuclear explosion that had ever been detonated on the face of the Earth." And yet in 2005 the United States showed signs of capitulating to the United Nations' attempts to smooth Hezbollah's way into mainstream Lebanese politics—a sign, some say, that the United States is currently too depleted by its involvements in Iraq and Afghanistan to risk toying with the puppets of Syria and Iran. With over one hundred million dollars in annual funding from Iran and flourishing black-market and intelligence resources, Hezbollah has ballooned into the world's premier terror network; even Al Qaeda looks to them for training and advice. They are, after all, considered the leading experts in the kidnap and torture of foreigners—particularly Americans—for political advantage.

Nasrallah picks his moments well. Having successfully ended the Israeli occupation of Lebanon in 2000, he won the support of 87 percent of the Lebanese population during the war he essentially started in 2006. Since then he has focused on building Hezbollah's influence as a political party. They won 14 of Lebanon's 128 parliamentary seats in 2005 and have forged opposition alliances with Amal—another Shia faction—and the largest Christian bloc in parliament, led by former military commander Michel Aoun. In a 1985 manifesto Hezbollah made its agenda plain: they sought to eject Western colonialism from the country, bring the Phalangists to justice for the atrocities committed during the civil war, eradicate the "Zionist entity" of Israel, and bring the Islamic revolution lockstepping through Lebanon.

Nasrallah has lately stood down on that last item. His more immediate concern is acquiring veto power for Hezbollah in the cabinet, a provision that has thrown the government into chaos. Lebanon will come in at number eighteen on the Failed State Index for 2008, just two down from North Korea, two up from Yemen. Months have passed in the parliament without agreement on the makeup of a national unity government, each party cleaving to its demand for greater power. The cabinet is unwilling, in other words, to stay together for the kids. They won't even share custody.

———

Felicia suggested a second drink at an old Beirut beach club, where we could sample some of the city's ruined glory. The journey began with a common error in judgment—the decision to drive—and we spent the better part of an hour making excruciating, frame-by-frame progress down a few blocks in Felicia's car. We had plenty of time for pedestrian-gazing on Hamra Street—mostly women of aggressive glamour, the head of every fourth or fifth one wrapped in a hijab. "You never used to see that," Felicia said, nodding her big sunglasses toward the street. When it's completely unavoidable, on assignment to Saudi Arabia, say, Felicia will wear a hijab. She'll even take a little pleasure in picking one out, mitigating the annoyance with maximum cuteness. But the sight of them here at home made her wistful.

Today the club where Felicia says all of fabulous Beirut would come to show off their new sun hats and sip brightly colored drinks looks like a shelled-out bunker. The seating area is a couple of green plastic tables and chairs scattered across a vast slab of concrete. Though it feels like taking a seat in a condemned public lot, discreet waitstaff appear before long. Our waiter regretted to inform us that there is no longer a working kitchen, so we ordered sodas and a bowl of the house's salted soybeans. The wind was sharp off the water, sucking our hair and voices relentlessly back into the city.

We didn't stay long. The club seems resigned to accommodating gestures of patronage rather than actual patrons, fond visitors like Felicia who come to pay respect to what is essentially a tombstone. On the way out Felicia pointed to the spot where an anti-Syrian member of parliament had been killed by a car bomb in June of 2007. He died between the lighthouse rebuilt after a 2006 Israeli bombing at one end of the corniche and Hariri's 2005 assassination site at the other end. The guided tour of Beirut's latest misfortunes is nothing if not compact.

Felicia was convinced that traces of mineral-hardened water in the previous night's fattoush had done me in. Even natives aren't immune to its devilry, she said. After a few months away, her homecoming might include a good puke as well. She dropped me off at the hotel, and I flopped out on the bed, assuming the sad, crampy little z I call "downward-facing tourist." There was a party in Felicia's honor later that evening and I was resolved to go.

A few hours later four of us—me, Felicia, and a pair of her friends—were in a blue BMW and headed for Gemmayzeh, a Christian enclave known for the clubs you won't find in its Muslim counterpart. Like many of the young Lebanese I met, Felicia is well-connected, geographically: she has already lived in more countries than many Americans will ever visit, including the United States, where her family waited out the civil war. Her stunning, raven-haired girlfriends were also raised primarily in the U.S. and could toggle between frankly accented American English and the rhythmic, glottal flow of Arabic.

The empty streets clapped out our footsteps as we approached Kayan, a low-lit pub that serves bad music and big, strong drinks. We commandeered a corner and waited for Felicia's guests, including a BBC News producer, a former *Daily Star* reporter, an NGO worker, and Neill, a mysterious, British ladies' man with a nonprofit day job none of them could quite fathom. Before his arrival it was speculated, by people I can only assume count him as a friend, that their Neill might be a spy.

Within an hour the bar was packed with heads nodding in time—improbably, I felt—to Cornershop and Roxette. Two drinks in I was struggling to explain myself to Rob, the NGO worker from Florida. Rob was rangy and kind and made jokes about whether it was too early in the evening to send a booty text. Dipping in and ducking back in the birdish choreography of a first, loud conversation, he told me that even a year ago, even right after the war, he would have said the entire country had a 10 percent chance of spinning out of control on any given day. "Now," he shouted, raising his eyebrows and working his palms like pistons to ensure I got the point above the music, "fifty-fifty."

A young Lebanese man with a blazing white bandage fitted across the bridge of his nose was seated at the bar. A punch-up seemed unlikely for such a slickly drawn boy; Rob said it was probably a nose job. Beirut has become the plastic-surgery capital of the region, a Middle Eastern counterpart to its similarly middle-class-less, expatriate satellite country, Brazil. Last year Lebanese banks began offering multithousand-dollar loans specifically for plastic surgery, and it is currently the investment of choice; bandages are worn like Hermès scarves. "It makes no sense!" I yelled over Rob's shoulder, as Felicia bounced to the beat at the next table. It was Friday night and everyone was glad to be alive and in good company. And yet it makes perfect sense: in the face of astronomical disarray, perhaps the sanest impulse is to fix what you can.

Felicia invited me to join the group on a ski trip the next day, and I had to confess that I have never been on skis in my life. "I'm a big fan of traction" is what I always say when the subject comes up, and I said it then.

Instead I began that Saturday the way I would the next

several mornings: calling a tour company to see if they had attracted the single other customer needed to merit their running a day trip into the countryside. I was still the only taker. A few floors up, in the hotel's hushed dining bay overlooking the sea, the continental breakfast spread had been reduced to coffee, a few squares of poreless bread, and a fruit salad spotted with black olives. I plucked one up with a pair of small, serrated tongs, then dropped it through a salutary puff of fruit flies.

I decided to walk over to Gouraud Street and sip away a few hours in Le Rouge Café. It was the weekend rush; chattering couples and families filled every table of the small front room. A bar at the back opens onto a galley kitchen, and English literary quotes are stenciled onto the walls in various fonts and sizes. From Günter Grass: *The job of the citizen is to keep his mouth open.* Oh really, Günter?

I was close enough to the three old-timers beside me, merry chain-smokers who received staff members throughout the meal with copious kisses and handshakes, to feel a part of their fun. In fact I sat through an entire service without catching my waiter's eye. After a further half hour spent wondering if I had managed to offend, something about the polite sweep of his gaze across the empty chair opposite me every time he passed suggested it had not occurred to him that I would be dining alone. When I told him just that, he popped up straight with a mortified look, quickly slipping me a second Diet Pepsi as consolation.

This is where the Parisian influence ends: one does not eat alone in Beirut. It's seen as a rather sad, confusing thing to do. To be alone signals misfortune or just misjudgment—in any case a kind of defeat. I had asked Felicia if Beirut had any movie theaters, and she told me they were all on hiatus; people were too afraid to go out at night. But today the mood is almost jubilant, defiantly so. When the restaurant falls to darkness and the kitchen's whirring cuts out with a kind of needle drop, the waiters don't break their step and no head turns. Eventually the owner, a hale and gracious gentleman named Hamil, stopped by my table to wonder if I had any quotes to add to the wall. I had been pretending to write in my notebook to keep from collecting looks from my fellow diners that could as easily have passed between us at the funeral of my firstborn son. I couldn't think of a quote for Hamil, or at least I didn't tell him what came to mind: *Oh really, Günter?*

After lunch I walked south into Ras El Nabaa, where I had Lebanon's National Museum to myself on a Saturday afternoon. One guard was on duty, and we played a lethargic game of cat and mouse as I lingered over two floors of mosaics, Bronze Age baubles, and Roman sarcophagi. Every thirty feet or so I heard the jingle of the guard's keys a respectful distance behind, as he rose to limp toward an adjacent corner and continue his surveillance. This kind of thing would usually make me laugh, but it was one of those days when I can't understand how anyone makes it down the street with all of the shit they have inside them. So it just made me want to cry.

We were leaving Beirut, circling into the valley beneath the nasty gap in the middle of the Mdairej Bridge. "We're about to get a terrific view of what accurate munitions can do," said the Irishman sitting directly in front of me. From the low angle of our detour, the damage to the Middle East's tallest bridge was even more spectacular. The Palestinian woman beside me began taking pictures, centering the long blank space in her digital monitor. The Israelis had bombed the bridge in 2006, taking out a two-hundred-foot support beam and crippling Beirut's supply traffic.

After a week of early-morning calls, there had finally been enough people for a trip to Anjar and Baalbek to go forward, and so four of us were in the back of a minivan: Peter, the Irishman, and his wife, Margaret; Nisrine, the Palestinian; and me—along with our Lebanese guide, Raaida, and Bilalo, who was huge, bashful, and drove like the blazes.

Nisrine had not been to Lebanon since she was three years old. She felt the odds that her sponsor—the producers of a documentary she was working on—would secure a visa were almost nil, so the trip was sudden and a considerable surprise. Now she was cramming her schedule with sights like Godard's *bande à part* racing through the Louvre. The Irish couple had toured Damascus the previous day and enjoyed the city very much. "Maybe I could borrow your passport," Nisrine said, with what would become her trademark, edgy deadpan, "and see it for myself." Over fortysome years she had traveled the world, but never entered the countries bordering her own. Nisrine seemed surprised and a little pained by the green of the mountain vegetation bordering the Bekáa Valley; she had almost forgotten how Palestine used to look. When we hit a patch of scrubby, desert bush she muttered about this being more like it. Earlier she had turned to me, by way of introduction, and asked if I was interested in seeing the Jeita caves with her the next day. "If there are two people," she said, eyebrows all but waggling, "they have to take us." I liked Nisrine immediately. I would go; I wouldn't let her down. She kept asking throughout the day, just to be sure.

Raaida was wide-mouthed and willowy. Wrapped in sunglasses and two wool sweaters, she chatted about our itinerary while the rest of us exchanged dippy comments about the weather, the food, the countries of our birth. Late into his sixties and all but retired, Peter was in Beirut consulting. He had spent a career as an electrical engineer building power plants around the world; his accent seemed diluted by equal parts travel and time. "You've come to fix our power!" Raaida exclaimed, twisting in her front seat to face us. Peter chuckled. "God himself couldn't fix the power here."

President Bush was in the region, but he wasn't coming to Lebanon. He had been photographed goofing off with Saudi sheikhs and exchanging backslaps with Israeli emissaries. These images, Nisrine said, confirmed Bush's unseriousness about the Palestinian cause. President Clinton—now he almost got there. There might be peace today, she said, had it not been for that chubby tramp and her big, red lips. Here Margaret chimed in from behind her massive sunglasses for the first time that morning. It was unclear if her approving murmur was meant to affirm the tragic subversion of the Clinton administration's agenda for peace in the Middle East or the notorious sluttery of young American women.

Less than fifteen kilometers from the Syrian border in the east of Lebanon, Baalbek is the birthplace of Hezbollah. The first members began training there in 1979, and today it is considered the group's strategic headquarters. The ruins at Baalbek are devastating. The site encompasses the largest Roman temples ever built and evidence of a settlement dating back to the Bronze Age. Excavation in the area—like all excavation in the archaeologically larded Lebanese countryside—halted with the civil war and has not resumed. Tourism, once a lifeblood industry, is increasingly untenable. There were no guards, no barriers, and no other visitors. We drifted through the heady sprawl of this minicivilization, picking and wobbling and jumping back at the treacherous drop that divides the temples of Jupiter and Bacchus. The noon call to prayer began to sound throughout not just the city but the valley, the loudest and most plaintive I had heard. It wended through the towering pillars below, in no rush to reach our ears.

On the way back to the van we were beset by four or five grizzled, older men hawking gum, scarves, and green-and-yellow Party of God commemorative gear. They tugged at our elbows and shook Chiclets under our noses, surrounding us in an impressive formation. When it became clear that they were going to follow us the several blocks back to the van, a mixture of embarrassment and a more complicated tension overtook the group.

"Well, I decided against the Hezbollah T-shirt," Peter sighed, breaking our heavy silence as he strapped back into his seat. We all laughed, delivered by Peter's perfect delivery.

We six finally faced each other over lunch—platter after platter of traditional food served by the fireplace of a large, drafty family restaurant in Zahlé. The minor revelations of a shared meal eased the way into franker talk: Nisrine tolerates Americans and reveres the Japanese; Margaret doesn't drink and never has; Raaida is off carbs and was so tickled by Peter's use of the expression "a moment on the lips, a lifetime on the hips" that she made him write it down ("It's really true," she said, wiping her eyes); Bilalo smokes between courses; and I can eat my weight in baba ghanoush.

Raaida called to me from the far end of the table as the bitter candied fruit arrived for dessert, rhyming my name with *seashell*. "Bilalo has something he's been wanting to ask you," she announced. I leaned over my plate to catch our driver's eye two seats down, but Bilalo had shrunk into the back of his chair like a kid refusing rice pudding. Raaida is a teaser, so his discomfort was her delight.

"He's curious about your name," she went on. "Do you want to know why?" Bilalo had wondered if I was aware that Lebanon's opposition leader was a man by the name of Michel Aoun, and that Aoun's party color is orange. There is even, I would learn, an "Orange TV" channel, the premier network for Iranian jihadist propaganda. Bilalo finally looked down at me, blushing to the rafters. I assured him, a little flushed myself, that I was Orange in name only.

Raaida and Nisrine had been cordial, almost careful with one another throughout the morning, often lapsing into Arabic, but spoke more freely over lunch. Raaida is Greek Catholic—basically Greek Orthodox plus pope, she said—though the concept of "taking the pin," which Margaret did at her confirmation at the age of twelve, felt bafflingly foreign. There was needling throughout the meal: *Just a sip! Come on, Margaret.* As though a lifetime's commitment might topple because a Lebanese tour guide thought it was the stupidest thing she ever heard. Margaret still wears the Pioneer pin, with its emblem of the sacred heart, and won't touch chocolate liqueurs or certain medications. At this point it's just stubbornness, Peter added reflexively, forking through a sour grape leaf between sips of beer. Nisrine's brother is making a film about Palestine's fledgling network of microbreweries. She mentions more than once that Christians make up less than 1.5 percent of Palestine's population.

"We built much of what is here," Nisrine said, during a discussion of Lebanon's faltering infrastructure, and Raaida allowed it. Today Sri Lankans and Filipinos make up the country's sorely unregulated underclass, and Palestinians are official pariahs. After a few moments' deliberation, Nisrine put down her glass and declared that four days spent meeting and speaking with the people of Beirut had made it clear to her that the Palestinians were better off than the Lebanese. "In an occupied country there is a solution," she said. "Get rid of the occupier, get rid of the problem. The people still have *hope*." But in Lebanon, she went on, the problems are so treacherous and densely intertwined that there is no path out, or none that the people can see, and that is a far worse place to be.

This was more than Raaida could bear. Being pitied by a Palestinian was definitely not on the itinerary. Her eyes filled with tears and the fragile good humor that had borne us all through the day gave way.

"If you want to know the truth," she said, looking around the table, "if I can speak openly—I am miserable." She made a sharp, helpless gesture, as though momentarily waiving her professional veneer. "I am very depressed. My whole country is depressed. We are frightened. Everyone is trying to leave but there is nowhere to go—there are no jobs, no money. We don't know what will happen. For us this is a terrible time."

Nisrine was the only one who spoke. "Yes," she said, nodding. "Yes."

During the ride back over the mountain we were buoyant again. Raaida told jokes circa the summer of '06, including the one about the vain women of Achrafieh, and another about a pneumatic Lebanese pop star named Haifa being traded for the Israeli port town of the same name. Peter told a story about his daughter's recent attempt to buy a house in Northern Ireland. Hers was the top bid, but the seller turned it down when he saw the spelling of her last name. Not Kelley but Kelly, as in Catholic. These things take time to resolve, was his point, if they ever do.

Beached in the hideous traffic of rush-hour Beirut, we all lost steam and were silent. Cars surrounded us two and three deep on either side. Beyond them, the curious profile of the city: for every structure that is newly built or merely intact, there is a stooped shadow building at its side, kneeling in its own ruin. Raaida leapt from the car with barely a goodbye, following a complicated acceptance of some money from Peter and Margaret, who departed soon after with polite good wishes. I was next.

Down by the corniche Nisrine shuddered as we drove across Beirut's latest ground zero. It was not goodbye, she said, extracting one more promise about the next day's trip to Jeita. I awoke early the next morning and called the company from my bed to confirm. They told me Nisrine had called even earlier, to cancel.

Beirut's boardwalk is as pretty as any on the Mediterranean, and I was determined to make the most of it. I moved along slowly, stopping every few feet to lean against the railing and look out across the sea. It is a rare stretch of the city where lingering is permitted, and one can behave and even begin to feel more or less like a tourist. German warships sit in the middle distance, patrolling the waters for the Israelis. These things take time.

The men don't bother unescorted women in Beirut, when they bother with them at all. I wasn't concerned when a young man wearing jeans with a complicated wash and embellished pockets drew up alongside me at the railing, then slid a ways down. I turned to the mountains, slipping into a paranoiac reverie and rehearsing for the fifty-third time what I would tell the American agent at passport control when he asked me what I was doing alone in Beirut in the middle of January. Before I left, a friend had put a terrible reentry scenario in my head involving German shepherds, tax returns, and a porn sweep of my laptop. I went over the straight story and then I considered the truth, amassing as it was out there over the water. I thought of telling the officer, as he looked over my visa—my life—that Beirut doesn't give a shit about either of us, or what we think. It didn't care when I came, it didn't care when I left, and I respected that. I'd tell him that it's gorgeous and battered and tired and awful, that the mountains are exquisite, the sea as lush and blue as any you'll ever know, that the sky is silky and bright, that the fishermen casting rods, smoking hookahs, and casually wizzing on the rocks below are charming and picturesque—even the warships look sort of beautiful, carving dread into the horizon—and that none of it means a thing. I'd tell him that Beirut did not let me down.

Eventually I turned back to the boardwalk, where the young man in the ornate jeans had attracted a small crowd.

He was standing against the railing with his back to the sea. His chin was tucked in sharp and both hands were shoved deep into his pockets. Four soldiers in red berets were flanking him, two to a side. The shortest, strongest-looking one was questioning him with what seemed like tenderness; they were probably the same age, could have been brothers. He put his hand on the young man's cheek, then pushed up under his chin. The young man refused to look at him. The soldier spread his hands over the young man's temples, tilting his forehead back with his thumbs. Again the young man resisted, keeping his eyes closed and his mouth pursed. I thought maybe he had tried to jump. But how had I missed it? After about half an hour the crowd dispersed, the soldiers went back to wherever they came from, and the young man stood alone again, his back to the sea, his fists in his pockets, and his eyes squeezed shut.

That afternoon I headed toward Al Hikmat to visit the Sursock collection of Islamic art, maybe walk home along the port. It had taken several tries to get the museum's eccentric hours straight. I didn't hear the explosion, but within moments it was clear it had happened. There was an uptake in the streets, an intensified version of things I had seen before: groups of seven or eight narrow-eyed toughs emerging from nowhere, bumping and pushing down the sidewalk; unmarked Hyundai vans filled with kerchiefed men leaning hard into the corners, jumping in and out at stoplights.

I walked back over to Charles Helou Avenue, where army trucks were amassing and dispersing. Ambulance peals were sounding, but I couldn't tell from where. A handful of local security guards had gathered on the corner and were pointing out over the coast. I moved in closer and followed their gestures: a bloom of smoke was rising off to the right, to the north, where a U.S. embassy car was burning in the street. The bomb had been detonated a breath too soon; the car's passenger and driver were injured but alive. The three people who happened to be passing by, however, were dead. A soldier from a nearby checkpoint came to join the men and eventually turned to me. After a scan through my bag, he told me to clear out, that it wasn't safe.

That seemed to be my cue—permission, finally, to panic. Yet even for me, even after just a few days, the moment was not unexpected. When a city is wound this tight, the ambient strain of apprehension rivals any single vicious note plucked upon it, those brief vibrations absorbed by a further tightening of the strings. The soldier was used to telling people what to do, and I was clearly waiting to be told. In truth nothing felt that different from before.

Earlier, on the boardwalk, I had moved to leave the scene gathering around the frozen young man but found myself taking a seat on a nearby bench. The crowd was swelling with each passerby, until real commotion encircled his silence. No one tried to move him; everyone just wanted to talk. A wide-set, older woman in a thick wool coat dropped back from the soldiers and the scrum. She sat down beside me and let spill a few tears. One woman and then another stopped to console her, so that a satellite crowd soon amassed to mirror the larger one across the way. We looked on together, waiting for some kind of outcome, some progress. Every few minutes a commuter plane swung in low over the water, making its way into the city.

War and Well-Being,
21° 19'N., 157° 52'W.

I am wonderfully and fearfully made,
and such knowledge is too excellent for me.
             —Psalm of David 139:14, 6

We are sick! We are sick!
We are sick, sick, sick!
Like we're sociologically sick!
—"Gee, Officer Krupke," *West Side Story*

1

The top reasons for visiting Hawaii have been broken down by its Department of Business, Economic Development, and Tourism in this order: Honeymoon; To Get Married; Pleasure/Vacation; Convention/Conference; Corporate Meeting; Incentive Trip; Other Business; Visiting Friends or Relatives; Government or Military Business; To Attend School; Sports Event; and Other, which leaves a one-inch line for elaboration. I handed back the form that all incoming island visitors are asked to fill out blank but aware of my first sensation of the place: it did not seem unusual that someone with a long history of near-complete lack of interest in Hawaii was on the brink of availing herself of more or less its full spectrum of attractions.

Visiting the fiftieth state a mere eight years into one's American education feels a little like skipping to the end of a story with only the wispiest grasp of the plot. Or at least it felt that way touching down in Honolulu, which is farther from my current home in New York City than any point in my native Canada. And yet, as I was careful to confirm, despite traveling five thousand miles west, the sudden ubiquity of sarongs, and a wicked case of jet lag, I had not committed the cellular sin of "roaming." Whatever the future of territorial boundaries might be, one of the best ways for an American (or even a resident alien) to recover a sense of them at the beginning of the twenty-first century is to enjoy the outer limits of her satellite privileges. Welcome to paradise.

A couple of weeks before my flight to Honolulu, where I had traveled to attend the annual conference of the American Psychiatric Association, President Obama had crossed the East Room of the White House, looked into a camera, and announced that Osama bin Laden had been killed during a Navy SEAL raid on his compound in Pakistan. The news satisfied the craving for a clear victory that has only seemed to intensify in recent years. Positive military PR bursts have been especially scarce throughout the Iraq and Afghan wars, despite the efforts of a team devoted to generating them. Those efforts have not gone unnoticed by the APA, an embattled body about which more in a moment, though for now it may give you a sense of their predicament to learn that they recently recruited a public relations guru away from his perch at the Department of Defense.

Among the first such efforts was the military's assurance that DNA technology would be a part of these new campaigns, meaning every casualty would be properly identified and accounted for—no American left behind. In a parallel effort, national cemeteries were being combed for unmarked graves and remains exhumed for testing. Among the first of these was one of the four famously unknown men laid to rest in the most visited tomb in Virginia's Arlington National Cemetery.

The tradition that came to define the Tomb of the Unknown Soldier began in 1921, when a World War I veteran was flown to France to select an unknown from unknowns. The ceremony was initiated by the British several years earlier. Faced with four identical caskets taken from different French cemeteries, after a few moments' consideration the veteran signaled his choice with the placement of a bouquet of white roses. The selected casket was shipped to Arlington, and on Veterans Day of that year the monument housing the body was unveiled to the public. In 1956 the process was repeated: several unidentified bodies from World War II and the Korean War were exhumed from cemeteries around the world, and a veteran of each war was asked to select, according to an intuition known only to him, the body that would be placed in the Arlington tomb.

By the time a Vietnam casualty was chosen, in a Pearl Harbor ceremony in 1984, the ritual had taken on an indelible significance. It is said that military brass have gone so far as to suppress or destroy evidence that might identify one of the men. Rumor has it that service in the twenty-four-hour honor guard over the tombs requires a pledge to maintain both eternal sobriety and a thirty-inch waist.

It was even suggested that the Pentagon had a good idea

about the Vietnam unknown's identity when he was chosen. By the spring of 1998, that kind of deception was tough to maintain; it was the first days of the Internet, and the idea was just taking shape that information, like the mediating sweat from our pores, wanted to be free. A veterans' rights activist named Ted Sampley had worked online to piece together a case for the Vietnam unknown's identity. The story was picked up by the media, and soon after that the advances in forensic science that arrived too late for the murder prosecution of a faded football hero and too early for the sitting president reached the tomb.

In June 1998 a bone fragment of the last of the unknown soldiers was tested for mitochondrial DNA and identified as the remains of twenty-four-year-old Michael Blassie, an air force first lieutenant whose plane was shot down over An Loc during the Easter Offensive of 1972. His body was returned to his family in St. Louis, Missouri, and the Vietnam tomb at Arlington has remained pointedly empty ever since.

Between 1972 and 1984, Blassie's remains were in Honolulu, home of the National Memorial Cemetery of the Pacific, a majestic burial site located atop a volcanic crater. Called Puowaina, or "hill of sacrifice," in Hawaiian, after its original, pagan function as just that, it was rechristened as the Punchbowl in English, I was told, because it looks kind of like a punch bowl. Despite a legible map and the clear instruction of the Frenchman manning a table full of his large-printed local-history texts in the vestibule of the U.S. Army Museum of Hawaii, I spent the better part of my first afternoon in Honolulu searching for the Punchbowl.

The museum, set along the cool, dark corridor of a defunct munitions battery at Fort DeRussy, was all but empty at late morning. Because it tells the story not of the island but of the United States on the island, the museum's overwhelming mood is that of a double failure. The first, made plain by the fort itself, is treated more euphemistically in a brief description of the slingshots used by the natives "before the arrival of western technology." The second is laid out in a relic-strewn installation detailing the Japanese attack on Honolulu's Pearl Harbor in December of 1941. A few photographs are among the maps and recovered shards of metal. Seventy years later, the main emotion flowing through the museum's retelling of the story of that "peaceful" morning is still wounded surprise, as every attack on American soil is in some sense a surprise. Farther down the hall, after the Pacific war has been ended by an "overwhelming show of power" at Hiroshima and Nagasaki, a certain relief is expressed about the return to conventional weapons and tactics in Korea. General "Hap" Arnold, whose remarks are posted near the images of a decimated Japan, sums it up: "Destruction has become too cheap, too easy!"

The museum's designers brought the bulk of their creativity to bear on Vietnam. The "Back to Nam" corner is accessible via a kind of disco bridge, inlaid with bamboo, where footsteps trigger flashing lights and arcade-style explosions. Nearby a vintage Coke can is spotlit beside an explanation of improvised grenades titled "It's the Real Thing." The story of Vietnam, in case you are still wondering, ends this way: "The disengagement was honorable; United States forces had not been defeated on the battlefield. But there remain lasting scars for having paid such a price to accomplish so little."

I was checking out the gift shop's array of four-color books about Pearl Harbor movies when I spotted Pierre Moulin, full-bellied and gray-bearded, sweating lightly through his blue linen button-down as he schooled an old-timer about a local war monument. Pierre left his native Bruyères, France—site of one of the ten most important battles in American history, he informed me, and with no movie to show for it!—for the islands almost thirty years before, and since that time he had written a book to address my every Hawaiian concern. Pierre noted my French Canadian lineage favorably, though even he had forgotten the significance of whether *Meunier* is spelled with an *i* or a *y*. Europe had offloaded its rubbish to the United States during the great migration, he confided, whereas Canada attracted a higher order of immigrant.

And who winds up on Hawaii?

I had but one day to burn in paradise, where the days have been burning for those who wind up here since Captain Cook crashed the Polynesians' thousand-year reign in 1778. (Pierre says the Spanish beat Cook by three centuries; he's writing a book.) And it would seem we all wind up on Hawaii, eventually. If Hawaii has learned to expect us, it is no longer with fresh lilies and dashboard-surfing beauties—we are too many to stand on that particular ceremony, though self-purchased synthetic leis are a suitable nod to it. Instead Hawaii greets its guests with the cool accommodation of algorithm, a paradise theme park with bodies to move. Somewhat late to its own game, in the fall of 2011 Disney opened its first Hawaiian resort. The Aulani, set on twenty-one acres of beachfront seventeen miles outside Honolulu, promises immersion in local culture "through Disney magic."

The question of how you wound up on Hawaii and the desire for a sense of being *in* it are subsets of the same, so-close-yet-so-damn-far problem. It had me blotting out the mimetic shopping strips to glean the distance, leaning into the thick, misted morning air for some situating, bone-alarm frequency, tilting at the ocean for a sense of stubborn place, and typing at night to friends who would receive my words in the same form and at the same speed no matter their origin or how often I told them, or myself, that I was but a dot in the ocean, a comma between continents. For those temporary, those airborne fleas, it's easier to be Hawaii than be in it.

That first morning I had woken up with military business on my mind—a visit to the Pearl Harbor memorial, where over a thousand servicemen are still entombed in the sunken USS *Arizona*. Brochures in the lobby of my Waikiki hotel, a high-rise the same, minimally varied shade of Cheerio of all the others comprising the "10,000 bookable rooms" I see advertised throughout my stay, described *NEW* and *AMAZING* "Pearl Harbor Heroes Adventure" tours. Each tour emphasizes the visceral pleasures of re-creation, so that to choose between them means choosing whether to *relive*, *experience*, or *immerse yourself in* the moment in American history that *will live in infamy*. There is also the option of doing any one of those things *while also* exploring the island of Oahu *in all its grandeur*, but that costs a little more. Some might prefer to walk *in the exact footsteps* of America's most courageous heroes, others to *stand in their shadows*. These are things each consumer must figure out for herself.

The concierge told me that there was no point in my trying to stand in anyone's shadow at Pearl Harbor: it's the most popular tourist attraction in Hawaii. "If you get there after nine, it's a four-hour wait," he advised. "And they close the lines at noon." I cast my eyes back to the pamphlet trolley advertising sixty-dollar bus tours, all with a memorial-hogging pickup time of 6:00 a.m. And then resolved to find the Punchbowl—where buses can only pass through—on foot.

In theory the walk to the Punchbowl, a straight shot two miles from Waikiki, lacks intrigue. But clues to the old volcano's whereabouts are few and the craters are many. I scaled two of them, deep in Honolulu's suburbs, before pulling a local out of his home to help set me right. I was still guessing right up to the gates, which open onto a vista-skimming view of the beachfront enclave below. It was five in the afternoon, the oppressively direct sunlight had given way to a precious-metal glow, and a windward breeze was brushing grass and leaves over the grave markers of thirty-four thousand bodies. The names and the states differ, but the age—nineteen, twenty, twenty-one—is almost always the same. The crater covers over a hundred acres, and I seemed to have them all to myself.

More unknown soldiers are buried in the Punchbowl than in any other American national cemetery. Its centerpiece—a court of ten marble monuments—is dedicated to the nearly thirty thousand with only a name to lay to rest. For the last decade the Pentagon has been scouring the grounds for suitable DNA candidates. Earlier this year the five bone fragments that remained of a USS *Oklahoma* casualty were the source of a successful identification. It made for a nice press item, even if the only remaining relative of Machinist Mate First Class Charles H. Swanson didn't know he had a cousin at Pearl Harbor.

Magnificent institutional structures are designed to evoke an unknown or maybe just unsuspected emotional response.

I did not know, for instance, until I stood inside the balustraded arms of the Vatican, that God's perfection did in fact rule over my mortal, sinning soul. I hardly guessed, until I sat at Abraham Lincoln's massive, marble-booted feet in Washington, D.C., that the blood of a patriot could pump through my maple-syrup-sucking heart. And yet, sunk deep into the silent core of Puowaina—where President Obama's grandfather rests in mile-deep ash—moving across the vast lawns and through the engraved marble theater, gawping at the Byzantine mosaics that translate the story of the Pacific wars into cave-wall tableaux, and kneeling over a grave to pencil-rub the word UNKNOWN into a notebook page, I didn't feel what I was meant to. I could not seem to submit. Even at the urging of Lincoln himself, whose letter of condolence to the famously, unfathomably bereaved Lydia Bixby is quoted at the foot of an apparitional statue of Lady Columbia.

I thought only of the dead—the known dead, named and unnamed—who never imagined their bodies filling the crater of a sea-speck volcano. The dead who died anguished and light-years from home—at last I felt the distance—pleading for its safeties as the life was blasted from their bodies. I thought of the living—not the bereft, oddly, but those intent on suspending their lives at the age of these young men, who had no choice. I thought of how Lydia Bixby lost two sons in the Civil War—not five, as Lincoln was told. No one cares about that now. The truth of his words about *the solemn pride that must be yours*, the nobility of *sacrifice*, and *the altar of freedom* outweighed the truth of the situation. I thought of how often the same words are now used to jam the scales to suit political will. The way that these new wars have been shoved into the shadow of a larger monument, eroding the ground where it stands. I wondered if it's possible to memorialize a war that was itself conceived as a kind of reminder. I listened to the wind blow and all I heard was wind blowing.

"Every war is ironic," Paul Fussell wrote in 1975, "because every war is worse than expected." Sixteen years later, teenagers like me wrote earnest diary entries on the eve of the Gulf War. We wondered what was going to happen, what it all meant, what war *was*. In fact it seemed not at all as bad as the movies would have had us believe—a kind of inverted irony. This was tidy and precise, combat by remote control. Were the experience of war ever remotely comprehensible by those reading the papers and manning their own remote controls, digitizing and disseminating its enactment lost it to us forever. We absorbed information in seemingly comprehensive terms—even watched aerial bombings in real time—and yet the enemy had never felt quite so unknown.

Fussell called the Great War the most ironic war in human history. The gap between what the participants thought they were doing and what actually happened had never been greater. The result was mass disillusionment, and the birth of modern irony. Such illusions as lingered on toward the end of that century were sustained by a kind of artificial respiration, where we breathed in the promises of brands or passing beliefs and breathed out part of ourselves with them, choking the atmosphere with unsynthesized desire. The ideals of freedom and prosperity grew strangely dichotomous, dividing within and without. Confronting literal limits had lost its nation-defining purpose; Hawaii was as far west as we were going to go in the postnuclear age, and the space program was foundering into irrelevance. Prosperity too faded into cherished abstraction, even as the freedom to consume became the metaphor of modern life.

On the morning of September 11, 2001, as the towers were still burning, a white-haired woman stepped into my Toronto apartment building's elevator with four words—"We're going to war"—and I realized I still didn't know what they meant. But then the meaning of war was about to shift again, we were told, this time to accommodate an untraditional combatant, an enemy that seemed to come out of nowhere, out of the sky. The national self-drama of absolutes—us versus them, known and unknown, before and after—resurged just as we were settling into a sense of private omnipotence. So that when Donald Rumsfeld talked about "the unknown unknowns" at provocative large in Iraq, beyond their use as instant grist for digital chortlers, instead of forming a caution the words found their meaning as a dare.

In the chapel a guest book is filled with direct addresses to the dead. Most favor two of Lincoln's words: *freedom* and *sacrifice*. Drawing a causal connection between them was a popular choice. "It is incumbent for all of us to always remember the price we pay to fight the wars this great country has, is, and will be fighting for in the name of the precious freedom we all enjoy," one woman wrote. "We are in an eternal debt of gratitude to all these men and women who unstintingly give their lives in the cause of freedom. God Bless America!"

It gives me no pleasure to admit that I can't read the inscription of a God-fearing woman without feeling the chill of irony. It becomes exhausting, all this parsing, to the point that one begins to envy that kind of certainty, if only as a relief from the constant searching, through a mustard fog of rhetoric and reflexivity, for one's own response. Irony imposes its own kind of innocence—the swaddling of detachment, which only intensified as two wars were waged on terms so ironic they broke through to postmodernity. Like "reality," *freedom* now threatens to arm itself permanently with double-barreled quotes. Say "9/11" in a crowded theater and watch it divide into gleaming masks of conviction and rictal expressions of the grimmest doubt. The simplest and most obvious response—deep, enduring sadness—has somehow become the most elusive. Instead, my first sensation while reading through the guest book is the quill ripple of apprehension. This might be the most American feeling I have all day.

2

Of special interest to the state's Department of Business, Economic Development, and Tourism are your intentions toward the Hawaii Convention Center. Over its four-year construction, begun in 1994, two hundred dollars were spent for every one of its million square feet. The idea, tourism-wise, was that if large institutional bodies held their conferences in paradise, conference-goers might pad out their stay to make the trip worthwhile. State-owned and privately operated, the Hawaii Convention Center is a meringue-tufted monolith about a mile from the Waikiki shore in Honolulu, and for five days in the spring of 2011 it was reserved to host the American Psychiatric Association's annual conference.

Officially I was press. Having requested a pass, I was told, after peeling a teal-blue tote bag off a shawarma-like pile of them in the general registration hall, that I had complete access to the symposiums, sessions, seminars, keynotes, and classes that began at six every morning. I felt a little sheepish about this: APA members paid hundreds of dollars for the privilege I was granted with an e-mail. My press badge was an index card printed with my name and slipped into a clear plastic sleeve bound by a thin nylon string. It hung, ignored, around my neck over five days of wandering into general and registered events. Second-tier film festivals run with Pentagon-grade clearances by comparison.

Unlike, say, the bunkered labyrinth in Austin, Texas, Honolulu's convention center is filled with light and open air. A warm, saline breeze wends through its wide-slung corridors. The word is *pleasant*, which is about as excited as it's possible to get over a convention center. Turning through the halls the afternoon before opening day, as the APA constituency began to file in and form migratory patterns, it seemed a safe and secluded enough place to air out what was festering in our darkest closets back home. As sedentary-workforce members go, psychiatrists have a specifically underutilized look. Moving as a thin, toneless herd through the building's ceramic-tiled, multitiered savanna, they took on an antelope-like vulnerability: the greater their number, the more defenseless they appeared.

The APA, a body still adjusting to its own tremendous and unforeseen influence, had come to Honolulu to reveal the shifting outline of its signal creation, the *Diagnostic and Statistical Manual of Mental Disorders*, commonly known as the *DSM*. Over its sixty-year history the manual has charted our changing relationship to what is considered normal—socially and individually, emotionally and behaviorally. That its value as a historical document has threatened to outweigh its practical use—helping doctors help patients by identifying and diagnosing their mental illnesses—places the *DSM* very much in the psychiatric tradition.

There has always been a conspicuous connection between a culture's shortcomings and prevailing self-interests and what it defines as crazy. In seventeenth-century Europe the first pangs of globalization seemed to manifest in a Swiss doctor's diagnosis of *nostalgia*—Greek for "homesickness"—in students and soldiers who experienced crippling melancholy after time spent far from home. In the mid-1800s, an American doctor named Samuel Cartwright proposed that runaway slaves were suffering from something called *drapetomania*. "Normal" blacks, Cartwright argued, displayed a childlike love of their masters, and the urge for freedom was "as much a disease of the mind as any other species of mental alienation."

The publication of the first *DSM* in 1952 promoted a new and central scientific order in the taxonomy of mental illness; Joe Doctor could no longer go around fashioning Greek fragments into words and calling them diseases. But consensus didn't necessarily equate progress: the first *DSM* classified homosexuality as a mental disorder, as did the second. If the evidence of overt social biases has eased somewhat, the power of putting a name to something inconvenient, uncomfortable, or plainly fraught and calling it a sickness has only intensified in the decades since the *DSM* was forced to expunge its homosexuality diagnosis. The decline of rigid social roles and rituals reopened the question of what it means to be normal just as the idea of better living through science and technology took seed. If you were looking for answers about what was wrong with you or how to realize some ideal self—and it seemed many of us were—psychiatry was more than happy to oblige, and with the benefit of a shiny new scientific veneer.

To the extent that a belief in self-direction and personal freedom stands in rejection of collectively defined limitations, inflation of the one equals shrinkage of the other. The less willing we were to acknowledge limits, however—starting with death and working backward—the more desperately we seemed to pursue a sense of them, directly or indirectly, as individuals. The APA's role in public health is both an example and a reflection of the paradox of personal satisfaction, where the refusal of limits pretty much ensures you will be bound by them in some defining and highly screwed-up way. By the time of the publication of *DSM-IV*, in 1994, the number of diagnosable disorders had tripled, indicating a rate of about five new mental illnesses a year since they started keeping count.

The APA has gone by several names over its 167-year history, including the American Medico-Psychological Association, and before that the Association of Medical Superintendents of American Institutions for the Insane. In 1840, shortly before the APA formed under the latter name, a first attempt was made to try to count the number of insane people populating the United States, as part of the census sometimes cited as the origin of the *DSM*. Statistics, quite fashionable in the mid-nineteenth century, were promoted as a clearer, less biased—that is to say, less political—resource in developing social policy. The 1840 census's methods were crude and tied largely to mental institutions, and the results were used to demonstrate successful rehabilitation rather than inform diagnosis or classification. At that time, the treatment for insanity reflected a belief in the connection between a rising rate of mental illness and a rapidly modernizing society. Remove the patient from a frenetic environment, the theory went, and her craziness would clear right up.

Despite endorsing the idea that modern life made people nuts, Edward Jarvis, a psychiatrist involved in guiding and interpreting the census-derived statistics over the next several decades, argued that the fact that mental health facilities were filling up as fast as they could build them didn't necessarily reflect an increasingly deranged population. Jarvis believed that an easing of the social stigma attached to mental illness and the rise in transportation and availability of treatment indicated that the troubled were now more willing to look into treatment.

Working backward in pursuit of causality, Jarvis used statistics to speculate about the connection between mental illness and everything from education to sex, race, geography, and marital status. Using data derived from already institutionalized patients, the 1880 census identified seven types of insanity: simple, epileptic, paralytic, senile dementia, organic dementia, idiocy, and cretinism. Where medicine's move into germ theory meant a fever was increasingly no longer just a fever—a treatable affliction with an unknown cause—insanity was still a judgment call made case by case, and population studies remained the most reliable source of information on the when, where, and why of going mad.

Early in the twentieth century it was war—specifically the connection of circumstance to psychiatric distress—that created a need for a classification system that existed outside the extremes of institutionalization. Having staggered off the battlefields of rural Europe, boys still shy of voting age were suffering in ways previously unknown to humankind.

It was a new reality, and homesickness didn't cover it. Advanced Weaponry—poison gases, machine guns, and artillery shells—was unveiled across trenches of massive, chaotic breadth. The First World War's seventy million soldiers had little relief from combat, incomprehensible carnage, and gruesome living conditions, and the result was psychic trauma on an unprecedented scale. The psychiatric community earned precious public trust when it moved in to join the effort to help fragile young veterans recover and reintegrate.

Institution-based psychiatry had ghettoized its practitioners—then called alienists—and the First World War helped expedite the shift to outpatient care and a more open role in public health. It also created a new language that continues to reverberate through the English vernacular. *Shell shock* lacks the romance of *nostalgia* or *soldier's heart*—a diagnosis used to describe the severe anxiety observed in American Civil War soldiers—but it fit the times and the men, including my great-grandfather, who might rather have died in the mudflats of France than be perceived as weakened by the fight. Perhaps the most famous diagnosis to emerge from the First World War was that of Adolf Hitler, who was determined to be suffering from *hysterical blindness* long after the effects of a run-in with a canister of mustard gas had worn off.

By the time of Hitler's war, psychiatry had undergone a medical makeover. To Sigmund Freud's dismay, psychiatry was acknowledged as a medical science in the 1920s, this being considered a strategic (and largely American-led) victory within the profession. The new influx of traumatized soldiers formed a platform for psychiatry's reinvention in the United States, where younger doctors—many motivated by war experience—opted to enter the field. Psychiatry had stagnated between the world wars, suffering from its undifferentiated approach to diagnosis and continued focus on the institutionalized, so that the army and the navy came up with their own classification systems during World War II to treat the disorders manifesting in their troops.

The first *DSM* used the armed forces classifications as a kind of cheat sheet, deviating from them only slightly and in some cases not at all. It divided mental illness into two broad categories: impaired mental function due to brain pathology, and general inability to adjust to the world due to psychiatric impairment. Inflected by psychoanalytic theory, which holds that the defining task of a human psychology is to broker between biological drives and the pressures of the external world, *DSM*'s military heritage also suggest a fundamental interest in the pathology of mental disturbance—its symptoms *and* its causes—in otherwise healthy individuals.

As well as setting down the first official record of our collective psychiatric history, *DSM-I* elevated the role of diagnosis as part of the psychiatric method. As then chair of the APA's committee on nomenclature and statistics, George Raines noted that sound diagnosis "is possible only with a nomenclature in keeping with current concepts of psychiatric illness." Because words were ultimately all the committee had, a huge part of the challenge would simply be finding the right ones to capture the psychosocial zeitgeist. Once a set of intangible symptoms and subjective observations could be reified, in print, as a mental illness, psychiatry's strange, self-defeating ambition to merge medical certainty with the art of personal storytelling could be pursued in earnest.

At the end of the century that began with Freud's vision of psychoanalysis as a form of narrative excavation only tangentially concerned with medicine, descriptive language was still the heart of psychiatric diagnosis. Its nomenclature had, however, come to reflect a more general tendency toward easily repeatable acronyms and the triple-processed language of market branding. That shift began in the mid-1970s, when psychiatry's image problem reached critical mass. Beyond the homosexuality snafu, research had shown that the diagnostic process had reliability issues beyond what any legitimate medical practice would allow. If a patient walked into five different doctors' offices presenting the same set of symptoms, the odds that he would walk out with five different diagnoses were intolerably high. Diagnostic patterns also seemed to be consistent with location: British doctors, for instance, tended to see manic depression where their American counterparts saw schizophrenia. Psychoanalysis had already completed a cycle of cultural acceptance and repudiation. By the 1970s, factions within that school were recording sessions and scanning transcripts for algorithmic patterns in the race to prove validity. By the time I was in university, in the late 1990s, Freud's case history of "Dora," the nubile hysteric, was being assigned in fiction courses and studied as an example of the unreliable narrator. Modern psychiatry sought to avoid a similar fate.

The 1980 publication of *DSM-III* is widely acknowledged as a turning point for the APA. A task force led by Robert Spitzer sought to rewrite the *DSM* in the language of checklists and codes, eliminating theories of causation altogether and redefining diagnosis in terms of criteria, traits, and axes derived from statistical patterns and identifiable according to a clear and ostensibly less biased system of evaluation. The more binary approach was well-suited to a health- and numbers-crazed culture at home, and the new standardized formulations went international. The media was now doing much of the filtering for the public, which learned to speak OCD and ADD before it could spell the acronyms out. While psychiatrists agreed to use its labels and codes to set insurance mechanisms into motion, the new five-hundred-page manual proved too unwieldy for scrupulous use. As Allen Frances, the chair of *DSM-IV*, told me, "*DSM* is like the Bible or *Origin of the Species*: much discussed but little read."

That few of us have taken a good look at it might explain how the manual became a load-bearing pillar of the pharmaceutical industry. *DSM-IV* marked a new era in our understanding and treatment of mental illness, one that rewarded psychiatry's desire to be recognized as a medical science and Big Pharma's dream of filling the Aral Sea basin with cash. Although we have adopted the language of war to describe the nature of modern well-being—how we fight and struggle and battle with ourselves, win and lose, face demons, destruct and rebuild—the *DSM*'s military origins, along with their vested interest in causality, have been buried deep under half a century of proselytizing for mental health as a biomedical concern and its treatment a medical transaction.

This new framework for understanding how we feel had rational lines but plenty of interpretive room, and a renovated psychiatric infrastructure was inlaid with its first prescription. Not even the interested parties predicted what happened next. Depression, especially, proved to be a pandemic gold mine. Since Prozac was patented in 1988, antidepressants have become the fourth-biggest-selling drug in the country. Alone in the market in the early days, Prozac sales jumped 20 percent in 1993. At its peak, Prozac outdid Eli Lilly's projections forty-five times over, bringing in three billion dollars in a single year. Last year Americans consumed over ten billion dollars' worth of antidepressants.

Like every other late-twentieth-century capitalist enterprise, the mental health industry was soon in cancerous thrall to perpetual growth. Soon pharma-sponsored studies were indicating antidepressants as an effective treatment for "generalized anxiety," "social phobia," and all manner of compulsive disorders and substance addictions. The search for new disorders was consolidated, so that scientific studies, the illnesses they identify, and the drugs designed (or retrofitted, as the case may be; the why and how of the way antidepressants work are that rare *unknown known*) to treat them might debut together. After "pre-menstrual dysphoric disorder" was introduced in *DSM-IV*, Prozac was quickly rebranded as Sarafem and marketed to women whose severe menstrual cycles now fell under the rubric of mental illness. Billions of dollars were funneled into advertising campaigns after the Food and Drug Administration let out its already generous direct-to-consumer advertising legislation in 1997, and doctors were the targets of separate but equally extravagant marketing blitzes. Outside of New Zealand, the United States is the only country in the world that allows such advertising, and millions of Americans were diagnosed by their television sets during the evening news or an episode of *Road Rules*. Just ask your doctor.

The fifth version of the *DSM*, in the works for over a decade, is at least a year behind its original publication schedule. After a series of delays, the APA has committed to a drop-dead of spring 2013. The psychiatric community is bitterly divided over revisions that will shape both the culture and a multibillion-dollar business. The problem is the APA claims its first allegiance is to scientific research; whatever comes of that research cannot be their concern. They shouldn't be punished for relaying the story of who we are and what we have; is it their fault that story now serves as both a holy text and a guide to surviving the world we've created?

From a narrative standpoint, it's tough to argue with that. The APA is subject to the insanity it documents—if anything, its confusions are highly symptomatic. The story and the storyteller have merged into one big book of crazy, and now we're all mixed up in this thing together. The writers of *DSM-5* have claimed that the switch from Roman to Arabic numerals reflects its status as "a living document" subject to frequent updates, like software, to five-point-one and so on. In the name of transparency, the APA opened up a comments section on its *DSM-5* site, and throughout the conference the eight thousand comments logged thus far are frequently cited as valuable to a process that is described in terms of consensus and yet defined by the convolutions of soft, commercial science.

The plight of the *DSM* reflects that of psychiatry's bedeviled identity: driven toward scientific validation despite essentially humanistic aims and means, the field has come to embody the modern refusal of art and science to meet for anything but a fight to the death. If War is the only winner when two great nations seek to destroy each other, Business appears poised for victory in the battle between psychiatry's polar interests. That they were supposed to be fighting for us seems easily forgotten.

Something about the Aqua Waikiki Wave, my hotel on the strip, did not agree with me. Every morning in Honolulu I woke up with marbled, swollen eyes and a body that appeared to have been baked in ruby sprinkles overnight. If this was paradise's idea of a rejection slip, I had to admire its gothic flair. I would begin to recover human form by late afternoon, around the time I was expelled from the convention center's great glass facade, with nowhere to go but back to my mysterious allergen chamber, and no way to get there but through Waikiki's gauntlet of high-end stores.

In general these stores sold prohibitively expensive versions of what could be had on the cheap two blocks away, on Kuhio. Long, floral dresses and thin, sequined tops, mostly, themselves selling the ineffable stink of quality and the ersatz rewards of retail piety. Every evening, as I made my doleful way down Kalakaua Avenue, I considered whether I had acquired the need for its wares since passing them by the previous day. Every evening the answer was: *Possibly. Let's see.*

Along with Sephora and Prada and Bottega Veneta, there is a Macy's department store. Straddling the sidewalk in front of Macy's, a sandwich board flanked by two whiskery men advertises the Hawaii Gun Club. Their sign says SHOOT REAL GUNS. Their sketchy, lupine look says, "I shoot real guns." From a block's distance they're a Hells Angels mirage in the midst of a flip-floppy tourist frenzy. An olfactory berth had formed around them despite the heavy flow of shoppers. Upon first sighting, I cut in close in the hopes of a hard sell, or at least the handoff of some literature. But the one was absorbed by the other's private ranting as I passed. This is all I could make out: "Five, six years old—and in *fucking therapy*!"

That morning, my first at the conference, I had decided to attend a three-hour session called "Mood Disorders Across the Lifespan: Implications for *DSM-5*." A ballroom designed to hold hundreds of people was tipping toward capacity when I shuffled in a few minutes late. The conference's program was packed with workshops and lectures with names like "Cluster B Personality Disorders and the Neo-Noir Femme Fatale," "Spies and Lies: Cold War Psychiatry and the CIA," "Faith and Resilience: Carl Dreyer's *The Passion of Joan of Arc*," and, perhaps most beguiling, "Children of Psychiatrists."

Those and several military PTSD research sessions were taking place that morning alone. The choice was an object lesson in the modern difficulty of making even the most trivial commitments. All through the afternoon's discourse on the difference between bereavement and depression (there will be no difference, according to *DSM-5*), dismantling the connection between self-cutting and suicide (the former will no longer be a criterion for a borderline-personality diagnosis and may graduate to becoming its own disorder), a new mood disorder called late-life depression (they have little data about the unique presentation of major depression later in life, but will try to do better in coming years), and a danger to clinical practitioners called "the fallacy of misplaced empathy" (i.e., relating to a grieving patient instead of diagnosing her with depression), I felt the conference-goer's remorse flowing strong. Are they having a better time over in "Adult Sexual Love and Infidelity"?

The *DSM-5* task force—a group of about two dozen psychiatrists, academics, neuroscientists, and researchers—chose early on to define their work against *DSM-IV*, which meant that those associated with its writing were relegated to the sidelines of the conference and often to another site entirely, where a shadow conference made up of *DSM-5* rejects was taking shape. The new guard was in full effect for the mood-disorders session, which began at the beginning: a psychologist named Ellen Frank's discussion of "stressors in early life."

Each presentation opened with the same PowerPoint slides identifying the speaker and his or her conflict-of-interest disclosures. No one had current drug company ties, if only because they were required to sever them in anticipation of moments like this. Frank focused on the changes being proposed to the criteria for bipolar disorder in children. In thirty years, she said, she has never treated a patient who met all of the diagnostic criteria for bipolar disorder. And yet Frank felt the *DSM-IV* criteria were not too broad but too restrictive; with more mixed specifiers it would be easier to identify the kids at risk of moving from a unipolar to a bipolar disorder. She made what was essentially a usage argument for the descriptive value of *energy* over *mood* when diagnosing young people with bipolar disorder. She cited one bit in particular— patients must report "a distinct period of abnormally and persistently elevated, expansive, or irritable mood"—as an insufficiently objective variable. An objective variable, it would seem, is just a turn of phrase that patients will cop to more readily. The words *elevated, expansive, or irritable mood* felt imprecise to Frank, maybe a little judgy. Why not "a distinct period of abnormally and persistently increased activity or energy"? The appearance of excessive but benign futzing is the most deadly aspect of these semantic shell games; what look and sound like glazed distinctions can have consequences as enormous as they are elusive. My heart might have gone out to Ms. Frank were it not sack-weighted with envy.

Next was David Shaffer, a pediatric psychiatrist at NewYork-Presbyterian and the ex-husband of *Vogue* editor

Anna Wintour. Shaffer, a Brit with recessive white hair and a typically awkward take on the "aloha casual" dress code, affected a wry tone while describing the psychiatric community's response, in the 1970s and '80s, to the discovery that depression was rare to obsolete in children. They just shifted the criteria around to make it so, he said, and began calling things like bed-wetting and nail-biting "masked depression."

With symptoms like disinhibition and irritability, childhood itself is a cause of attention-deficit/hyperactivity disorder, a diagnosis first associated with children and then extended into adulthood as the first wave of patients grew up. The opposite was true of bipolar disorder, which was drawn back from adulthood into childhood after a child psychiatrist named Joseph Biederman proposed that certain ADHD-diagnosed kids were actually suffering from bipolar disorder, the latter generally held to be a lifelong illness. Because those kids could be wedged into a *DSM-IV* diagnosis for bipolar, a mood disorder, rather than ADHD, an anxiety disorder (sidestepping *comorbidity*, which is the medical way of saying you have two disorders at once, and it is impossible to tell which one flows from the other), they could be prescribed the standard complement of antipsychotic and antiseizure meds. Adolescent bipolar diagnoses have increased 400 percent since 1994, Shaffer told us; more youth are now diagnosed than adults. Young adulthood is the prime onset stage, although most of those diagnoses follow a first encounter with drugs or alcohol, further complicating the question of causality.

Of all the overlaps discussed that afternoon, to me the most compelling was the "get 'em young" mentality that the APA shares with every other big-ass brand in the country, including *Vogue*. More and more children, those mysterious miniatures, are being evaluated for their risk of mental illness and medicated according to prophylactic wont. Biederman's pitch hinged on the idea that ADHD kids sometimes develop into bipolar adults.

It was an argument over a new *DSM-5* disorder then called psychosis risk syndrome, since renamed attenuated psychosis symptoms syndrome—the "maybe your kid will be crazy but at the moment he's just unbearable so how about some Depakote" disorder—at the APA's 2009 convention in San Francisco that caused *DSM-IV* chair Allen Frances to light the torch he has since been waving in the general direction of everyone involved with *DSM-5*. Retired for almost a decade, Frances now spends much of his time thumbing off blog posts on his BlackBerry (he claims not to understand computers; his wife handles the back-end labor) and giving interviews about where psychiatry went wrong from his beachside perch on San Diego's Coronado Island. By far the most authoritative, consistent, and specific opponent of *DSM-5*, Frances claims that the current rate of bipolar and autism diagnoses resulted from the exploitation—mainly by drug companies and social programs—of a manual he spent much of his career devising.

Another *DSM-5* proposal, something called disruptive mood dysregulation disorder, is designed to offset the epidemic bipolar numbers. DMDD is an increasingly common example of a symptom of a more serious diagnosis coming into its own, as "hoarding" is being emancipated from OCD to acquire disorder status. Its full name will be misremembered and misrepresented many times throughout the conference, presumably because it was known as temper dysregulation disorder until that name bombed in a parental focus group. (My heart still lies with oppositional defiant disorder, a fabulously butch variation on the theme.) A key part of introducing new classifications is nailing that perfect combination of prosody and mouth feel.

Midway through some oppressive ADHD statistics, I realized that staying upright while riding the Olympian half-pipe of learning curves in extremely windy conditions would be the secondary challenge of the next five days. The first would be dodging a diagnosis myself. It's a not-uncommon fear where *DSM-5* revisions are concerned: instead of locking down existing diagnoses, the APA is extending their bounds by adding disorders, making the criteria for existing ones less specific, and furthering the idea that mental illnesses are defined on a spectrum. Introducing shades of gray has created a future scenario in which half of us will be diagnosed with an anxiety disorder by age thirty-two. Although the spectrum helped give shape to broad diagnoses for depression, autism, and bipolar disorder, it also opened up a stretch of bad road in the thinking about such things as schizophrenia, compulsive disorders, and our atomized attention spans. The resulting diagnostic creep, some say and studies suggest, will ultimately land on one spectrum or another anyone who has ever gone on a bender, had a bad month, or drifted through the day transfixed by cat videos.

By way of introducing his talk on removing the so-called bereavement exclusion from the diagnosis for major depression, Dr. Sidney Zisook asked the room to diagnose a patient reporting a persistent lack of "get-up-and-go" and an inability to think straight. The room played along and was soon prepared to confirm that this imaginary fellow was majorly, clinically depressed. What if, Zisook then ventured, we learned that the patient had just been diagnosed with cancer? Would that change things? After some concessionary points about medicalizing a "normal" person, Zisook's conclusion was: not really.

Dr. Zisook then cited his own experience with grief as an example of healthy bereavement. "I don't think I was ever funnier than I was at my mother's funeral," he mused, adding that he had missed his deceased parents "for about two minutes" at a recent event honoring his child. This, it was implied, was a normal response to the loss of a loved one. You make the best of a tough situation, spend a couple of minutes with your memories on major occasions, and get on with your life. It sounded clean and hygienic and a little unhinged. It must be odd, anyway, observing and managing your own mental health, ensuring your civilian counterpart makes good time transitioning from acute to integrated grief. I imagined Dr. Zisook reflecting on his own emotional journey through his daughter's birthday—on the drive home or maybe in the shower the next morning—and feeling soothed by the results.

The data suggests removing the bereavement exclusion so we can call depression depression, Zisook said, and get on with it. He also noted that patients are generally relied upon to decide for themselves whether they are bereaved or clinically depressed. This makes sense for a number of reasons, but chiefly because once you wind up in a doctor's office, the diagnostic process—in this case by making a clear rejection of causality—will sink you every time. If you have been feeling lower than a flea on a sewer rat for more than two weeks (the current time frame for a diagnosis of major depression), it doesn't really matter what's happening in your life, or if the natural course of grief or other stressors have adaptive benefits. You may as well have caught pinkeye and will walk out with a prescription. I drifted into a daydream about Dr. Zisook killing at his mom's funeral that was interrupted by his offhand but memorably phrased observation that everybody knows "being female is a validator for depression."

A few minutes into the Q&A, a psychiatrist in the far reaches of the auditorium stood up to tell us that he has been suffering from what he called "complicated grief" since the day his wife died, seven years ago. His mother's recent passing had triggered a relapse, and he was terrified to feel himself slipping away. The room grew more cavernous somehow; there was shouting for him to speak up. As his monologue continued, the audience began grappling with a secondary concern—whether to obey the impulse to turn their eyes onto this poor creature. A middle-aged Indian man, he appeared exactly as distraught as he said he was. The misery began at day one, he insisted. It turned on like a switch and now he can't get past it. How is that depression? Who will help me?

Technically that was his question. As a keen approximation of the kinds of crises presented in psychiatry offices thousands of times a day, it couldn't have felt more out of place. You could sense the hostility that prickles through a room when someone has shown bad form, in this case bringing his own, impossible problems into a tidy discussion about data and outcomes. In reply Dr. Zisook mentioned the study groups looking into the possibility of including "prolonged grief disorder" as a new diagnosis in *DSM-5*. I would soon learn that the suggestion of study groups is the APA version of a brushoff. And yet this news was more important to the widower than it might first have seemed: putting a name to his suffering had become its own imperative. It was at least a point of order in the chaos.

Although David Kupfer, the chair of *DSM-5*, had congratulated the presenters for hitting all the major controversies, "Mood Disorders Across the Lifespan: Implications for *DSM-5*" was a pretty sleepy affair. When mildly challenged by questioners from Brazil, Finland, and Canada during their Q&A sessions, the presenters had been quick to defer to an absence of full knowledge about everything up to and including the topic they were discussing. By contrast, the next day's personality-disorders symposium was a straight-up riot, where practicing psychiatrists bared hind molars over *DSM-5*'s plan to wipe half the PD diagnoses from the books.

Tougher to understand and more comprehensive as diagnoses, personality disorders as they are defined perhaps get closest to Freud's psychic schema of id, ego, and superego—a trio that threatens a kind of moral chaos when out of balance. Like psychoanalytic conflicts, personality disorders emphasize a patient's inability to exist peacefully in the world, as opposed to her own skin. The names—antisocial, avoidant, borderline, histrionic, narcissistic—suggest a failure to engage and consequent crisis of identity. Freudians claimed successful psychoanalysis as a safe passage into adulthood; Carl Jung believed the personality only reaches perfection in death. It's classically rich terrain, but as psychiatry continues to narrow its focus on the individual and his scientific profile, the whole concept of having a personality—a way of being formed symbiotically, over time and in relation to others—is politely being ushered to the land of the obsolete, where it will rest between chivalry and laser-disc players.

Five out of the ten personality disorders are currently on

the cutting block: narcissistic, paranoid, schizoid, histrionic, and dependent. The proposed changes and consolidations left angry clinicians like Thomas Widiger, the head of research for *DSM-IV*, trying to illustrate major ideological points with frustrated micro-critiques of the newly proposed dimensions, traits, and criteria. What, for instance, does a weird, self-canceling criterion like "(lack of) rigid perfectionism" have to do with the diagnosis of schizotypal personality disorder? With fewer disorders and blurry criteria, all personality disorders will blend together—which, in a system built around the appearance of discrete classifications, amounts to a form of sabotage. But giving up on the category, Widiger told us, means giving up on a branch of psychiatry that has devised successful treatments for patients with strong suicidal tendencies. If anything, why not get rid of "personality disorder not otherwise specified"—a junky diagnosis used to capture those who don't fit cleanly into an APA mold. Most disorders, including depression and bipolar, have NOS contingencies that ultimately negate all the tortured wordsmithing that goes on at conferences like this one.

NOS can also be used as a weapon. In the last decade, thirty-one thousand troops have been discharged from the U.S. military on the grounds of a personality-disorder-NOS diagnosis. *The New York Times* reported in early 2012 that military commanders have specifically requested a PD-NOS diagnosis in order to purge unwanted individuals from their ranks. It's also a money-saver: because personality disorders are treated as preexisting conditions (if anything can be said to have an early onset, it's probably your personality), veterans' benefits are waived and the military is no longer responsible for the treatment of service-related injuries, including the costly and pervasive post-traumatic stress disorder. With its clear delineation of cause and effect, PTSD is the most prominent vestige of the *DSM*'s roots. Treating it the modern way—including powerful opiate and psychotropic prescriptions—has been a conspicuous, catastrophic failure. A couple of months after the Honolulu conference, the army reported a record high of active-duty and reserve suicides. A 2009 study found that an American veteran commits suicide every eighty minutes, doubling the combined total of Iraq and Afghanistan casualties each year.

Practically speaking, it may not make much difference to responsible clinicians if personality disorders and their criteria are cut in half. With experience and an engaged heart, psychiatrists develop their own Tao of disorder, what Jung called "a real knowledge of the human soul." Everything from familiarity with Woody Allen types to first gut impressions were cited as valid litmus tests for neuroticism—or "negative emotionality," as it's now called—a trait of almost every personality disorder. ("If you give me a pony," one presenter offered by way of example of a classic Debbie Downer–ism, "that means I'll wind up shoveling horse shit.") The problems begin, another presenter noted, when you have to put this stuff into a book. But for *DSM-5* to be accepted by insurance companies, general practitioners, and the public, as Widiger ruefully pointed out, *it has to make sense*.

One of the new criteria proposed for borderline personality disorder was singled out for PowerPoint scrutiny. The checklist will now inquire into the patient's "sense of a self that is unique and grounded in personal history." What's tricky about people who fit the profile for a personality disorder is that they are often—you might even say by definition—not the best judges of their own character. More so than other mental illnesses, to have a personality disorder is to be perceived as having a personality disorder. Alone in her room or with her thoughts, a toxic narcissist gets along just fine. It's when she tries to exist out in the world that things go pear-shaped.

For those still reeling from the reclassification of a category-four dickhead to a sufferer of mental illness, the shifting of a personality disorder's terms away from social dysfunction and toward impaired self-image is further bad news. In the same way that the descriptions of these disorders can also be read as guidelines for how a person should be, to define a personality outside of a social context or a shared reality is to change the definition of what a person *is*. We were told that a focus group of nurse practitioners had revolted against the idea of refocusing personality disorders around a self-directed, self-reported checklist. The nurses called interpersonal function the "bread and butter" of a PD diagnosis. The study also raised the intriguing but rather hopeless question of whether a social worker would define "self" and "identity" differently from, say, a neuropharmacologist, or a psychotherapist, and on and on and on.

"That's not my reality" is already the mantra of the self-involved. Most of us have a hard enough time overthrowing the idea that we are located at the center of the universe—I don't know about you, but everything about my experience of the world would seem to confirm it. Personality and the terms of a social, adult existence are really all that are keeping us from becoming a race of self-reinforcing oligarchs. Must they now become their own privately experienced realities as well?

The next week, on a train from Los Angeles to San Diego,

I listened from across the aisle and against my will as a young man described and defended the terms of his personality. He was a kind of public broadcaster, speaking to his seatmate without pause and with the diaphragmatic gusto of someone certain that everyone within his signal radius was interested in whatever he had to say. Had I not been so wrecked by an overnight flight, I would have obeyed my instinct and switched seats. After about fifteen minutes another woman did just that, and it really ticked the young man off.

"I bet you one hundred million dollars she left because of my talking," he interrupted himself to complain. I hadn't noticed the exit-in-progress before that point. Though he feigned oblivion to putting on the foregoing performance, the young man was closely monitoring its effect, all while eating Maruchan instant lunch out of a cup. The woman with the blond bob's escape was an insult to his personality, and further evidence of the declining state of "social etiquacy." You got the feeling this had happened before.

"Honestly, this is me," he sighed, tired of explaining an obvious point to a world too slow or too stupid to grasp it. "And we're in public. This is not like a freaking movie, this is public transportation." His friend, a young woman, replied softly, "Yeah, but nobody else is talking."

"It's not just her," he snapped. "I'm expressing myself about people who are like that." The way he saw it, Blond Bob would be talking too if she had two friends in the world to rub together. That Blond Bob had relocated with the stealth of a navy SEAL, making the opposite of a scene, wasn't the point. Maruchan felt judged, and that was wrong. He fielded creditor calls throughout the trip. After losing his job during the recession he ran up a sizable debt, mostly on clothes made necessary by a move into California's convoluted weather patterns. The creditors were threatened with lawsuits and bankruptcy, alternately; he had done the research. He couldn't find a job, and whose fault was that?

In San Diego I mentioned the most unsettling part of the personality-disorders symposium to Allen Frances: Very often someone with a personality disorder will shed the terms of the illness—the criteria that led to diagnosis—without improving her social or professional function. Frances shrugged. "Compulsive features of the personality tend to mellow out with age," he said. "People, as they get older, get less tense; the rough edges are smoothed by time and experience. Their expectations go down, so that may be part of it. The Sturm and Drang, the suicide attempts and all of that, get better with time. But that doesn't mean they feel completely comfortable in their skin or will have great interpersonal relationships."

In other words, with treatment and the considerable passage of time, you too can transition from meeting the psychiatric definition of antisocial to merely embodying that of your peers and the *Oxford English Dictionary*.

I washed out of "Cities as Creators of Madness," but you may be interested to confirm that urban centers are considered risk factors for mental illness. Only the Europeans seemed interested in telling this story. I made it through a Dutchman and a German before replacing my sunglasses and heading for the door. There was something profoundly dejecting about finally hearing what I'd been longing to hear—we live too alone, too quickly, too incoherently—only to realize I wanted more. The Netherlands—where they treat heroin addicts with heroin;

it's mostly the tourists who OD, anyway—is currently dismantling its public-health care, which means its studied and socially conscious policies are soon to follow. I was in low spirits going in, having been particularly blighted overnight by whatever detergent, pollutant, or local heavy metal was tormenting my lymphatic system, but this news bottomed me out.

Following the "Cities" session I drifted onto the convention center's exhibition floor, where a wall of psychiatry texts gave way to a kind of pharmaceutical wonderland. As far as the eye could see, twenty-foot mobiles made slow, serene revolutions high above the village of branded pavilions below. The uniformity of the logos suggested a gold aesthetic standard had taken shape: copious white space set off by hushed primaries and Easter-egg pastels. They advertised the bigger names—Eli Lilly, Pfizer, Merck, GlaxoSmithKline—and showcased star products with soothingly abstract insignias and, in the case of Nuedexta—a new drug for chronic weeping and/or laughing—an inscrutable nesting-doll theme. Extensive carpeting gave the space a soundless, sealed-in quality, enhancing the exhibit floor's vacuum-sealed futurity. Marketing literature flowed, but few drug reps patrolled the stations. This battle had been won, and the drowsy mobiles appeared less like representatives of contending products than coolly presiding flags planted in Hawaii's heavily scarred soil.

The exception to this deceptively soft sell was the most ambitious display on the floor, for a drug called Latuda. Another antipsychotic, Latuda is made by Dainippon Sumitomo, a Japanese company recently expanded into the United States. The tunneled centerpiece of their display was designed to create a "virtual" experience of mental illness—specifically schizophrenia. It was more immediately successful as an answer to the question of what would happen if The North Face attempted to build a giant, Gore-Tex vagina.

About forty feet long with a curve in the middle, the tunnel was dark enough to conceal the speakers rigged throughout the passage—above your head, by your feet, and at points in between—each one blasting a different voice. As the chanted symptoms of schizophrenia ricocheted around you, various actors on various screens testified to the pain of mental illness, and the miracle of Latuda. I stood alone in the middle of the schizophrenia tunnel and closed my eyes for a moment. Dumped together the voices formed an aural hash, and the rapid-fire words flashing on yet more screens registered as faint white bursts through my eyelids. If this was insanity, it did indeed feel a lot like Times Square on a Friday night.

Upon exiting the tunnel I circled, semiconsciously, back to its start. As I stood gawping into the abyss, a pale teenage girl in a Latuda golf shirt asked me if I had enjoyed the ride. An import from some mall's accessories kiosk, she was taller than I am, which is kind of rare and vaguely irritating, with dark eyes and even darker eye makeup. I asked if the tunnel was really meant to mimic psychosis.

"Totally," she said, nodding gravely. "It's just to remind you of . . . *you know.*" We looked at each other, and she stopped nodding. "But I'm sure it's not like that. I'm sure it's much more . . . *intense.*"

Along with Archbishop Desmond Tutu, one of the conference's big-ticket speakers was Lorraine Bracco, the Brooklyn actress who played a mob boss's therapist on the previous decade's most celebrated television series, *The Sopranos*. The grand ballroom's stage had been decorated like a psychiatrist's office (or perhaps its more famous relation, the talk-show set) for her appearance, complete with symmetric ferns. The scheduled chat with an APA point woman, sponsored by AstraZeneca, drew a crowd of a couple hundred to the convention center's airy top floor.

Bracco is more of a Pfizer woman herself and made frequent mention of its biggest seller, the antidepressant Zoloft—a pill she has also endorsed in Web and television ads. I remember two other things from the hour, the first being that the actress's bare, glossy legs gave off a retina-singeing glare. Rather than actual Lorraine, many of the camera phones held up in the audience were pointed at her blown-up image on the thirty-foot screens flanking the stage. On the smartphone screen in front of me, her shins had turned to lightning streaks. The second thing I remember is that, despite the conversation's general cushiness, Bracco managed to graze every pressure point on psychiatry's embattled body.

Throughout the interview, Bracco demonstrated the earnest, understandable confusion that characterizes a larger attitude toward mental health. She was careful, for instance, to explain the story behind the depression she suffered over the past decade: divorce and a custody battle had overshadowed her success; her parents had died within ten days of each other. It sounded painful and complex, but from there Bracco segued into the idea that "mental illness" (a term she implored her audience to soften) is no different from a toothache—a medical problem with a medical solution. She hailed the miracle of pharmacology and discussed her resistance to talk therapy before citing an Oprah gem about self-awareness as her mantra. When the interviewer asked if Bracco could tell the audience how to better do their jobs—a peak in the afternoon's refractive irreality—she was adamant that the psychiatrists in the room treat their patients with affection and love, like family members, ideally.

"I think that's very, very important," Bracco said, turning to address the fifty or so rows of rapt, sunburned shrinks. "I think *you* being vulnerable was very helpful for me." And a century's worth of debate over the psychoanalytical dynamic passed by with a wave of her bangled arm.

Coming out as mentally ill has become an endorsement boon for the famous. In one of that spring's heavily rotated television commercials, a reedy-voiced rock star urges anyone who was diagnosed with ADHD—attention-deficit/hyperactivity disorder—back in childhood to check that they don't (i.e., do) still have it now. "It's *your* ADHD," he says, alternating between moody profiles and meaningful eye contact. *"Own it."*

Curious about the six-question website quiz (where the presence of the commercial's sponsor, the drug company Shire, is consigned to a modest corner logo), I selected "sometimes" in response to questions about difficulty getting organized, beginning or completing tasks, remembering appointments, or sitting still when stuck in one place for long periods. My result: "ADHD may be likely." Two short paragraphs of conditional jujitsu explained that people who answered as I did have been diagnosed with ADHD, and that although this result was most definitely not a diagnosis, it would be "advisable and likely beneficial" to seek out "further diagnosis" from a doctor.

The doctor's intake form wouldn't look much different from Shire's point-and-click checklist. Devised to restore an aura of reliability to the field, a few minutes with a *DSM* checklist emphasizes the extent to which symptoms of a mental illness are synonymous with the disorder they describe. The first symptom is often the helplessly obvious one: Are you depressed? Do you binge eat? Are you sometimes distracted? Have you been ambushed by the producers of *Hoarders*?

DSM-IV checklists are how Ted "Unabomber" Kaczynski, a man who spent seventeen years maiming and murdering people with homemade bombs before his capture in 1996, was diagnosed as a paranoid schizophrenic. Kaczynski, who objected passionately to a psychiatric defense ("Science has no business probing the workings of the human mind," he said, echoing Freud), refused to submit to the evaluation his lawyers sought to help stave off a death sentence. However, to dismiss his defense team, Kaczynski had to be deemed competent to represent himself and was thus subjected to the process he had sought to avoid. Dr. Sally Johnson made the diagnosis, the same psychiatrist who helped ensure that President Reagan's would-be assassin was found not guilty by reason of insanity.

Thirty years later, John Hinckley still spends his days strumming a guitar in a Washington, D.C., mental hospital, but the insanity defense was tightly restricted in the wake of his nonconviction. Kaczynski, anyway, would rather have died than be called crazy: although he was deemed competent to represent himself, the judge denied his request; he decided to plead guilty rather than be portrayed as a lunatic in court. Justice seemed to have been done, which has always been the most we can ask of the legal system. Symbolically, however, the case of Ted Kaczynski—by almost every account an exceptionally intelligent, coherent, and remorseless criminal—furthered the idea that rejecting technology's course was an act of insanity, as the Hinckley case enforced the idea of confronting authority as madmen's work.

As the APA conference began, back in Arizona the latest high-profile criminal to receive a schizophrenia diagnosis—the twenty-two-year-old college student who killed six people in his attempt to assassinate Democratic congresswoman Gabrielle Giffords—was resisting the forced consumption of antipsychotic medication that psychiatrists claimed would allow him to stand trial in a state that doesn't much care for the insanity defense. (The APA no longer cares for insanity either. Like *neurotic*, the term was exhausted by decades of being bounce-passed throughout the culture, becoming too plastic for a field that depends on perceived authority.) Conferring legal competence is a new side effect for antipsychotics with brave new brand names like Abilify and Seroquel, but it's not as if they need the boost. In a nation filled with unruly children, unloved criminals, and untended old people, antipsychotics are among the highest grossing class of medications, clearing sixteen billion dollars in 2010.

Now might be the time to mention that the seventeen years since the *DSM*'s last major revision encompassed the most radical technological and psychosocial shifts in human history. Along with the Internet and its rampancy—of information, gaming, social networks, pornography—we have invented new and strikingly metaphorical ways to manifest the same old human sadness and invert pursuits of happiness into grim, pellet-seeking perversions of themselves.

If we have created a fresh and unfamiliar reality, we still lack a common poetry to describe it, and the *DSM* has filled that void by default. The idiom of dysfunction, disorder, and addiction—the action nouns of modern life—has become a shared language. "Internet, Video Games, and Mental Health," a seminar that touched on "Facebook sadness" and other aspirational toxicities in its discussion of online addictions, was the only time the psychiatrists in the audience asked not about best practices or problem patients but their children. Just how worried should they be?

"I won't get into it," said neuropharmacologist and chair of the *DSM-5* addiction committee Charles O'Brien during his "Behavior Addictions: A New Category" talk, "but we've figured out what a mental disorder is."

This is not as uncommon an admission as you might imagine; because the APA habitually tweaks the meaning of words like *addiction* and *disorder*, task forcers tend to float possible definitions like test balloons. The small room holding the seminar was crammed back to the doors with young faces and the odd soldier in fatigues. Behavioral addictions, a newly proposed category, is conspicuous in part because it would seem to ratify the connection between the way we live and how messed up we feel. Sex, food, shopping, work, exercise, and Internet addiction were all considered for inclusion; although the latter earned a spot in the appendix, only gambling will be included in *DSM-5*. The inception of "gambling disorder" was largely dependent on the finding that opiate antagonists have the same effect on the brains of compulsive gamblers as on the brains of alcoholics.

O'Brien told us that behavioral addiction is an intuitive frontier for neuroscience. A variety of biomarkers have been identified for substance addiction—animals model well for the studies, dopamine patterns have been established, and successful drug treatments have been developed. It's convenient to just carry them over. Because the time/money/will wasn't there to validate the other candidates, several of them are destined for *DSM-5*'s appendix, referred to elsewhere at the conference as "a respectable graveyard." *And if you don't like it*, O'Brien said in conclusion, *get out there and do your own research*. In the meantime, maybe begin memorizing the insurance code for behavioral addiction (NOS).

Copresenter Ken Rosenberg opened with his own definition of addiction—"a failure to bond"—and the announcement that we are now dealing with behaviors that didn't exist in 1991. Rosenberg's beat was sex, and he was sorry to tell us that he has seen the future sitting in his office, and it's hairy as all hell. "We have a tsunami coming," Rosenberg said, citing statistics about eleven-year-olds switching between homework and online porn as a matter of course and warning of the addictive neuro-pathways that kind of behavior creates.

As the gap between the kids' learning how to control their impulses and the guardians' trying to figure them out widens, the idea of what's normal threatens to find a new level inside it. Can we stop that from happening? Should we? "We as a profession cannot duck it," Rosenberg said of the coming wave of misfits, if not the culture creating them. Yet treating apparently "new" emotional and behavioral disturbances like biological events would seem to be another evasion of a problem the 12-step program makes plain. It feels significant that the first thing someone seeking that program's help does is walk into a room filled with other people.

Another *DSM-5* revision seeks to collapse "alcohol dependence" and "alcohol abuse," two separate diagnoses, into "alcohol use disorder." Where *DSM-III* defined addiction in terms of dependence (clearing the whiff of conversion and transience that surrounds *alcoholism* and *alcoholic*), *alcohol use disorder* reconceives addiction more explicitly as a brain disease, even as it spreads open a diagnostic spectrum. If it feels like the culmination of a blame-conscious trend in the nomenclature, the fine-tuning of alcohol use disorder's criteria is potentially infinite. On the table now is the removal of alcohol-related legal trouble from the checklist (since state laws differ about things like drunk driving, it is seen as an unreliable marker) and adding alcohol craving. Consensus on what constitutes "craving" is already proving elusive, which might indicate why it was left off the list for so long. An Australian study published in *Addiction*, a scientific journal, and presented at the conference suggested that adopting this new classification would lead to a 60 percent increase in diagnoses; in the United States that number has been estimated at up to twenty million newly diagnosed addicts.

Because a second *DSM* diagnosis often accompanies their addiction problem, substance abusers offer a stark example of how close psychiatry remains to its predicament of a century ago, where symptoms and diseases refuse to separate and assume their proper order. Did the anorexic stop eating because she was depressed, or did malnutrition cause her mood to plummet? Was depression a response to stress or molecular mutation? Was a gene marker for compulsion turned on by circumstance?

The Greek idea that personal identity derives from what we do and how we are perceived has been adjusted for an inward-facing culture: you are what you have, and you have what you do. Instead of reckoning with the world, reckoning with your illness is the path to self-discovery. But what if *owning* your ADHD and responsibly re-upping your Adder-all scrips is actually hindering the passage into self? What if we are masking the mysterious cause of so much spiritual and emotional suffering by calling it a psychiatric disease? What if we never stopped being what we do, and that's the better part of the problem?

Separating symptoms from disorders—those who feel de-pressed from those who *are* depressed or *have* depression—according to a keenly intuitive discretion is the clinician's job. As waves of psychiatrists forsake traditional forms of talk therapy in favor of the lucrative prescription-writing business, the issue of causality recedes from "a philosophical problem with no defined answer," as one conference presenter put it, to an afterthought defined by default, once a drug treatment is found to suggest that a mental illness is based in bio-pathology. But psychiatry's sibling worship of science is critically flawed: the biological basis of disease is self-evident; it doesn't need to be proven. At stake is the cause—of diabetes, of heart disease, of lupus. Only by understanding a cause can cures be deter-mined and vaccines developed. It's why cancer treatments are so brutal and imprecise. It's why my thirty-six-year-old uncle, an immunologist, died of a heart attack after sloppy radiation treatments for lymphoma weakened his brachial artery. We still don't understand cancer's causes, so we do battle with its effects. By turning to science to prove the existence of sad-nesses, compulsions, darkened or deluded minds, and dis-ordered behavior our own experience has already confirmed, we are denying a complexity of self that only language and the continuum of lived experience can contain.

Allen Frances thinks money and hubris have corrupted the APA, that it can no longer be trusted to define the terms of mental health. "They overvalue what they think they know," he told me. "There's a certain lack of humility for the great unknown, particularly with the impact of this new neuroscience." Frances doesn't believe there's a new wave of reactive pathologies and takes a question about that possibility as an opportunity to reiterate that the one thing that hasn't changed in the last twenty years is clinical psychiatry—certainly not based on anything brain scans have turned up so far. So why change its handbook?

"Once you write the book, it can be easily distorted," Frances said, "and you have no control over it. We had every reason to think that autism would *not* become an epidemic, that ADHD would *not* become an epidemic, because we did cautious—fairly cautious things. And that thing blew out of control." He paused. "These suggestions, they slope the curve of normality."

When I told Frances that post–*DSM-IV* autism numbers have altered my thinking about having children of my own, his answer was immediate: "I don't think you should have children for other reasons, but autism isn't one of them." He looked away. "The world's too crowded."

It was fixing to rain on Waikiki. Having checked out of my hotel and blown off the conference's final-afternoon dregs, I had eight hours and nothing but beach until my flight back to Los Angeles.

It was like breathing wet T-shirt on the strip, so I headed into one of the nearby outlets—a Billabong, if you must know—with nothing in particular in mind. This used to be a fairly safe option. The part of the retail world not geared toward my concrete desires, which were finite and never extended far beyond food, travel, and clothing, was busy proposing possible aspirations, which were infinite, and involved things like hair extensions, handbags, and expanding every part of my physiognomy I wasn't obsessed with shrinking. No part of it was not interested in some present or future part of me. We existed in a kind of mutually reinforcing harmony that way.

Inside the store, carefully curated indie-punk-ska fusion droned from corner speakers and a backwash of sand covered the floor. The salespeople appeared as polished preadolescents, and within a minute two of them had addressed me as *ma'am*. Except for the sand, which I may have imagined, all of these things have happened before. At some point, though, while moving between rack after rack of what suddenly looked to me like clothing designed for sub-life-size sculptures made by intelligent aliens working from rumors of the human form, I realized what was happening. Determined to drop myself from this thing's greatest height, I pulled a fitted, many-pouched jacket and what looked to be a reasonable pair of cargo pants from their hangers and headed for the changing room.

I can't really describe what happened next, except to say that I faced the inconceivable, and it was *not cool*.

I took the only retail job I've ever had during a summer at home in Toronto, after my first year in New York City ended with what I came to describe as a nervous breakdown.

I had always been curious about that phrase. It sounded both mysterious and meaningless—the refuge of Victorian romantics, maybe, or the girls at my grade school who went around, to my voluble scorn, proudly announcing their PMS. And yet there was nothing else to call it, and no way to leave it unnamed. Symptoms: incapacitating loneliness, exhaustion; extreme susceptibility to common viruses, anemic chest pains. Onset: sequoia slow, then all at once.

A couple of times a week that summer I walked over to the high-end boutique where a friend of a friend had offered me a twelve-dollar-an-hour gig doing inventory and stocking shelves. The boutique, since deceased, exemplified a new kind of retail: the concept of the old general store rarefied to scale. They sold their parent company's boot-cut jeans and plush peacoats alongside towels in unexpected colors and designer stemware; Italian kitchen implements mingled with seasonal-print pajama bottoms.

I had asked to stay mostly in the back, where I stacked seat covers and reorganized shelving units filled with scented candles and camisoles. Too much time in public, with people I didn't know, felt dangerous. There was this hideous fragility. An incident in a sandwich shop had left me in a heap on the bathroom floor. For weeks, even small unkindnesses spelled chaos. I appreciated the calm of the stockroom, where I could bring order to the merchandise, stepping onto the floor now and then to watch the show. I was grateful for a place to go.

Cracking up meant asking for help. Deciding that I had, in fact, cracked up was liberating in this regard. Dreading my own company, all summer I followed family and friends from room to room, auditing weekend trips and errands to the hardware store as though they might save my life. I tried therapy, briefly, but it was too late for that. It was too late for a thumbs-up in the dike.

At its core it was a problem of context. Flailing around

inside my own poorly defined limits, I had lost my place. The rituals of youth no longer mark our passages with any authority. We reach maturity any number of times—biologically, religiously, legally, academically, socially—before the age of twenty-one, but the imputation rarely sticks. The world will not be informed of your various arrivals, the world informs you. It probably always did, though multiplexity means better hiding places, more ways for the contingencies of time to splinter into crisis. It seems obvious to me now that tribal coming-of-age rituals are often designed to be searingly painful so they won't leave any doubt. Because cut as many ribbons, engrave as much parchment, pound all the Jäger shots you like, the long and largely spouseless, childless, asset-free stretch of one's twenties and thirties is not the ordered march into adulthood it has been.

And so, at some point, the options are made plain. The longer you wait to address them, the more basic they become. The world informs you and then you must decide. Slowly, sometimes moment by moment, small choices about whom and how to be beget bigger ones—shading in background, scaling out the continuum; striking out villains, fleshing in the overlooked—until the story begins to tell itself, with a fully fledged hero at its center. Here's the gist: at twenty-nine, I broke down and became a woman.

Because the boutique was near a cluster of office buildings and a grocery complex, at lunchtime it teemed with working women. Wearing bright pedicures and the face of drift, they moved absently about the floor. It's one of the most private rituals you will see a woman conduct in public: eye contact is discouraged and conegotiation strictly peripheral. Crossing domains—kitchen to bathroom, beauty to fashion, work to home—the women reached out blindly, caressing a crystal decanter, briefly adjudging a mandoline, letting the synthetic but reasonably silklike fabric of a peach-colored blouse slip through their fingers as they passed.

"They don't know what they want," the store manager shrugged one afternoon, after I remarked on her deft brokering of the sale of a three-hundred-dollar leather jacket. "You just have to tell them."

I think of that summer in the stockroom when I see those women now—when I see us—arms outstretched, passing through the material world in a waking trance. I wish I could tell her what she wants. I wish I knew.

The sky was pouring as I hurried out of Billabong, youth officially over, and ran toward an open, sheltered structure on the beach. I sat at the third of its seven stone picnic tables, where one muttering woman was quickly replaced by another—a Hawaiian for a blonde. At the next table five men were playing bridge. The blond woman pulled a woven mat from the green milk cart fastened to a set of wheels and spread it out on the ground behind me.

"You gotta be in by nine, out after six," said the bald, mustached man with the Carolina accent. "New house rules." The men murmured. "But you know what? I'm gonna break 'em." He giggled like a Nick Ray delinquent, a real juvie. The blond woman in the pink floral dress pulled white wool and needles from the pink-and-black plastic suitcase beside her crate and began crocheting an infant's skullcap. The chess game at a far table had attracted a crowd.

A gaunt, shirtless guy in orange shorts changed tables

every fifteen minutes, bicycle in tow. The Hawaiian with the dangling cigarette and HANG LOOSE trucker hat had placed a blue cushion between his butt and the stone slab. A stringy blond hustler blew through the shelter, talking up a designer-sneaker windfall. The bridge club ignored him and he skittered away, sorry for their loss. The Hawaiian snorted, "Wasn't he the one with the coffee yesterday?"

I had been sitting there for about an hour when a shoeless man with bursting-blue eyes and a badly scabbed face and hands took a seat directly across from me. His thick head of eggshell-white hair was well combed with pomade on one side, but mussy and crusted with bird shit on the other. He was small and shambling with bright, vaudevillian features and hid a minibottle of vodka in his right hand. We looked at each other for a second or two.

"I am *des*-per-ate," he announced, watching me. "I am *desperate* . . . for some intelligent conversation." It was a great opener and he knew it. I smiled, setting down my pen, and inquired as to how I had qualified for the job.

"You have no computer," he said, waving over my belongings. "You have a notebook, and a pen—longhand, that's the way to go." I laughed by way of agreement. There suddenly seemed an awful lot to laugh about.

"Everybody has a story," he said with a topic-changing rap of the table. "I'm an alcoholic. What's your story?"

I told him I'd bet there was more to it; he shrugged, then said that he used to be a writer too. Is that so? It is, he said, for a show called *Cheers*—maybe I knew it? I laughed—again—and said maybe I did. After some prodding he recounted the best joke he ever wrote, a slow burn for Sam Malone involving a gas station, nasty cologne, and a botched seduction. The punch line eluded me but I gave it up anyway. He was a Vietnam combat veteran, he mentioned in passing. He used to edit fiction for hire.

"Have you ever tried to write a novel?" he asked, spreading both hands out and dividing the space between them into three with his left one. "I show them what they're doing wrong, almost like a schoolteacher."

I wanted to know what happened in California; he only grew maudlin about the money Ted Danson had shrugged off for one last season of *Cheers*—a decades-old refusal still at the forefront of all the things he couldn't understand. Patricia Richardson—same thing. And to think, she wasn't even that well known.

"Not much to look at. Nothing up here," he said, cupping his hands over his chest. "She should have taken the twenty million and run." He shook his head. Who wouldn't? He talked about Andy Ackerman and David Angell, the *Cheers* producer who was on American Airlines Flight 11: "We lost him."

My companion went on quickly, with no time for follow-ups, tacking in a new direction when I asked for more detail. He was a gambler—twenty-one and Texas Hold'em, mostly, and followed a show called *Poker at Night*, where a woman—again, not much to look at—had just cleared close to a million dollars. He confused the show's name but remembered the exact number: $930,000. He'd never bet more than eighteen hundred.

From there it was back to comedy. "I'm not a racist," he said, naming off his favorites—Woody Allen, the Marx Brothers—"but these are all Jews. They're the best at comedy: you just can't beat 'em."

When a friend at the next table offered a sandwich from

the ABC Store across the street, the man squeezed my arm as he stood to leave. I asked his name—still dazed by his absurdly improbable appearance and hoping he might hang around—but couldn't make out his reply. I asked again, and he frowned.

"I'm *fay*-mous!" he sang, shuffling past. "*Everybody knows me.*"

About an hour later, when I rose to leave, the man in the inside-out, oatmeal sweatshirt was too far gone to talk. He had sent his friend back to ABC for more vodka. The bridge game had broken up, small bills were exchanged, parties dispersed. I told him I wanted to say goodbye and thank him for the conversation. Would he give me his name? I don't know why but I was stuck on it.

"What would you want with me?" he asked miserably, propping his head in both hands. "I'm a piece of garbage." I said it wasn't true and pushed a piece of paper with my e-mail on it in front of him. Again, I don't know why. He'd mentioned having an e-mail address but it was submerged in vodka by then. A young black man watching from two tables over gestured for me to come speak with him. He had heard the city was sending out homeless relief—was I it?

Who winds up in Hawaii? Statistically, it has one of the ten lowest rates of depression in the country. It was named America's happiest state for the third year in a row in 2011, according to something called the Gallup-Healthways Well-Being Index. Statistically, alcohol hospital admissions are trending downward, while methamphetamine use has seen a 20 percent spike. Hawaii is in the top tier of drug users with "unmet treatment needs." Its rate of patients admitted to the ER with secondary psychiatric problems has doubled in the last fifteen years. These are the numbers.

"You really want to talk to me?" The old man seemed wistful, as though I'd just fanned out Danson's millions. I said I did. What was his name? With his head hanging low, he began grappling blindly with his wallet. I stood puzzled, then pained, by his objective. At length he pulled out a pristine twenty-dollar bill and lifted it into the space between us. I said no—please. No, thank you. I squeezed his arm. And goodbye.

Just to the left of the picnic shelter is the Waikiki strip, ever streaming with tourists carrying ABC bags on their way to their next meal, or purchase, or rest in between those two things. To the right is the beach, where a family of three, a toddler and her parents, were camped for the day. All afternoon a ritual played out: The little girl let out an icy scream each time her father returned her to the ocean, sometimes permitting submersion, sometimes not. Always she reserved the right—between burying her face in his neck and turning to contemplate the waves—to reconsider. You didn't need to hear her cries to know them: *Don't let go of me, Daddy! Daddy—don't let go!* You heard him too: *Button, have I ever?*

Beyond the family is shoreline, then a stone breaker. Beyond that are dozens of surfers, small and silhouetted, like penguins riding on personal floes. They wait and wait and intermittently rise up. Finding their footing, they stand like *inukshuks* on the horizon, under a perfect ceiling of cloud. One at a time they crouch and twist with the waves, more than human, bypassing the human altogether. Beyond the surfers are the sailboats, beyond them the warships, and beyond those the thin, levitating line between sea and sky.

Pixelation Nation
Photography, Memory, and the Public Image

History is embedded in every inauguration-night image of President Obama, but for me only one says it all. Three years later, the original of this particular image was hard enough to turn up that I briefly wondered if I had imagined it. Cropped for clarity, it would look much the same as what you're envisioning now: Barack and Michelle Obama, the first black president of the United States in the arms of his black wife, smiling and slow dancing as they are serenaded by Beyoncé—the world's foremost pop star, who also happens to be black—on a proscenium that seemed to have lowered from the sky for the occasion. It's a campaign manager's dream, the very picture of hope and change. At last!

It's the uncropped version, though, that vexed me. Granted, the margin of context in the Obama photo I'm talking about has more in common with, say, a moment-killing pan from Elizabeth Taylor and Montgomery Clift kissing in *A Place in the Sun* to the nearby grip wiping mayo off his shirtfront than it does the sinister element hidden behind Vanessa Redgrave in that *Blow-Up* shot, or Hitchcock's camera showing us a knife rising behind a soapy, unsuspecting Janet Leigh. And yet, the scene beyond that proscenium seems like a pretty essential clue; without it you get a nicer picture but only half the story.

But then as trained aesthetic consumers we prefer our defining public images well composed and to the point. For instance, were it not similarly cropped for clarity, the most notorious image of the torture perpetrated at Iraq's Abu Ghraib prison between 2003 and 2004—of local community leader Ali Shalal Qaissi balancing on a wooden box with his arms outstretched, his fingers wired for electrocution, his head hooded and body draped in black cloth—might have made an even more horrifying impression. Edited out of the shot that inspired its own Banksy stencil and landed on the cover of *The Economist* below the words "Resign, Rumsfeld" is the schlubby outline of *some guy*. Standing in profile, maybe three feet in the foreground and off to the right of the hooded, electrified prisoner, *some guy* is a brush-cut brunet in belted khakis and an olive-green golf shirt. The wedding ring on *some guy*'s left hand is poised just above his gently thickened middle, and he's peering down into a digital viewfinder of his own, as though he's just taken a snap of his four-year-old twins posing with Pluto on the Magic Kingdom promenade and wants to make sure everybody's eyes are open.

On the morning after the January 20, 2009, inauguration, I was most struck by an image of the presidential waltz taken from deep in the crowd: Barack and Michelle embrace like lacquered wedding toppers in the middle distance; between our photographer and the first couple stand a phosphorescent crop of cameras, phones, and camera phones, all raised high in a kind of holy gesture of affirmation. The aliens might assume the cameras are part of a blessing ritual, glowing amulets bestowing good luck. That assumption would be close but ultimately too kind. The aliens would probably figure that out when they discovered the same ritual surrounding the fatal beating of a Chicago kid in junior high, or the gang rape of a Vancouver schoolgirl. Or when they got a load of *some guy* scanning his camera's screen while a torture victim teeters nearby.

If cameras were originally used, as Susan Sontag memorably put it, to collect the world, the atomic device known as the digital camera has more of a self-reinforcing quality, sucking a fluid moment in at one end and spritzing its owner with *eau de permanence* out the other. Whether the images are moving or frozen hardly matters anymore. That only a thumb-toggle divides the two introduces a kind of interchangeability; each one can become the other at your command. Especially when they are held out blindly in big crowds, the screens that have replaced the traditional viewfinder appear to function as a kind of second subjectivity, a third eye to cope with a world that is less often collected with any kind of discretion than amassed in daily reality dumps. So that to raise a camera is mostly to remind yourself: *Right now I'm here; I'm here right now.*

I suppose it goes without saying that, even as I shook my head over the inauguration-night photo's landscape of pale, Promethean torches, their same periwinkle shadows painted my face. Sitting at my laptop, I wondered what difference it made, when technology offers such persuasive surrogates for seeing the world, whether you experienced that night with the help of a three- or a thirteen-inch screen. After all, that was kind of the point of communication and broadcast technologies—bringing us together, eliminating obstacles of access, equalizing an experience or event. But images like that of the new president and first lady make me wonder at the thoroughness of the job. What difference does it make that I wasn't able to actually witness this historic event when it appears the majority of the people who were there couldn't quite bring themselves to show up.

Is that unfair? Very well then it's unfair. But even if we are to agree that inserting a camera between yourself and your immediate surroundings, or raising that surrogate eye, does not in any way affect the experience of those surroundings—does not swaddle you up in a sense of impartiality, or shift the burden of action—the question remains, *What's the deal with that?* What's the deal, especially at public events inevitably recorded by professional equipment and pinged instantly around the world, with the compulsion to add your funky G3 shooter to the mix? Are trophy pics even possible in a world where all is photographed?

In the digital age, everything survives in an equal perpetuity, so that to experience the world through images is less and less to be rewarded by pleasure or insight and more and more to be afflicted with a kind of hysterical reality blindness. Some claim digital celibacy—we'll call them *liars*—while others end their days with the numbed insensibility of a triage nurse on Flickr's teeming front lines. Even the most cheerful digital creators and consumers are sometimes overcome by the odds of a race between infinite content and their two little eyeballs.

But then getting eyes onto every image is no longer the point. Or at least, a post-Soviet case of inflation has caused any given image's valuation to plummet. Those of us compelled to slog through every one of a friend's seven hundred wedding photos, or each album of a weekend away, need not worry so much about hurt feelings. A complete lack of audience will hardly inhibit a steady upload stream, any more than it stops us from living our lives. For every personal photo disseminated through some form of media, dozens more are the result of pure reflex and languish until giga-space is needed for more like them. The act of shooting, not necessarily its smeared result, is now in many ways the point of photography, which has become more medium than message. I can only imagine that the bulk of the cell-phone videos shot on inauguration night now rest in unvisited digital tombs.

At the 2011 SXSW music, film, and interactive festival in Austin, Texas, the Q&A session that followed the world premiere of a documentary about a crappy year in the life of talk show host Conan O'Brien was lit in part by the audience's hoisted iPhones. The energy of a room changes when this staggered, Lite-Brite wall goes up; we move from audience members to viewers, a seemingly minor but when you think about it kind of massive shift. It is as though—as we so often feel with celebrities and indeed as celebrities often feel themselves—there would be little point to an event that was not photographed. Instead of helping to create a moment, we insert a remove from it; instead of feasting our eyes, we make a formal claim on what they see.

After ninety minutes of listening to Conan O'Brien bellyache about the hardships of high-stakes showbiz, I didn't feel bad for him until he stepped out onto the stage of the Paramount, and a theaterful of journalists and partisan moviegoers lifted their phones in a kind of inverted salute. Tiny images of Conan and his director filled the theater like backward mirror shards; on a screen hovering next to me, he looked much farther away than the Gumby-legged figure a few rows off. Another MPEG to fatten up the old blog, I guess. Another thing that happened, if we still agree to the barest terms. It is considered more accurate and more interesting to say "another thing that happened *to me*."

All right, then. After all, in at least one sense it *did* happen to you. You flew to freaking Texas, where for five days in March junior Google techs attempt to spawn in Austin's Red River District; you braved the melee at Madison Square Garden ("Put your cell phones away and put your cameras down," pop minstrel Lady Gaga commanded during a recent—and televised—concert there, "'cause this is only going to happen once"); you murdered that plate of buttermilk fried chicken; you boned a B-lister in a Reno hot tub; you were the point man in a brutal and sustained frat hazing; your first flight was to Baghdad, and anyway at Abu Ghraib, as Ali Qaissi told *The New York Times* in 2006, "All the soldiers had cameras." Things happen to us as they ever did. It may be just as obvious to note that the way we experience those things, and the way we then frame that experience, and the way that those framed experiences are remembered has changed.

The still camera's earliest shills endowed it with the power to create memories. If such claims were to be believed—and it seems they were—the more photographs taken, the richer our individual and collective memories. The iPhone promised not only to create but enhance its owners' memories: "If you don't have an iPhone," went a 2011 ad, "movies aren't this dramatic, maps aren't this clear, e-mails aren't this detailed, and memories aren't this memorable." And, well—who wants shitty, unmemorable memories?

As a marketing strategy, tapping into memory anxiety has only looked smarter as we develop more ways to record and transmit reality. The smartphone camera may be the ultimate cause of and solution to all such anxieties; from here on out, both can only be perfected. The way we relate to images reflects the two kinds of memory: systematic recall and documentation—these things happened in this order—and the strange, slow emulsion that brings the invisible ink of experience into clearer view. The first lends itself to search-able cataloging; the second is completely unpredictable. Nei-ther is entirely reliable, though one would seem more likely to harbor meaning. Yet it is the former type of image—if not memory—that has flourished. If the digital camera, with its promise of perfect recall, both reminds and relieves the shooter of the burden of being present, the resulting images often have more of a social than a subjective or individual purpose. The most common modern image is consciously about display and dissemination, giving a public order to one's persona and ex-periences. It's more about representing a certain reality than remembering it, although looking through carefully curated Facebook albums one often senses the longing of the subject to remember herself the way she would have others do.

The thing about memory, though, is that it's like a beauti-ful woman: you have to pay attention for a shot at its full reward. Part of being overwhelmed by the surplus of whip-lashingly lovely women stomping the streets of New York City is the contemplation of the world of attention that must be built around each one. Every indelible face is the center of its own ecosystem of enchantment, or bloody well better be.

The whole thing can tucker you out in a glance. Facing the deluge of social-media images can feel the same: by their nature each one—especially the self-portraits—seeks a spot in your dreams, despite being designed to die a quick, mosquito-like death. The digital image has presented memory with a paradox: infinite but transient choice makes it both more and im-possible to remember well.

Consider DailyBooth.com (slogan: "Your Life in Pictures"), a social network composed solely of photo updates—image statements that crawl across the bottom of the home page in real time. With few exceptions, the photos are classic laptop pics—pictures taken by the camera now built into almost every computer. These cameras have a slight fish-eye effect and bathe the subject in an eerie, deoxygenated blue. DailyBooth's live feed is essentially a gallery of puckering young girls, each obeying an instinct with ever-expanding possibilities for exploitation. Faces pass as soon as they pop up, glancing bids for attention that seem frivolous in one light, crushing in another. Who will love them all?

There's something unnerving about a social network composed almost entirely of self-portraits, of kids pulling in their chins, pointing a cheekbone to the ceiling, and staring into a pinhole while their hand goes *click*. Within the first dozen or so photos, you have trouble telling the faces apart, so similar are the boudoir backgrounds, the spooky lighting contrasts, the flagrant moues. What at first feels revolutionary—dispatches from the private, teenaged sanctuaries where so much of what has defined the last sixty years of Western culture was incubated—begins to look more like what it is: a vacuum of random, repetitive self-exposure, the mutation of a process that was turbulent enough when it was conducted in relative privacy. Your life in pictures turns out to look a lot like your life at a computer.

God knows I did hard time in front of the mirror as a girl. Had it been an option, I might have cleaved to the communal glass, where young and old now search for the features of a viable self. But I'm not sure I could have mistaken it for a social activity, and I feel certain that the mirror cannot be a source of memory.

Photography was conceived not to create memories but to record and represent beauty. Specifically nature's beauty. "In many ways," John Fowles writes in *The Tree*, his sharply unsentimental 1979 treatise, "painters did not begin to see nature whole until the camera saw it for them; and already, in this context, had begun to supersede them." And yet the world's forests and seas "cannot be framed. And words are as futile, too laborious and used to capture the reality." We only truly encounter nature's fearful symmetries, Fowles believed, by way of consciousness, the subjective foregroundings and recessions of response, memory, and imagination. We must submit to her before nature will slip out a shoulder.

In this way, perception forms a kind of secret passage: the first, submissive step into an unrecordable reality is a first step toward the self. For Fowles, a certain quality of subjectivity defies sharing or re-presentation. It is unknowable the way the mind of an old, tail-whapping lion is unknowable. It is that unknowability which makes its near-penetrations—in art, in life—so terribly moving.

"It, this namelessness," he writes of the ancient, stunted oak trees in southern England's Wistman's Wood, "is beyond our science and our arts because its secret is being, not saying.

> Its greatest value to us is that it cannot be reproduced, that this being can be apprehended only by other present being, only by the living senses and consciousness. All experience of it through surrogate and replica, through selected image, gardened word, through other eyes and minds, betrays or banishes its reality. But this is nature's consolation, its message, and well beyond the Wistman's Wood of its own strict world. It can be known and entered only by each, and in its now; not by you through me, by any you through any me; only by you through yourself, and me through myself. We still have this to learn: the inalienable otherness of each, human and non-human, which may seem the prison of each, but is at heart, in the deepest of those countless million metaphorical trees for which we cannot see the wood, both the justification and the redemption.

Leaving Wistman's Wood, Fowles was resigned to the erosions of his own impressions: "Already no more than another memory trace, already becoming an artefact, a thing to use. An end to this, dead retting of its living leaves."

The Tree might seem like a strange memo from a fiction writer, whose business is finding a way to represent the world and what it's like to live in it. But much of Fowles's writing wrestled with the nature, as it were, of that business. In his most celebrated novel, *The French Lieutenant's Woman*, a filtering of Victorian tradition through postmodern prisms seems to forgo reality in favor of a self-consciously literary world. George Eliot and the rest of the social realists Fowles was tweaking saw human perception's lonely paradox as a challenge, not a red herring.

In conceiving Dorothea Brooke, the heroine of *Middlemarch*, Eliot developed a style of near-microscopically descriptive realism to illuminate the ways that a woman can remain unknown even to herself. Describing Dorothea's maiden voyage to Italy, Eliot acknowledges the Fowlesian, fleeting nature of pure perception, but offers the curious yields of memory as a kind of compensation:

The weight of unintelligible Rome might lie easily on bright nymphs to whom it formed a background for the brilliant picnic of Anglo-foreign society; but Dorothea had no such defence against deep impressions. Ruins and basilicas, palaces and colossi, set in the midst of a sordid present, where all that was living and warm-blooded seemed sunk in the deep degeneracy of a superstition divorced from reverence; the dimmer but yet eager Titanic life gazing and struggling on walls and ceilings; the long vistas of white forms whose marble eyes seemed to hold the monotonous light of an alien world: all this vast wreck of ambitious ideals, sensuous and spiritual, mixed confusedly with the signs of breathing forgetfulness and degradation, at first jarred her as with an electric shock, and then urged themselves on her with that ache belonging to a glut of confused ideas which check the flow of emotions. Forms both pale and glowing took possession of her young sense, and fixed themselves in her memory even when she was not thinking of them, preparing strange associations which remained through her after-years.

Now consider the modern tourist making a quick swipe of St. Peter's with her Flip cam and moving on. Or a young man interrupting a conversation with an unknown partygoer to Facebook-friend her on his phone, skimming her likes and dislikes for offense, noting their mutual acquaintances, and appraising her profile photo as she stands mute beside him.

In her extreme youth, Dorothea Brooke is not a character in touch with what we might call "reality": the ossified Casaubon's powdery marriage proposal makes her swoon, and she soon finds herself wedded to an empty idea of intellectual apprenticeship. Yet Dorothea is fundamentally awake to the world, a creature whose "deep impressions" will eventually furnish the richly appointed inner life she was so desperate to inhabit as a girl. Through Dorothea, Eliot suggests an ideal of memory as the bedrock of human understanding—a home for the self—rather than an act of acquisitive personal recording, where new experiences form a novel backdrop for an ongoing picnic of self-celebration. She and Fowles, who was born and lived much of his life in provincial England, shared at least one conviction: true memory is a forest; remembering is just the trees.

There was this too: they were both deeply ambivalent about photography. George Eliot set *Middlemarch* almost four decades into the past when she began writing it in 1869. It was set, in fact, in the two years before British inventor and nature-sketching hobbyist Henry Fox Talbot dreamed up the still camera during an 1833 trip to Lake Como.

Italy's beauty had struck again, this time as Fox Talbot

pondered a camera obscura's projection of the Mediterranean landscape he was sketching. The "inimitable beauty" of the projected image gripped him, along with the idea that the same image might somehow be permanently imprinted on the paper where it hovered. Though he referred to the still camera he eventually invented as "nature's pencil"—a fortuitous but organic combination of glass and light—Fox Talbot's idea had something of science to it, not just a trick of chemical solution, but a way of seeing reformed by objectivity. Here was reality, recorded with a fidelity that matched and perhaps succeeded that of the human eye.

Reform and realism were much on Eliot's mind as she wrote *Middlemarch*, which sets the overhaul of England's political system and a shift toward science-based medicine into an intimate social relief. Some of photography's early critics vowed that it would spell the end of not just painting but writing: Why labor over intensive description when a photograph can tell us all we need to know about the world?

As if to refute the previous forty years of fretting over the future of the fine arts and nullify the competition for the most truthful rendering of reality, Eliot devoted herself to describing human experience with scalpel-like acuity. The author's partner, a philosopher and biologist (in a time when the two disciplines were often and intuitively bound together) named George Henry Lewes, noted that no response to *Middlemarch* pleased her more than that of surgeon Sir James Paget, who marveled that reading the novel was like "assisting at the creation—a universe formed out of nothing!"

As a young woman, the author was beguiled by phrenology—a "science" that connected character to the topography of the skull—going so far as to have a cast of her own head made. That interest seems reflected in her writing, where Eliot sketches faces, outfits, postures, and attitudes so closely they seem to yield a moral essence. Eliot has been included in a school of close description dubbed literary pictorialism, and indeed, portraits hang on many of her characters' walls, often serving as false reflections or otherwise improbable ideals. Though we are encouraged to universalize her characters (Eliot's suggestion that the picture of young Mary Garth is available in any crowd comes to mind), her descriptive scrutiny distinguishes the weight and consequence of every soul. (It's a technique, curiously, that now marks the work of no one more than nonfiction paragon and sometime photography critic Janet Malcolm.) Like Whitman, Eliot insists on the greater connections between us, on the least of our goodnesses as the highest human achievement—that is the progressive cause that most interests her.

In *Middlemarch*, the odious Naumann's proposed portrait of Dorothea drives Will Ladislaw, who doesn't believe her beauty can adequately be represented, to protective distraction. In *Daniel Deronda*, Eliot's final novel, set after the dawn of photography, the extraordinarily self-conscious, self-admiring Gwendolen exhausts the narrator, who considers the photographer's comparative ease in representing such a girl: "Sir Joshua would have been glad to take her portrait; and he would have had an easier task than the historian at least in this, that he would not have had to represent the truth of change—only to give stability to one beautiful moment."

A Google image search of many of Eliot's generation of writers—Charles Dickens, Whitman, Herman Melville, Nathaniel Hawthorne—returns a gallery that, arranged chronologically, documents a gestation that delivers the author from the smudgy womb of vignetted oil portraiture into the ass-spanking world of the photographic image. The transfiguration generally occurs in the 1850s, when instead of another tinted cameo—bam!—there they are.

Dickens was an uneasy subject, wary of compounding the problem of image fraud that followed photography's inception. "I feel it will not be in my power to sit," he replied to photographer John E. Mayall's 1856 request for a session. "I have so much to do and such a disinclination to multiply my 'counterfeit presentments.'" It took twenty years for Dickens's earlier Mayall headshot to make it to George Eliot in 1871, and it pleased her both for correcting the "keepsakey, impossible face" given to him by painter Daniel Maclise in 1839, and for preserving the youth that had since been worn from his features.

When Mayall and his daguerreotype got to Eliot herself, in February of 1858, she was so disconcerted by the result that she vowed never to be photographed again. Mayall's three-quarter profile is now the only existing photograph of the author, though as with many of her portraits, its translations have raised suspicions of fraud and defamation. Eliot was not considered a beauty, and though Eliot was not many of the things convention required of a Victorian woman, it is said that even she was not free from the agonies of self-image and felt little better about her painted portraits than she did the blasted photograph.

A pseudonymously male novelist who insisted on more realistic portrayals of women but didn't believe in her own right to vote, of her many contradictions Eliot's faith in the physical image as a tool of realism—subject to its own doubts—and her disappointment in every visual rendering of her own face are, to me, the most easily reconciled. Her attraction to physical detail is only one facet of a heightened quality of perception—the capacity to perceive the inescapable surface in worldly terms, then push beyond that surface for meaning.

Consider the rather brutal first strokes of an Eliot likeness Henry James offered his parents: "She is magnificently ugly, deliciously hideous," he began, but "in this vast ugliness resides a most powerful beauty which, in a very few minutes, steals forth and charms the mind." She may not have thought much of James during their first meeting in 1870, but in this he at least shows the potential for the kind of acute but considered observation—representing the truth of change; something jeopardized in the image-first age of social profiles—Eliot favored on and off the page.

Toward the end of her life, Eliot expressed reservations about photography's claims on realism. Writing in 1879 about a portrait of her recently deceased friend G. H. Lewes—also taken by the apparently unstoppable Mayall—Eliot questioned the dark alchemy of photographs: "My inward representation even of comparatively indifferent faces is so vivid as to make portraits of them unsatisfactory to me. And I am bitterly repenting now that I was led into buying Mayall's enlarged copy of the photograph [of Lewes] you mention. It is smoothed down and altered, and each time I look at it I feel its unlikeness more. Himself as he was is what I see inwardly, and I am afraid of outward images lest they should corrupt the inward."

For Eliot, photographs do the opposite of what they claim to: record a subject's reality, which is to say preserve its memory. At best photography footnotes what the attentive mind already knows; at worst it bullies the imagination. Again and again, Eliot's novels suggest the extent to which handwrought portraiture forged social identity and defined a way of seeing and not seeing in nineteenth-century Europe—most often in her native provincial England. More insinuating than traditional portraiture, photography offered its own reality, one that over the next century would proliferate beyond the question of whether its replications might rival those of the arts, and on to the point, as Eliot feared, of supplanting a subjective experience of memory and even reality itself.

This new reality resists distinction. Networks like Facebook, Flickr, DailyBooth, and Instagram have forged a new standard for social realism, and though they are designed to promote individuality, what jumps out immediately is the organized, ticky-tacky sameness of the profiles—personality portals that members groom and prune like geometric rows of royal shrubbery. Beginning with the vaguely photographic dimensions of every computer screen, in any attempt to recreate a society within the physical confines of a 2-D square, aesthetically the jig is pretty much up. We're all going to look like variations on a pretty banal theme, which I suppose is realistic enough. The variety is in the human detail—of gesture, of voice, of pheromonal profile—something sacrificed in the transmutation of social life into the flat-screened exchange of images and occasional, captionary bursts. The sameness and placelessness of that life is reflected in the unification of much of the world into an interdependent monolith.

For Eliot, again, any amalgamation has a moral sting. She believed in the comforts of the physical world with a touch of the nostalgist's fever for the past. In *Daniel Deronda*, she describes the advantages of remaining on nodding terms with the place one first called home:

> A human life, I think, should be well rooted in some spot of a native land, where it may get the love of tender kinship for the face of the earth, for the labors men go forth to, for the sounds and accents that haunt it, for whatever will give that early home a familiar, unmistakable difference amidst the future widening of knowledge: a spot where the definiteness of early memories may be inwrought with affection, and kindly acquaintance with all neighbors, even to the dogs and donkeys, may spread not by sentimental effort and reflection, but as a sweet habit of the blood.

Eliot's ideals might seem quaint, or worse, to us now. They might seem as silly and antiquated as the pointed conversation opener a friend once overheard in mixed (and presumably fancy) company: "Who are your people and where do they summer?" In the twenty-first century we invent ourselves however and wherever we please, and maintaining ties to a "native land"—assuming, God forbid, you don't actually *stay* there—is a private, slightly embarrassing matter, when it isn't slowly crushing your spirit or cluttering the better portion of your dreams.

Complicating notions of rootedness and sweet habits of the blood further is the extent to which citizens of town and country, province and locality, suburb and inner city, east and west, north and south, and all points in between can now effectively inhabit the same space, subdivided into home pages. The excitement of this possibility was hardly unfounded, and to a great extent the results were as magical as their promise. Uncanny and salubrious connections were made; information traveled through unimaginable corridors and at an unthinkable speed; lonelinesses were averted; billions of online Scrabble games with strangers passed as many hours; the entire planet was mapped for instant reference, and most of its knowledge too. The world began to reform as one nation, and though it was many things, it emerged, foremost, as a country of images.

Early on, Web historians like to remind us, the Internet was made up solely of language, or at least the alphabet of code. Making it "work" meant tapping out some kind of communiqué with the intention of reaching someone far away. In this, its inception had the same, miraculous quality of every communication system yet devised, from printing press to telephone. The lay public's first experience of the Internet was as a kind of techno-social chimera, where the phone line and the postal service combined to create e-mail, and the next era of communication was lit with the butt end of the last one.

The first advantage claimed for any aspiring mass technology is its democratic nature, and the Internet was no different from photography in this regard. University campuses, libraries, and other learning institutions were among the first to wire up, and fifteen years later charity programs such as One Laptop per Child are founded on the ideal of access to technology as a basic right. Photography was first embraced as the class-immolating antithesis of formal portraiture. Where for centuries only the elite could afford or would presume to have their portraits painted, and possession of one's own image was the rarest of status symbols, in good time picture-taking—an instant seized in an instant—would be available to anyone with some pocket change to spare.

In theory the camera was a great equalizer, depicting whatever stepped in front of it with a consistent and dispassionate gaze. By the end of the nineteenth century, some found the whole thing a little *too* democratic: the "pictorial" movement was mobilized to rescue photography from the mugging plebs and arrange it—via experiments in lighting, form, and exposure—into a more painterly art.

But the battle over photography's cultural turf was ultimately too great to be fought in the provinces of Alfred Stieglitz and his photo-secessionists. It was, perhaps—like the other great twentieth-century cage match between high and low culture—no battle at all. Anyway it seems that way from here—just as a cultural economy run on the production and consumption of "realistic" images looks like a foregone conclusion, the argument over art versus documentation feels mostly irrelevant, and the question of whether, in generating the most prolific human records to be created with no real notion of posterity, we are making history or preening like Melville's *dayalized* dunces appears somewhat self-evident. North American culture in particular—founded in a meritocratic spirit but nourished by a democratic one—now feels defined by a free-market, deeply individualist mentality. More is not only always better but always necessary; and if you're not either taking it in or putting it out, what are you doing?

As we cultivated a boutique experience of the world—where cable channels and Web niches and food franchises became available to cater to particular interests, reinforce particular views, and make Afghan airfields feel more particularly like "home"—the digital camera offered one more way to consume our own lives. Given the right tools, we became masters at entertaining ourselves, an expression that has shed the suggestion of private diversion or introspection. Maintaining even the most basic Web presence can quickly start to feel like running a small celebrity empire. To leave the house unprepared to be photographed is to risk being captured and preserved that way forever and for all who'd care to see. (In a city like London, England, it has been estimated that the average commuter is photographed by surveillance cameras over three hundred times a day.) If anything, images have gained the advantage over "reality" first associated with people like Madonna, who became so used to the camera's attention that she was accused of not wanting to live without it. Rather than freezing a moment, digital cameras effectively unfreeze reality; more and more we exist in a pre-represented state, and only what is photographed can be said to have actually taken place.

The creation of a parallel, virtual society in a fact-obsessed culture has put reality into something of a bind: in privileging the self and its expression we have reduced it to something flat and static and yet wholly unstable, infinitely changeable. Persona and subjectivity are now easily conflated, especially when it comes to the display and consumption of images—of ourselves and our lives, of others and their lives. The former is designed to be elastic—just ask Madonna. The latter is an innate sense of the world and one's own experience that can be pursued to its own end. From the novelty of developing public identities to the telephone-pole flyers selling a thousand "likes" for Facebook photos to the pseuds we dream up to nudge the comment count on prized blog posts, the endgame of we waxen stars wandering through our empty mansions and performing the old hits for the end tables doesn't seem that far off. Hegemony is already here, it seems safe to say, and it looks a lot like last night's meal.

I don't know. It's not that I think that things were somehow *better* when a person could live his entire life without ever seeing a single photographic image of himself or anyone or anything else. No—how could I believe that? I was the child who, when lacking in any other suitable occupation, would spend evenings poring over old family albums, imprinting and installing them, in the case of my father's early photos in particular, into the part of my mind still deliberating over what childhood looked like. I could tell you the color and texture of each of these albums, the sound they made when I opened my father's closet and edged them off the top shelf—the sound *I* made when they finally tipped into my arms. The sound my father made when he found me bent over them for the seven hundredth time. In this way and so many others I was raised on images, I was drawn to them from the start in the most intimate way, and now they are all mixed up inside me.

If my interest in family photographs was obsessive, as a pint-size subject anyway I had an easy coexistence with the camera. Now when I see a child open his face for the lens, serenely accepting the conceit, I marvel at how seamlessly the moment translates. Or I wince at her self-consciousness, the way she moves in a millisecond from regular life to junior catalog posing. Or I am startled by his lunge for the camera and eager self-appraisal the second after a photo is taken. Or, finally, I feel for those kids who reflexively balk from the one-eyed machine, dart a corner of their mouths in displeasure, or face-plant into the nearest lap. For although the copious photographs from my childhood suggest what Roland Barthes, in describing a picture of his own mother as a girl, described as "a sovereign *innocence*"—pure, unmediated personality—today when a flash is set off within thirty feet of me my instinct is to enumerate every available exit. I mean, there is *very little*, down to like Madagascan spiders and the speaking voice of Bashar al-Assad, that provokes in me a similar balance of fear and loathing.

I suppose the albums themselves tell the tale. As most teenagers do, I tired of posing for family photos. At fourteen I identified the full complement of frauds I was participating in and began a process of elimination. Smiling for my mother was either first or second to monthly confession. But my disenchantment with being photographed persisted beyond the awkward years. It seemed the more images I consumed in a given day, the less readily I would sit for a picture. This was all easier to manage in the days when everyone leaned in over a festive groaning board a few times and called it a year.

The upshot is that every photograph taken of me as an adult that wasn't an outright theft has involved capitulation. After a few such surrenders in my twenties—including a *heroic* submission to a professional sitting—I felt sufficient images were available to prove my existence and satisfy everyone seeking its reminder. Having fulfilled a reasonable quota, I effectively retired. Timing-wise, it was like Churchill hanging up his jowls while Poland fell. Just as I issued a blanket "I prefer not to," the digital-camera bomb went off and the whole world mobilized for deployment.

By 2011, social-media sites were absorbing hundreds of millions of personal photographs each day. That these images are conceived and then live as a combination of light and code makes their numbers particularly unintelligible; it's like counting cloud particles. In the new social reality, to refuse to be photographed is not only to be antisocial but in some sense to negate one's own existence. The potential for every human being on earth to confront the existence of every other has arrived—George Eliot's global moral economy realized as a data swap.

But there too Eliot's remarks on the limits of human connection seem prescient. Eliot makes us aware, for instance, that when the artist Naumann is first captivated by Dorothea in the Vatican museum, she has just realized the grim reality of her marriage to Casaubon while lingering beside a Hellenistic sculpture of the ravishing Ariadne. Naumann gasses on to Ladislaw about capturing the "antique beauty" and "sensuous perfection" of a woman we know to be in the depth of a private misery.

But then a lot of people see a lot of things in Dorothea—Eliot herself compares her to several of God's favorite saints—each impression a riff on the feminine ideal. Naumann may have rotten timing, Eliot suggests, but he's not wrong. He's just limited by human subjectivity, our gift and our curse; he sees what he sees. Having moved her heroine to tears, Eliot pauses to reflect on the weight of a few drops in a larger balance:

> Some discouragement, some faintness of heart at the new real future which replaces the imaginary, is not unusual, and we do not expect people to be deeply moved by what is not unusual. That element of tragedy which

lies in the very fact of frequency, has not yet wrought it-self into the coarse emotion of mankind; and perhaps our frames could hardly bear much of it. If we had a keen vision and feeling of all ordinary human life, it would be like hearing the grass grow and the squirrel's heart beat, and we should die of that roar which lies on the other side of silence. As it is, the quickest of us walk about well wadded with stupidity.

Often, scything through the streets of New York, the physical frustration of negotiating the city's endless stream of bodies forms a kind of psychic buffer. It's only on those rare occasions when you're penetrated, in a glimpse, by the entirety—the person-ness—of each of those bodies, that the meaning of *overwhelmed* appears, at full gallop, on the horizon. "Perfect" perception would be the end of us. The handful of people on the planet with flawless, unexpurgated memories—who can tell you which episode of *St. Elsewhere* was airing on November 14, 1985, or the exact shitty thing that their sister said between the second and third course thirty-seven Easter din-ners ago—strike me as tragic figures of particular modernity. Gathered for a recent television interview, a number of these individuals commiserated about the impossibility of main-taining close personal relationships, and the way that access to shallow detail across a deep stretch of time had cluttered their minds to the point of dysfunction. Perfect recall is the enemy of memory, which relies for its particular textures on the art—to say nothing of the mercy—of forgetting.

The brains of those prodigal rememberers have been lik-ened to computers. But all technology aspires to human ideals or ideologies—so that to have the memory of a machine is to be superhuman, and to appear photoshopped is to achieve perfection. And the Internet, in its infinitude, only fulfills the modern desire for mastery over time and space. It was built in our image, in other words, a reality in which the operational imperative of "saving time" forms a paradox: driven on the one hand by the wish to make minor and major interactions, tasks, and consumptions happen as quickly as they possibly can, the Internet is also designed to literally save each second as it passes, preserving every hour in coded amber with a diligence that might seem sentimental were it not so straight-up fascist.

If anything could, shouldn't images rescue us from such a fate? Is there not still an essential purity to what they show us about the world? In the United States, the first version of what became a clichéd allusion to the photographic image's enviable clarity appeared in a 1914 *New York Times* ad for real estate: "A look is worth a thousand words." In 1921, *Printers' Ink* writer Frederick Barnard repeated the claim as an advertising tip, then used it again in the same magazine six years later, replacing *look* with *picture*, thus shifting the burden of power from the observer to the thing being observed.

A flooded market has warped and depreciated that power. To make images of food and faces and bikini-clad flanks stand out, advertisers digitally whittle and polish to the point that presenting them as photographs—that is to say, as a reflection of reality—constitutes a kind of fraud. In the women's beauty and lifestyle industries especially, companies like H&M are forgoing the imperfect, inconsistent human form entirely, generating their models from pixelated scratch. Photographic scrutiny has become too intense for even the most beautiful bodies to bear, and a totalizing sea of images has produced a standard so strict it verges on uncanny. Representing this hyperreality, paradoxically, requires a digital paintbrush and a neo-mannerist take on human proportion, not an expensive lens and good light.

Civilian image-makers, having also felt the burn of ubiquity, seek new ways to set their photographic lives apart from the amalgamating effects of social media. The first and so far most ingenious attempt to capitalize on this anxiety was the 2009 debut of a camera application called Hipstamatic (slogan: "Digital photography never looked so analog"). The equivalent of an aggressive lens filter, Hipstamatic is designed to imbue the disposable digital image with the qualities of time and memory we now associate with earlier photographic eras. Hipstamatic spokesman Mario Estrada has admitted that technically the app makes crummy camera-phone images look even worse. But it's a gorgeous corrosion, Estrada claims, and the images are now crummy "in the most beautiful way."

Different settings yield different patinas and color schemes, all meant to mimic both the limits of early mass-market cameras (the designers claim to have nicked the name Hipstamatic from a disposable camera manufactured in the early 1980s) and the numinous effects of time on print photographs. A century or so into photographic history, those effects were already apparent. Black-and-white photos from my father's childhood seemed romantically careworn to me as a kid—the paper albums, the adhesive corners that protect the photo and hold it in place, the white-picket frame built into every image. Because my grandfather was gadget-prone, all of my father's early home movies are also shot in crisp, color-saturated

16 mm. Scenes from my own childhood were recorded on fuzzy Super 8, then transferred to VHS in the mid-1990s. By the mid-2000s, *that* transfer had been transferred to DVD, so that now the white-lettered words PLAY and PAUSE occasionally appear in the upper-right corner—ghost traces, along with a damnably lachrymose pan-flute sound track, of the VHS layover.

While chaptering through the DVD with my cousin and her twentysomething boyfriend recently, searching for rare footage of my cousin's long-deceased mother, I was dispirited by the third-generation hemorrhaging of the images I remember chiefly as scenes I've watched before. But as my cousin and I squinted for signs of ourselves and our loved ones, her boyfriend fell into an aesthetic swoon. For him the failing images were incredible—realer than real, more authentic for their desiccated veils. He's a Hipstamatic fan, naturally, and therefore a connoisseur of the distressed look that, until our home movies, he knew chiefly by facsimile. I found myself more moved by his passion for the texture of the images than the grainy, pan-fluty hologram of my own first, thundering footsteps across the old living-room floor.

Camera apps became the center of a mild controversy in early 2011, when a photo taken with an iPhone using the Hipstamatic app won third prize in an international competition. The photo, taken by the *New York Times* photographer Damon Winter, depicts two American soldiers on an Afghan patrol: the helmet of the closer one looms in the center of the frame; the farther soldier is poised to return fire and appears above the nearer one's right shoulder, pointing his M16 into a vale of trees. The composition is striking, as is the color scheme, which blends the soldiers' camouflage and the surrounding flora into a corona of yellow and green. As much as the basics, however, the image's success relies on its *aura*: the vignetting effect responsible for the color wash is designed to give the image an antique-y look—a look, specifically, now associated with the war photography that came out of Vietnam.

The debate over Winter's award was scattered. Some picketed the fading line that distinguishes "professional" photographers from everyday snappers. Others discussed the ethics of using an aesthetic that references a past aesthetic to capture the "reality" of a given situation—in this case an American occupation. Clicking through Winter's Hipstamatic portfolio of his time in Afghanistan, I remembered my father's story about having to stop taking meals, in the late sixties, with the television news on. This was when my parents lived in New York, in the time before the draft notice arrived, which is to say before they hightailed it back to Canada. They'd never seen such carnage, real-life carnage, on any screen. Images like that have been withheld this time around, adding a darker sheen of irony to any appropriation, in the coverage of this war, of Vietnam's brutal confrontations. The ambivalence surrounding these particular conflicts seems to have driven an aesthetic that is both ultramodern and explicitly aligned with established war imagery. Did Winter's antiqued images seem more authentic because the Vietnam War somehow *feels* more real?

In Winter's defense of his Hipstamatic photos, published by the *Times* in the wake of the controversy over his win, he notes the public's naïveté about how images are made. For him the iPhone is just another tool in the photographer's ongoing excavation of the world—in this case useful precisely because it didn't spook the soldiers, who all carry camera phones themselves. Winter hoped representing American soldiers with the recognizably casual intimacy of a lazy-Sunday iPhone shoot with one's cat might have a de-anonymizing effect, rescuing the subjects from generic GI constraints even as it surrounds them with the familiar tint of the past. By bringing war into the aesthetic world we live in, the medium itself could help make us care. And, anyway, the iPhone seemed well suited to an atmosphere the photographer described elsewhere as "more like summer camp with guns" than a military operation.

Winter's images of soldiers horse-playing and sleeping in a pile *do* have a dreamy, summer-campy quality. Looking at them, arguments about declining standards and digital parameters feel beside the point: if there's peril in app-driven war photography, it involves the gentle death grip of nostalgia. If the compulsion to mediate our lives suggests a pathological remove from the present, Hipstamatic's insta-pastiche beggars Roland Barthes's belief that photography is important foremost because it helps us believe in the past. The present moment, ostensibly frozen by a camera, can now be distended to suggest any number of past realities. That distension is actually *built into* the thing taking the pictures, further layering the world with synthetic meaning in real time and fully, finally confusing the quality of authenticity that has obsessed our relationship to the image from the start.

The Bush White House claimed censoring images of military injuries and casualties was a matter of respect. It's hard not to wonder, ten years later, what difference it might have made. It's harder to grasp how fully the video games, war movies, torture-driven horror films, and Internet snuff buffets have informed and maybe even sated our curiosity about the realities of combat. Those doing the fighting deal with the far side of that influence. Again and again, in accounts of the Iraq and the Afghanistan wars, the disillusionment of young military subjects is defined by their media-fostered expectations.

The success of first-person shooter video games like *Call of Duty* inspired the military to step up their use of virtual-reality games in preparing soldiers for the experience of war. A 2008 MIT study concluded that *America's Army*, a *Call of Duty* knockoff developed by the military, is their most successful recruiting tool yet. Some say this kind of training is more about desensitizing soldiers to death and violence—quite a thought when you consider the preponderantly nonmilitary domain of video gaming. Older brass have noted that while the young, video-game-weaned recruits have startling console dexterity and hand-eye reflexes, they are less able—even unable—to distinguish between what's real and what's not. If there's any way to explain the glazed, incongruous glee of the soldiers in the Abu Ghraib images, it may have to do with this sense of irreality, of being there but not there—a feeling whose natural accelerant and antidote is the camera.

The initial response to the Abu Ghraib images was pretty universal: revulsion. Revulsion derived in part from the fact that these were not secondhand stories leaked by a mole or an intrepid reporter, but crimes that American soldiers documented themselves, as they happened, like for fun. As Susan Sontag noted at the time, not even the Nazis—obsessive archivists of their own atrocities—were known to cram a thumbs-up into the frame.

Sontag also used the Abu Ghraib scandal to point out that the purpose of every digital image is tied to its own dissemination, something reconfirmed by every new viral cell-phone video of a dictator's grisly lynching, or violation of an anonymous young girl. My mind goes blank when I hear stories about kids who grew up in a digital camera culture documenting their felonies and uploading them to Facebook. The horror is demagnetizing. The only sense to be made is surely tied to our desperation for the crisp sting of reality in an increasingly padded, prismatic world. If we've reached the point where what is not photographed does not count as "real," then in some situations the paradox may be that the camera is introduced to somehow complete or verify a moment that felt too surreal, as though it weren't really happening. And yet the most pervasive reality to emerge from camera culture meets only the most basic—which is to say legal—parameters. Pics, as they say, or it didn't happen.

In their respective 1970s meditations on photography, Roland Barthes and Susan Sontag ground certain of their arguments in the physical nature of the photograph. Barthes seemed to revel more in what photography—"a carnal medium, a skin I share with anyone who has been photographed"—could do than what it might; Sontag contrasted photography favorably with the chaos of television, "a stream of underselected images, each of which cancels its predecessor." Barthes preferred the still to the moving image because it asked and allowed for more of us—only subjectivity can develop, create, complete, the well-selected image. Sontag felt the physical fact of photographs was the source of both their power and their manageability, making them more given to a governing "ecology."

Although that hope seems far off indeed thirty years and

untold trillions of images later, a basic question behind it persists: Is there anything that should not be photographed?

Celebrity-photographer Eve Arnold has described the photographer's ecological responsibility as a matter of "gatekeeping." The death of a famous subject—and the subsequent surge to their living image—tests the photographer. Arnold calls Bert Stern's incessant republication of the photographs he took of Marilyn Monroe (whom she also photographed), known as the Last Sitting, a betrayal, especially given evidence of the actress's attempt to destroy a whack of them. But there is no privacy for the dead, and perhaps only the simulacrum of it for the living.

"As everyone knows who has ever heard a piece of gossip," wrote Janet Malcolm in "The Silent Woman," her 1993 *New Yorker* serial concerning the embattled literary estate of Sylvia Plath, the role of Plath's husband, Ted Hughes, in shaping her legacy, and the controversy surrounding the lengthening queue of Plath biographies, "we do not 'own' the facts of our lives at all.

> This ownership passes out of our hands at birth, at the moment we are first observed. The organs of publicity that have proliferated in our time are only an extension and a magnification of society's fundamental and incorrigible nosiness. Our business is everybody's business, should anybody wish to make it so. The concept of privacy is a sort of screen to hide the fact that almost none is possible in a social universe. In any struggle between the public's inviolable right to be diverted and an individual's wish to be left alone, the public almost always prevails. After we are dead, the pretense that we may somehow be

protected against the world's careless malice is abandoned. The branch of the law that putatively protects our good name against libel and slander withdraws from us indifferently.

In this light, Anthony Summers's publication of a photo of Monroe's corpse in his 1996 biography appears inevitable; the public prevailed. It was, Arnold felt, "the ultimate in horror, to me, of what can happen to a picture."

Today, it would seem, everything should be photographed, and everything that is photographed should be seen. It is a matter of maintaining our new social ecology; to resist is futile, as is the expectation of "privacy" as we have conceived of it since royal copulation as a spectator sport fell out of favor. What is it, we ask of the mother who complains about her child's photo being posted on another parent's social-media page, that you have to hide? What *exactly* are you worried about? Anyone who has badgered a stranger or even a good friend to stop posting his picture on the Internet has discovered the paradox of this new world of individuals living in a country of images: mutually assured solipsism means nothing is sacred. You'd think it would have created a kingdom of libertarians, stone-walled mini-fiefdoms as far as the eye can see. Instead we have chosen to believe that a self-interested society can run on the pretense of *sharing* and make a manicured production of living open and expansively represented lives online.

I take comfort, between dodging cameras and sending threatening e-mails to strangers, in the fact that Sontag was a reluctant subject herself. "Although reason tells me the camera is not aimed like a gun barrel at my head," she wrote, "each time I pose for a photograph portrait I feel apprehensive." Immobilized by the camera's scrutiny, she felt somehow hidden behind her face, "looking out through the windows of my eyes, like the prisoner in the iron mask in Dumas's novel." After considering the reasons for this apprehension—puritan anxiety, moral narcissism, plain self-consciousness—she decides it is mainly the dismay of being seen: "While some ninety percent of my consciousness thinks that I am in the world, that I am me, about ten percent thinks I am invisible. That part is always appalled whenever I see a photograph of myself. (Especially a photograph in which I look attractive.)"

Maybe that 10 percent is the place where serial killers hang out while hacking up their victims. I tend to think it's the portion that keeps the other 90 percent spiritually solvent. It must be the part, anyway, that maintains our connection to the whole of human history prior to 1850, in which lives were lived and identities forged without the benefit or the interference of photo-reflection. Those eras we now think of in terms of their "costumes," and an inherent suspicion of the dramatic fakery modern life has set right. All those hidden lives of Middlemarch, and their humble contributions to a continuum of social good.

But then, like the best novels, the best photographs remind the pure, invisible observer in me of the things I want to know, don't know, or have known, and the ways I want to be known myself. They remind me, in other words, of the world beyond images, and beyond me. But the rest—the vast majority—seep into me or slide by with the opposite effect, deflecting or confusing memory, canceling each other out, numbing my sense of the world beyond images, and beyond my own relentless consumption of them.

On a winter weekend several years ago, after heading to the Brooklyn Museum, I drifted from the usual panoply of impressionists to a retrospective of Annie Leibovitz's photographs. In making this transition I was reminded that the pleasure of looking at a painting combines the beauty of the image with the feeling that something of the artist lingers within the work itself: you are standing where the artist stood, and every brushstroke is tangible evidence of her life; the part of her memory embedded there seeks a place in yours. With photographic exhibits, the pleasure feels more purely aesthetic: the image was captured and in some sense abandoned by the artist. You look where she looked, literally, and try to place yourself where she stood, perhaps, but the emphasis is on what can be seen—on the image itself. I always laughed when a Dutch friend of mine referred to "making" a photo—a translation glitch he couldn't keep straight. I just thought it sounded funny, but there is something strange about the one art form we talk about in terms of taking, and not making.

Many of the Leibovitz photos were already well known from magazine covers and portfolios: celebrities and luminaries, each transformed by the photographer's signature, statued postures and bloodless pallor. Demi Moore, Arnold Schwarzenegger, John and Yoko arranged into a melancholy paragraphus. Then, at the far end of the exhibit, as the glossy photos ceded to personal snaps, there were a few shots of Susan Sontag, Leibovitz's partner of some years. Here Sontag appeared vital, that defiant glint of white hair taken up in her eyes; there she was stretched out on a couch, spent by sickness, as we had come to know. Then, arranged in the exhibit to punctuate those that came before, was a framed photograph of Sontag's corpse. The end of the story.

My first reaction was the basic one: here is another thing I did not care to see that I have now seen anyway. Here now my own memory of this woman—the feeling of having shared some space in her mind—would forever be presided upon by this bully, this empty body, which had nothing to tell me about its subject, though it spoke of some other loss, to be sure. It clarified the extent to which the modern image feels *taken*, representative mostly of its own theft. It didn't have to be digital to feel that way.

In my memory, anyway, Sontag seemed to shiver at the idea of images turning reality into a shadow. But my memory is overlaid with the compost work of time and distortions of perspective; it's what makes it mine. She might bristle at being thought anything but stoical and dispassionate about her own theories and conclusions. She might point out that it's highly unlikely that the tumbling, drunken toddler footsteps my father recorded in Super 8 during the years when she was coming to those conclusions were the first ones I took. The very first steps probably happened earlier that morning, or maybe the day before, and were re-created in the nicest room in the house, with my brother standing dutifully by. I don't have a memory to consult on that score and never heard the story. The images, being all that remain, have asserted their privilege. I'm grateful for it too. It seems close enough to a truth I wouldn't otherwise have.

It seems obvious, as well, that it was I who shivered reading Susan Sontag, standing where she stood and feeling her there with me. Because she was more right than she could have known when she said images are more real than anyone imagined. Reality itself now requires the gatekeeper, something to protect it from light-starved stagnation. Because a world mastered by images makes a conduit of human experience; we exist to serve the image, not the other way around. Anyone who has seen a camera's screen bobbing superfluously in a crowd, or realized that a subject's enigmatic smile was not directed at someone behind the lens because there was no one behind the lens, or imagined our millions of satellites and surveillance cameras carrying on long after we've all been evaporated, by the asteroid or the dino virus or some combination of the two, knows it would appear images can already take themselves. We take them in as automatically, ever turning to the next one and the one after that, scanning and scavenging, as though gripped by a hunger we don't understand.

More than our faces, our follies, or our plates of gourmet fries, the images reflect that famishment, seeming to tear through each other; it's a food chain in chaos, at the point of consuming itself. And so I wonder, Susan, and how I wish for your reply: If images have begun to eat their own, what might they do to us?

Do I Know You?
And Other Impossible Questions

A friend was grieving and had been gone. On the evening he returned to town I appeared at his door with a six-pack, some sweets, and a recently pilfered movie screener. It would be my second time watching Lynn Shelton's *My Effortless Brilliance*, having enjoyed it the first time with that particular zealousness that compels one to bypass recommendation and go straight to recruitment, chaperoned viewings staged as a most intimate gift. This was at least a place to begin, and the screening was a success: We laughed, we cringed, we were quietly moved. Most important, some time passed, and painlessly.

When it was over, my friend turned to me with a funny look. "That guy, the main character," he said. "Do you know who he reminded me of?" I did, but I didn't. It had bothered me all the way through the first time, this free-ranging recognition, so when my friend named its elusive source—a mutual acquaintance—the satisfaction was sonar deep. I'd only met this person once; there were no logical grounds for how fully I felt the justice of the comparison, which was physical, but not only. It just jived, it was yar—you knew it. It was also as if, simply by virtue of making the match, my friend and I had become the proprietors of a secret about this person, and a wicked one at that.

Turnabout, let's call it. Secret for secret, anyway. I seem to have one of those faces, see. Perhaps you do too, and you know what I'm talking about. The kind of face people think they know, or have seen before, or can easily conflate with those they have studied more intimately in two dimensions than we can ever hope to in three. Perhaps this isn't uncommon at all. In fact, in considering the phenomenon, I have imagined most of you reading these words and thinking, *Yeah, I get that all the time.* Indeed, the majority of participants in a recent, random polling on the matter affirmed that, yeah, they get that all the time. The possibility soon presented itself that on some level and to some degree we all somehow suspect we've encountered one another before.

So I—like you, apparently—get this a lot. Only occasionally do people suggest that we went to summer camp together, or that I played on their volleyball team; too rarely have I come to them in a dream. Most often it turns out I am someone, or remind them of someone, they have seen on the big screen, someone whose image or affect or ineffable essence, having refracted and settled into a murky, primordial quadrant of their memory, I have stirred and called to the fore. With strangers the conviction that attends the culmination of this process is especially tough to overturn.

A few weeks ago I was heading to Long Island City, on the N line around lunchtime, when the guy joggling his forearms with his knees beside me sought reassurance that our train stopped at Queensboro Plaza. I confirmed that it did, and we relaxed a little in our seats: one more of life's problems solved. Another issue quickly presented itself, however, and he leaned forward to peer at me again, this time uttering the words that have come to fire a sort of ontological dread in my belly: "Where have I seen you before?"

Lest you surmise the knee-joggling gentleman had any sort of *design* on his seatmate, let me assure you that the ratio of women to men who hit me with this big one is almost equal and in fact skews slightly female. "Have I seen you before?" he repeated, and I said no, I didn't think so. "Yeah, you're that woman—you were in that movie." I assured him that I'm not, I wasn't—I promise. "Are you *sure*?" he pressed, looking less suspicious than stone perplexed.

Am I sure? Too often, when I meet someone new, somewhere in the first few minutes they will get a sort of far-off, foggy look in their eyes as I'm banging on about the health care crisis or how I know the host. I have learned to recognize this look not as crashing boredom (though I can spot that too, thank you) but the prelude to my least favorite how-do-you-do. It comes in several variations: *Who do you look like? Do you* know *who you look like? Who do you remind me of? Do I know you? Where have I seen you before?*

The following is my attempt to get a grip on these questions and why they began to annoy, sadden, and then just thoroughly wig me out.

Let's start with the Greeks. Them or Larry King. "Perception is reality," the latter is fond of saying. Under that rubric, might we in fact *be* the amalgams of the different faces and performances that people impulsively map onto us? And might not that onion-skin atlas comprise our best hope of being known, if we are to be known at all?

A brief equation inspired by Mr. King's classical aphorism:

The essential unknowability of other people times the most sensational art form we have created to transcend it—the movies—equals the intense psychological and aesthetic intimacies we develop with the images and individuals we spend so much time watching more freely, closely, nakedly, than we can ever watch each other. That is to say, without being watched back.

Film in particular has become so much a part of how we absorb and organize the world, I would argue, that the mapping/comparative impulse is not a matter of art imitating life or vice versa, but art *mutating* into life, then setting off a series of elaborate and ultimately inextricable countermutations.

It was like a movie, a movie was like it—who can tell anymore? I wonder, if one were to empty out a brain and divvy up its critical, alpha-chip signifiers—this is a woman, this is a man; this is a man from nowhere, this is the kind of woman who can ruin his life just by walking into the room; this is repulsion, this is beauty; this is how a kiss goes, this is how you die; this is running for your life, this is rolling down a city street all exhilarated and shit—how many of them would come straight from the movies, how many from lived experience, and how many from some unholy genome splicing of the two, which becomes less an image or a visual phrase than a funny feeling in the old tummy.

I imagine most of us would prefer the second pile to be the biggest, but that's just not the world/perception/reality we live in; the moving image changed so much more than the way we spend our rainy Sundays. Sometimes I worry that I'm actually most alive at the movies, and that their primeval overtures to our most private selves are the reason we can't help but see them like lovers—which is to say everywhere we go, and in everyone we meet.

In the very French director Michel Gondry's 2008 film *Be Kind Rewind*, Jack Black plays a paranoid technophobe who accidentally destroys a New Jersey video-rental store's inventory, then attempts to restock it with homemade VHS versions of Cineplex classics like *Rush Hour 2* and *Ghostbusters*. Black and the video store's presiding clerk, played by Mos Def, tell customers these new films cost more and look kind of hectic because they come from Sweden. Privately, Mos Def worries that the customers will know the "sweded" films are fake—they won't be fooled—but Black doesn't see why: "Maybe I *am* in Ghostbusters," he says.

Maybe we all are, Gondry suggests. Maybe the act of watching a film not only completes but *activates* it, triggering a sort of psycho-sentient osmosis, opening a channel that allows a part of us to join the film and a part of the film to join us. Watching *Before Sunrise* a decade after I first saw it, I was struck by the feeling of having left a part of my former self somewhere within it; I could almost make her out between the bullet trains, down the cobblestone alleys, in the fresh faces of the actors themselves. Maybe I *am* in *Before Sunrise*.

When someone else does the recognizing, it gets trickier, by virtue of both engaging a foreign set of multimapped, memory-banked viewing experiences, and raising one of the most critical questions one human being can ask another: *What is it you see when you look at me?*

Consider the overlap between the way we normals and actual famous people field that question and its psychic fallout. Porn superstar Sasha Grey describes watching herself have sex on-screen as *surreal*. "I don't feel like it's me," she says. "It's just a weird feeling that's hard to describe." Early on in *Don't Look Back*, a young Bob Dylan laughs uneasily over a newspaper's claim that he smokes eighty cigarettes a day. "God," he mutters. "I'm glad I'm not me."

Forty years later, in a 2004 interview, Dylan described the kind of confrontation that keeps him from going out in public: "People will, they'll say, *Are you who I think you are?* And you'll say, *Ahh, I don't know.* And they'll say, *You—you're him.* And you'll say, *Okay, you know . . . yes?* And then the next thing they'll say, *Well no, like, are you* really *him? You're not him.* And, uh, you know, that can go on and on."

Lee Strasberg's daughter, Susan, used to tell a story about walking around New York with an incognito-in-plain-sight Marilyn Monroe. "Do you want to see me be *her*?" Monroe would say. Strasberg described the star dialing up an internal dimmer switch, slowly filling herself and the space around her with light. Within moments the people who had been passing by were stopping cold and scrambling for pen and paper.

Of course creating distance between person and persona is common among people whose faces and bodies and voices become commodities, if sometimes confusing for the public picking up the tab. (Apparently it's confusing for the celebrities as well, several of whom—most recently oblong national nightmare Kim Kardashian—have sued companies for using alleged doppelgängers in their commercials and trading on a look, the celebrities say, that belongs to them. As if to close the perfectly silly circle, Kardashian's ex-boyfriend, an NFL running back, began dating the model in question.) And of course normal people have personas too, themselves often in part constructed from the personas they have watched and admired on-screen, although we all want to be recognized, especially at parties where boys are present, as sovereign creations. No one wants to be unoriginal, or a type, or a screen of such accommodating blankness that pretty much anyone from Tallulah Bankhead to an animated lake trout can be projected onto it. But also, who needs their benign social interactions to segue without warning into not just an inappropriately intense eyeballing but a weirdly potent subversion of their individuality?

There was a point, two years ago, when I lost my patience. It happened as I was speaking with two gentlemen at an exceptionally civilized housewarming thrown by a lovely couple who happened to be my sole acquaintances in the room. As we talked about the space (grand) and the hosts' Florentine wedding (*grandissimo*), one of the gentlemen, a money guy, got the foggy look in his eyes. Something scrolled up behind my ribs in anticipation of what came next: *Wait, who do you remind me of? She reminds me of someone—who is it?*

I told him I hated this game and that it never ended well, but soon three others were pointing their noses in close to mine and shouting celebrity names like Pictionary clues. I followed what I'm pretty sure is the advised strategy in a bear attack: keep still, don't make eye contact, and wait for it to be over. But this guy was half-lit and wholly tenacious. Eventually he left the room to seek out a computer and google his mind to rest. He gathered his team around the monitor in the study, where they deliberated over the actress he had in mind. No one noticed when I pulled my coat from the closet behind them and walked out the door.

This bothered me for a long time. I complained bitterly about it to my dad, who seems to have one of those faces as well. All while growing up, I was advised of my father's resemblances—variations on the dark-and-handsome theme—by friends and strangers alike. He just looked like my dad to me. But then it happened: I was around thirteen when I saw *The Philadelphia Story*, my first Jimmy Stewart movie. "Dad!" I said. "That's *you*!" He smiled and said I was batty—a pretty Jimmy Stewart response, when you think about it—but I was adamant. It became important for him to recognize what I saw plainly for myself. How could he not? Hadn't people told him?

I have a better understanding of his befuddlement now, though I'll be damned if I'm wrong about Jimmy Stewart—especially in profile. It still happens: Last year my dad and I were piling up an A&P's conveyor belt with Christmas booty when he caught the checkout lady's eye. "You know, you look like someone," she observed from behind the register. "You look like that actor . . ."

"Abe Vigoda?" I offered, stacking fruitcake like firewood. She looked at me as though I'd just jammed a stick into a ten-speed's whirling front wheel, like that was my idea of fun.

My dad told me not to take the party incident so hard, that people sometimes fumble when they're trying to make frivolous social contact. I can understand that—*I am that*—and this was not that. It's not a misplaced generosity but a misunderstanding to write off the shift from cocktail banter to a ruthless round of Celebrity Whatsit as a clumsy attempt at connection. Generosity might involve a recognition of the impulse we earthlings have, when confronted with something perfectly ordinary and frankly terrifying—a new human being—to "solve" them, contain them in some satisfying way, avoid looking further into yet another wild abyss. In other words it's the avoidance of connection. Which I believe, dear Internet warrior, you might know well.

I suppose there's another option. I suppose there is the idea that we are meant to take comparisons to random and sometimes only faintly familiar celebrities as some kind of compliment. Though an ex-boyfriend of mine, who is often and straight-facedly told that he's a dead ringer for John C. Reilly, might disagree. Then again, this same ex-boyfriend practically levitated in a Las Vegas restaurant when our waiter, pausing between water-glass refills, told him that he looked like that guy—oh, that *guy*. *You know*, the one in that movie. Plays a vampire? *The Lost Boys!*

Um, we said, bracing for the worst. But the waiter was talking about Jason Patric, who was the best-looking man on the planet for about twenty-seven minutes in 1991. And yet it wasn't necessarily flattery—the waiter just wanted to get it right. In such cases the assumption seems to be that it's better to resemble someone famous than to drift along without a public antecedent, your bastard features displaced in a larger puzzle. A connection is indeed being made, it's just between you and a vast and agile ecology of celebrity DNA.

Computer science is working to mimic this kind of thing in cyberspace. Google and YouTube have partnered to create facial-recognition software that will map and organize the massive video hub's famous faces on its own. "The Internet is in a constant state of flux," Google's announcement of the project read, "and new 'celebrities' are constantly added to the popular culture even as the celebrities of the past fade. This ability to learn autonomously to constantly add to the existing gallery of celebrities is therefore a major design principle of our work."

From this angle what I call the *Compare and Conquer* looks more like a compulsive reflex than a deflective one. Certainly it's less personal. Which is not to say it can't be all of those things. The information-gorged brain resorts to pattern recognition, after all. We consume images, our primary cultural language, at a turbine-busting velocity, and all of those faces wind up forming a sort of alpha database that gets scanned like police software when someone like me comes into view. I'm not sure if the impersonality of the reflex will make those displeased with either the quality or quantity of the comparisons they receive feel any better, but it seems obvious that the only constant in subjective pattern recognition is the subject's inconstancy. Who can say whether that Las Vegas waiter had a brother who wore his hair in a feathery, Jason Patric mullet circa 1987, earning him a comparison that caught on despite the wiry glasses and dimpled chin that he happens to share with a certain restaurant patron, which patron then called up the original resemblance in his waiter's eye by a kind of pinball proxy? And who was I to bite my tongue?

Even if we don't always say it out loud, we have all done it or felt pinned under the weight of being unable to do it. Just in the past few days I have nailed down two matches between friends and celebrities that have been months in the making and, having done so, experienced the kind of vindication usually reserved for the foiling of rigged fairway games and landmark Supreme Court victories. The world, in all its sudden knowability, can feel impossibly opaque. The *Compare and Conquer* is often an involuntary response to that feeling, a crude mechanism that seems designed to maintain a sense of what's shared amid all this "sharing."

Which is why it makes sense that social-media networks were quick to translate the reflex into a feature. As of late 2011, Facebook was closing in on a billion members, each with an average of 130 "friends." Half of those members log in habitually, no doubt contributing to the 250 million photos uploaded to the site every day. Flickr, a personal photo-album site, now houses almost four billion photos, and Instagram, a social network that cut out the vernacular blubber to traffic solely in image statements, grew from one hundred thousand to twelve million members in the first year after its 2010 launch.

Of the many things one might then say about *that*, here I will only point out that (a) that's a shitload of faces; and (b) the way we look at photographs of friends or strangers or that new category of friend-strangers we've opened up has developed some key similarities with the way we look at celebrities.

The aptly named Facebook was the first to recognize and capitalize on these similarities. In 2007, Facebook introduced an application called FaceDouble, a facial-recognition algorithm that scanned users' faces with the purpose of matching them to a celebrity's. In a distant nod to Facemash—Facebook's progenitor, a program that paired the faces of Mark Zuckerberg's Harvard classmates for snap hotness judgments—your friends "vote" on the veracity of the resemblance. Alongside this function was the option of using FaceDouble to scan inside Facebook's millions for your civilian "twin," or twins. Though not as popular as the celebrity look-alike sites you now find all over the Web (weird: one of the biggest is found on the genealogy site myheritage.com), the "Facetwin" phenomenon is odd in the way that the trend of "friending" or "following" someone with the same name is odd: it literalizes social media's equation of connection with sameness.

All of this culminated, as so much of our culture now does, in a meme. "Doppelgänger Week" happened in early 2010, when all across Facebook users swapped out their profile pics for images of the celebrity they are said to resemble. Some upsold themselves as Robert Pattinson or J.Lo knockoffs; some went all the way downtown with Golem and Jabba. Others took the middle road of coy self-deprecation, unless posting a picture of someone like Ed Begley, Jr., actually represents a sincerely outdated frame of reference.

It must be said that I hear about these things secondhand. It must be said too that I don't have to ask. It became clear around 2007, when the site consumed my social circle like a Gila brushfire, that refusing to join Facebook was more of a gesture than a useful avoidance of its effects. In the weeks after old Jason Patric and I went our separate ways, I received updates about his Facebook-bound status (not yet "single") and epigrammatic regrets (phrased in German for added pathos) against my will, from friends who seemed to think they were doing me a favor, like smuggling code out of (or would that be *into*?) the Kremlin.

How to accept this new information, or at least this old information in its new encryption? The experimental nature of Internet discourse has produced some novel and baffling sensations, if not full-blown feelings. There's a kind of protocol, for instance, to carry us through real-world rejections; the emotional immune system recognizes it and either attacks or succumbs. But the ephemeral, punk-ass rejection of being followed, say, on Twitter, by a person whom one "knows" but has never met, and then unfollowed by that same vaguely acknowledged entity a few months/weeks/hours later, feels like a virtual sucker punch in part because there is no established pattern for dealing with it. Can there be any accountability for such a rejection? As with separating the refracted perceptions of others from the reality of your face, it can be so hard to tell what counts as personal and what's just managing information.

When it comes to strangers on trains and pleased-to-meet-you's at parties, I have made a philosophical peace with the *Compare and Conquer.* But those who know me well—friends, boyfriends, health professionals—aren't much better, and I hear regularly of the faces and performances that sent up flags of referential familiarity. I'm still working on that one. I once tried listing all of the names I have heard but stopped at sixteen, with one woman by far the front-runner. The others, when considered in a gallerylike format, share almost no distinguishing characteristics, save for their utter, abiding whiteness.

I feel oppressed by the spectrum. It makes me feel lonely, the opposite of known. And yet, in the same way that previously unremarked resemblances are discovered and sworn to at family funerals, it would seem as though I'm being told something important, so I keep my eye out for these unlikely women. I try to see what my friends see, but it's impossible.

It's most impossible, in fact, when I actually *do* see myself, briefly, in a laugh or a look or a pointy nose. It's just a weird feeling that's hard to describe.

One winter afternoon a couple of years ago I left my local supermarket feeling low after starting a fight between two stock boys. I became aware of it when I heard one loudly defending the honor of the former child star that the other had somehow seen in me as I was pricing strawberries. A stuccoed head of black hair peeked out from around the pasta display for a second look, then ducked back behind. "Naw, man—are you crazy?" he boomed. "That's my *girl*, that's my *chica*!" The other one stood his ground, hollering back. It was as though I weren't there at all.

This was 2009. Soon after the spaghetti-aisle incident I watched *The Girlfriend Experience*, Steven Soderbergh's moody neo-melodrama about call girls and the 2008 financial crisis. The film critic Glenn Kenny has a small part in the movie, and although I am on nodding and occasionally even speaking terms with Glenn when we meet on the howling heath of New York's screening rooms, not until I watched him in that uniquely uninhibited way—stripped to the image, a person projected outside himself—did I realize how profoundly he reminds me of another friend. A much closer friend. They look not a bit alike, and of course Glenn was playing a character, but on-screen it wasn't the image or personality of my friend that he captured but the *feeling*. I can't tell you how satisfying that two-toned ring of alarm and recognition was, that private zing of affirmation: There he is! *He lives!*

That night I came home to an e-mail from a different friend. He wrote to say that an actress in a film he'd just seen had reminded him of me. He wouldn't tell me her name though, or the nature of the role, aware of my long history of being driven bananas by such things. But also, he wrote, "because I fear that you might be like: 'Her?! Me?!?! NO WAY!' And then get mad at me."

I didn't press, and I didn't get mad. I don't think I would have even if he'd told me. For the first time it actually made me feel kind of good. *She lives!*

Soon after that night I made a trip to my local library. Passing through the revolving entrance doors, I noticed the security guard stationed at the turnstiles started to laugh when she saw me coming—not that unusual, I admit. But she kept smiling as I moved closer, prepping my bag for inspection. Waving it away, she asked if I'd forgotten something, then looked me right in the face. The security guard thought she knew me—had just seen me. I winked at her and slipped inside.

The San Diego of My Mind

The southwest corner of Scripps Ranch, a San Diego bedroom community named after the Midwestern newspaper baron Edward Willis Scripps, is a scrubby, dead-treed scab of land. This is more or less its natural state, though better living through irrigation, as signs posted around the area remind you, remains the California dream. When the twenty-one-hundred-acre parcel Scripps purchased for himself in the late nineteenth century was slated for residential development in the 1970s, vows were made to either preserve or parkify a majority of the land. Today the Scripps Ranch community, which numbers in the low thirty thousands, has a median household income of roughly 140 grand and includes what seems like a preponderant number of ex–professional football players.

A few more numbers: In 2003, a fire lit by a hunter lost in Cleveland National Forest consumed 350 community homes on its way to destroying upward of 3,000 buildings in the greater area. In late 2011, sixty-five Scripps Ranch homes, which begin at almost half a million dollars, were listed as having recently entered either foreclosure or default. Arguments among locals and armchair urban planners about whether Scripps Ranch can be defined as an exurb lead directly to arguments about the definition of *exurb*, which in turn lead nowhere, which seems fitting. The debate—diligently stoked and restoked across the Internet, like the Olympic flame—centers on issues of proximity. The qualifying distance between satellite community and mother city is under great and disgusted contention, as is the strength of the gravitational pull. Some measure from the city proper, others an adjacent corporate hub, still others from the nearest Starbucks. In being cradled by a chaparral moat, anyway, Scripps Ranch meets the most basic exurban criteria: exclusivity. In theory all that greenish space enhances property value and—though it might conduct a wildfire right to your door—keeps human unsavories at bay. Here history would like to note that Edward Scripps's turn-of-the-century, forty-seven-room Miramar Lake mansion—a health retreat built for himself and his rhinitic sister—was subjected to an epic and sustained looting as the first suburban frames went up.

I didn't know any of this on the late-May morning when I took a fifty-dollar cab ride from downtown San Diego to an industrial park clinging to what turned out to be the chin of Scripps Ranch. I just had an address and a rapidly aggravating sense of displacement. We were a disconcertingly long way from my room in a motel huddled in the Churrigueresque shadow of the El Cortez, the apparent destination of choice for nine out of ten San Diego prom-goers. It was far enough away that by the midpoint I had resigned myself, in an order I now forget, to both marrying and being murdered by my driver. It seemed implausible that two such disparate places could belong to one domain. But then San Diego seems determined to spread itself across as much space as possible; it's the young-male subway rider of the California coast. The city has a hard time filling it in: walking through the downtown during rush hour, an acoustic trick carries a laconic exchange between two Brink's guards across thirty feet of empty concrete valley and into your ear. New York City could jimmy five johns into the single-stall restroom of one of the city center's cavernous Thai joints, maybe a dozen more along the fifteen-foot runway and giant foyer that prelude it. Sprawl for sprawl's sake, weirdly, is crowding in the same way the bony, baggy-jeaned knees staked across three seats on the morning commute are crowding. We get it: it's big.

My instructions were to arrive at a tiny start-up marketing firm at 10:00 a.m. on a Friday. There I would speak to one of its founding partners about the future of focus testing and, if there was time, have my cognitive-response mechanism laid open like a morning paper. The outfit, called MindSign, claims to be home to the only privately owned, "market-friendly" functional magnetic resonance imaging (fMRI) machine in the world. The plan, hatched in early 2009 by college roommates and film-school graduates Philip Carlsen and Devin Hubbard, was to defect across the notional border between moviemaking and movie marketing. At the time both men were battling early-onset disillusionment with their Hollywood jobs (at DreamWorks and Sony, respectively) and looking for a way out of the development grind.

Their decision was eased by the fact that Devin's father, a research neurologist who made his mint patenting a Botox-related drug, had recently purchased a three-ton, three-million-dollar Siemens 3T Tim Trio—the new centerpiece of neurotechnology—as a retirement present to himself. Terminally formative contact with *The Fountainhead* had led David Hubbard to major in philosophy at Yale, and he nursed a desire to capture, vivify, and decoct the mysteries of human consciousness across a career that includes an M.A. in counseling psychology and an M.D. with a specialty in neurology. Having met the facility and management requirements for housing an fMRI machine under the auspices of a charitable organization in 2007, Dr. Hubbard was free to use it as he pleased.

Around the same time, in the mid-aughts, something called "neuromarketing" was being pitched as the new silver bullet in the market-research world. The high-tech alternative to feeding focus-group participants a few doughnuts, asking how they feel, and figuring out how to exploit the character chinks and insecurities they have unwittingly exposed, fMRI testing would reveal the effect of a product or campaign on key clusters of the amygdala, the part of the brain that registers fear and anxiety.

If the entire film industry could somehow be wrestled into a Tim Trio, on a good day its amygdala might appear to be engulfed in flames. Diffusing audiences, the rise of the home theater, and a bankruptcy-pocked exhibitor infrastructure have peaked the pressure on Hollywood to earn out and then some, every time. That pressure has made finding a reliable algorithm for success—a guarantee beyond formula or genre—the Holy Grail of Hollywood filmmaking, a shift that has long been reflected in the trend toward movies as brand-merchandising opportunities. In recent years it has become almost as expensive to market a major studio film as it is to make one—for every dollar spent on production between fifty and sixty cents is spent churning out ads and swag. With hundreds of millions in play and a global audience to consider, major studios run like risk-management firms. Rather than the threat of a jowly mogul recutting their masterpiece into hot-buttered pap, today's filmmakers must reckon with the tyranny of audience testing.

Intrigued with his father's retirement plans, Devin Hubbard moved home to begin an apprenticeship in 2008. Neuromarketing was catching on, and Dr. Hubbard proposed an entrepreneurial adventure: with access to the scanner and an in-house expert in the still-fledgling science of analyzing brain response, the boys could hang out a shingle and start fresh. After a persuasive L.A. lunch with Devin some months later, Carlsen began planning his relocation to San Diego as well. In my imagining both of them bombed down the 405 with only a Rolodex strapped to the roof. After four years of (again, I imagine) bong-enhanced blue-sky sessions about the places they'd go, the movies they'd make, and the universes they'd master, and a few more years after that of being ignored by greasy M.B.A.'s in soul-corroding pitch meetings, here, at last, was a chance to unleash their dorm-room bravado on the real world. A chance to master this new game and serve it back to their old bosses. Once installed in San Diego, the new partners lingered over the right name for their concern, staked a website, and decided on the cornerstone of the business—an offshoot of fMRI market research they would call neurocinema.

The Scripps Ranch Civic Association had just celebrated its fortieth anniversary the day I passed the desiccated corner of the wildlife preserve along Interstate 15. The flora on either side of the preserve's border is equally unimpressive, though only the freeway side is clotted with garbage. Some of it—a tenderized pack of American Spirits, a quarter bag of

Funyuns—cleaves, spread-eagled, to the fence itself. Nearby a metal sign that forbids passersby from entering, trespassing, loitering, hunting, and cutting or removing trees or shrubs is heavily Pollocked with rust.

Size-wise, anyway, it's a pretty healthy chunk of land. Speeding by it, I thought it might make a nice sanctuary for film journalism's fried first responders—those critics who, like me, have started to wonder if the next Adam Sandler picture might be the one to send them over the proverbial edge and into a palliative grazing-type situation.

Yeah, yeah: bad movies, *boohoo*—there have always been bad movies, I hear you say. And bad moods and silly critics and jobs that start to bore you senseless. It has always been a depraved business too—should anyone doubt it, there's an entire subgenre of meta-Hollywood movies and Raymond Chandler's deathlessly acid studio dispatches for handy consultation. I do understand these things, and I too have been watching bad movies and movies about bad movies and movies about how bad it is making bad movies my whole life. I can only say that things feel different and hope you'll trust me. Maybe you've felt it too. Maybe you are also unsure if bad movies—I mean really, like fog-up-the-joint bad—have ever done so well or stunk with this sort of alien enigma. Their inscrutability makes them difficult to align with a long and occasionally illustrious tradition of B-movie badness and straight-faced bombs.

In fact what's scariest about the neo-terrible movie is the way it eludes traditional evaluation, pointing ultimately and only to the riddle of its own existence. The viewing experience is akin to watching a carpet being rolled out at one end and up at the other—this kind of movie seems to consume itself as it goes, leaving only the fleeting impressions of an unpleasant dream or hypnotic event. The question posed by the worst of them is actually quite profound: Have we changed what it means to call something a movie, good or bad? Subset: If we ever got around to a general-use definition of good and bad, has that shifted as well? Sub-subset: How did this astonishingly stupid thing I'm watching even *happen*? Is this really happening? Wait—*what* just happened?

There's not a lot of sympathy to go around for those people waved into free movies for what is more or less a living. I'm not interested in sympathy; it's never looked right on me. Having spent a few years absorbing Hollywood's front line of fire at a rate of four to six new releases a week, I would only like to tell you that I have confronted and come to know quite particularly what we talk about, in the early twenty-first century of professional moviegoing, when we talk about burnout.

Ten minutes before we were scheduled to meet, Philip Carlsen painted the front of his button-down with freshly brewed coffee. Carlsen, now a Scripps Ranch resident, lives close enough to his headquarters that he was able to walk home, change his shirt, and walk back in time to greet me as I was milling about MindSign's doors. The office is part of an industrial park found at the juncture of Old Grove Road and Businesspark Avenue, an asphalt gully among a wealth of elephant-footed eucalyptus trees. Scripps legend has it that the mogul's gardener, one Chauncey I. Jerabek, believed eucalyptus wood to be a premium material in the production of railroad ties; he set out to line the ranch with free-market mojo. Though he was sadly mistaken about the wood, the spirit of Chauncey

"Always Thinking" Jerabek's enterprise lived on: Scripps Ranch's first residential contractor was caught passing off bum lumber as prime cut.

Freshly shirted, Carlsen entered the office ahead of me, pleading an eccentric alarm system, then returned to buzz me in. It's a modest office—just the two partners and the odd tech on-site on a given day—dominated by the presence of its engine. Built like massive mezzi rigatoni, the fMRI machine fills the center of its operating theater from floor to ceiling, a sculpted chunk of Tesla magnet, copper, and steel, coated in a smooth, white surface and stamped with the Siemens logo. It's glassed into its own chamber, like a neonatal unit for an unknown species. You can hear it breathing throughout the office, the endless, electric inhale of a thousand refrigerators. The 3T had to be lowered in through the ceiling of the complex, and the office was rebuilt around it. Scans are watched from an observational bay, reinforcing the feeling that something Plutonian is being incubated inside. As we passed the chamber, Carlsen opened the door for a better look, warning me against letting my bag dangle over a line of red tape on the floor. They've lost a few good iPhones that way.

Carlsen pushed back in his chair as I placed a lipstick-size Olympus recorder on the corner slice of table separating us in the small meeting room next door. A look of pity crossed with polite aversion passed over his face, and I wondered whether he had wearied of going on the record with presumed enemies or was just taking in the absurdity of the contrast between his gadget and mine.

In their brief existence, MindSign has aroused some predictable controversy. Where the advertising racket is supposed to be poised on the cutting edge of evil, in general we assume the film industry is guided by better angels. We still want to believe that a bunch of people who are smarter and better looking than we are are spending that awesome capital trying to figure out how to entertain us, even send us away with our hearts full and our heads rearranged.

Any movie not being watched with one's eyes pincered open is availed of this good faith. It won't surprise anyone who has sampled even a rancid sliver of an episode of *Bridalplasty* or the last *Saw* sequel to learn that the working definition of entertainment has made a sharp turn toward the atavistic. It may feel troubling that we now accept on-screen vivisections and survival-of-the-hottest tournaments as entertainment, but those are human appetites with long and inglorious human precedents. Whether we should be encouraging those appetites and clarifying them into high definition is the question. The kind of stuff Carlsen is talking about involves relocating the movie industry's creative command center into a lab like this one, where decisions about casting, character, plot, and style are determined according to a schema of diagnostic testing, a process ruled by what is referred to in neuroscience as *activation*.

Entertainment is the noun Graham Greene used to describe his lesser novels in the 1930s; David Foster Wallace imagined it as a velvet assassin in 1996's *Infinite Jest*. But the Ponzi scheme of Western culture has a wicked turnover: like *escapism* before it, *entertainment* has shed its pejorative stench, and in just a few decades. The nihilistic scenario of a nation of pinwheel-eyed automatons has been reconceived as an ideal— quality-of-life as unlimited data, the mastery of amusement over time and space. *Infinite Jest* was the name of a movie so exquisitely entertaining that viewers basically shit themselves and died. What came to pass over the years in which Wallace's novel is set is a sort of inversion of that scenario, where the quality of whatever you're watching or clicking or gawping at doesn't much matter, as long as it's something and it's always on. Like buying the right sneaker or living in the right neighborhood, it becomes a matter of keeping up.

Different media conglomerates and cellular-service providers have tried on different versions of Bell's proto-utopian 2010 slogan: "Be entertained anywhere." Every week this ambition is pushed a little further. After a meal at a Union Square restaurant on a recent Friday night, I passed a lone man guiding fork to mouth with his earbuds plugged in and his eyes trained on an iPad, where the mise-en-scènic architecture of a movie pulsed in holographic blues. Watching the latest *Transformers* sequel and hoovering meat loaf at a crowded diner may be closer to an act of *distraction*, the pyramid's late-twentieth-century ringer. Distraction and entertainment may in fact be the cochairs of the current culture, and the distinction between them gets thinner all the time.

I'd get so bummed out, back a few years ago when I was babysitting a six-year-old boy, watching him take all of his meals alone, in front of the television. *Kid*, I'd think, *you've got your whole life to do that*. It's the only way he'll eat, his parents said—he needs a distraction. But that wasn't quite true: the instant the TV came on, he fixed and dilated, reanimating only when you moved to turn it off. His previous babysitter had demonstrated her method of pushing chicken nuggets in when his mouth hung open, but I just couldn't do it. I'd try to watch the assaultive, crudely animated cartoons along with him and wind up asking, Do you like this show? Is it *good*? But this otherwise bright and extremely quick-witted little kid was in a place beyond value judgment and would grunt in reply. Activation is maybe the most basic marker of human response—anyone who has jangled house keys for a baby has observed it in its purest form.

Marshall McLuhan insisted, as the pshaw-ing Western world TV'd up and embraced the miracle of the microwave in the 1960s, that technology would retribalize man. The reconception of subjective cognitive and emotional experience in objective, neuroscientific terms will add another check in the man's running column of catastrophes foretold. The more sophisticated the technology, it seems, the more profoundly it reduces the human to the animal, a paradox that has served the sciences relatively well but seems poised to destroy what we think of as social and creative culture. To valuate even the broadest forms of entertainment in terms of fight-or-flight brain-activation patterns is to bring us into line with the cinephilic tastes of the common prairie vole. It is to begin a process that has the potential to turn our primary storytelling medium into the equivalent of a giant crib mobile, a rotating dangler of spring-loaded stimuli.

It would appear that we are still very much invested in the idea of what makes a movie "good." The entire industry is organized around a late-winter referendum on the subject; first just a show—the Oscars—now film awards comprise an entire season, if one crowded by industry politics and celebrity gawping. Yet the question of what makes a movie *bad* is treated as superfluous, snobby, or understood, i.e., not *good*. "Well, it's all subjective" is how we agree to disagree on movie quality. And that's true, to a considerable extent. But neuroscience is not just furthering a realignment of the culture with the principle that activation = good. It bears reminding that the first step of any scientific method is to eliminate subjectivity altogether. And what is a subject minus her subjectivity?

Carlsen has admitted it's the screenwriters who send him hate mail. The honest ones, anyway. For the rest, the no-brainer shortcuts of neuroscience, like the microwave, just make life that much easier.

The face, for our purposes, of this particular future is so improbable it feels, to the cynical para-brain, totally obvious. Philip Carlsen is fair with closely cropped blond hair, thirty-ish, and handsome in a slightly ruddy, wait-and-see way. He's friendly but watchful, with the invigorated look and equable manner of a young man who has finally cleared a field for himself. He's not worried, in other words, and in general. Carlsen describes MindSign as a family business—the Hubbards have all but adopted him—and he is free to hang around after hours and conduct pop-up experiments for fun. Instead of banging through a few *GTA IV* missions at home on a Friday night, he might stuff his head in the scanner to browse through high-end motorbikes, or use an Amazon couch purchase as an opportunity to see what his brain looks like when he clicks "buy." Dr. Hubbard, a longtime practitioner of Transcendental Meditation, had planned to spend his dotage making similar sorties to the facility. A neuromantic of sorts, he envisioned the meditating brain as a Bastille Day of brain waves, blood firing like Roman candles in every lobe. In fact the images looked more like a tranquil pond at midnight. Couch buying, however, is activating as all hell.

The machine exerts a magnetic force thirty thousand times

that of the earth's gravity; belt buckles and ballpoints become deadly weapons in its presence. Its lavish energy needs have an allegorical pang: once turned on the machine cannot be turned off, for fear of surging the grid. In the simplest terms, fMRI scans track the iron in the blood as it is called to various parts of the brain. Interpreting blood flow in response to external stimuli is a matter of decoding complicated and as yet largely mysterious patterns. Facial recognition and motor cognition, for instance, have been mapped more confidently than the difference between fear and agitation, or agitation and laughter, for that matter. When I ask Carlsen what fifteen years of fMRI science has clarified about the nature of human response, he quotes Dr. Hubbard: "We know more about outer space than we do about inner space."

But then the movie business has always been more interested in going concerns than in rocket science—and in terms of focus grouping, fMRI is the slick new thing. More comprehensive than the electric-signal capture of electroencephalography (EEG) and electromyography (EMG), and more accurate than galvanic skin response ("It can tell you a little bit," Carlsen says, "but I wouldn't change a campaign based on Subject 42 sweating") and standard MRI pictures, fMRI works in real time, revealing the parts of the brain where, as Carlsen says, "all the cool stuff happens." The machine takes a picture of the brain every two seconds, which happens to be the average length of a movie shot. Though Hollywood studios are hypercautious about confidentiality (political campaigns also demand DEFCON secrecy), MindSign hopes to insinuate itself into every step of the filmmaking process. At the moment they deal mainly in movie trailers; in this they are not far removed from their Hollywood clients.

Still gunning in start-up mode, MindSign has picked up a rogue assortment of clients. Much smaller fish than McDonald's and Warner Bros. are willing to shell out for what Carlsen calls "an expensive way to prove the obvious." They have dealt with lawyers looking to out medical claimants as malingerers, and women determined to crack the case of the husband and the Asian masseuse. Though a techno-gumshoe outfit called No Lie MRI provided a steady feed of clients, MindSign found the adultery racket a little tawdry. Even so, there's something comforting in the idea that the same old human messes were first in line at the future's door. If there is an unwavering constant between the days of savior-doubting, witch-floating, and last week's episode of *Cheaters*, it is the human obsession with gleaning, eliciting, and proving the "truth." In that sense, the relationship between technology and tribalism is a two-way parade.

The lie-detecting business will thrive with or without MindSign—the people who know about such things agree that fMRI lie-detection scans will soon be widely admissible in courts. Still waiting for the movie-studio lawyers to triple-caulk their nondisclosure agreements, in 2010 MindSign hooked up with Martin Lindstrom—a branding consultant and the author of a book called *Brandwashed: Tricks Companies Use to Manipulate Our Minds and Persuade Us to Buy*—to conduct more traditional neuromarketing research. Together they designed a study to determine how close iPhone users are to the truth when they talk about being addicted to their gadgets. Subjects were scanned while they looked at images of an iPhone with no service and an iPhone that read "Mom calling"; they listened to the chirp of a text coming in; they watched video of an iPhone vibrating with a new message.

The study predicted that iPhone stimuli would match the activation patterns associated with addiction, but in fact it engaged the insular cortex, the part of the brain believed to be associated with feelings of love and empathy. Carlsen cited this study as an example of how brain scans often prove surprising. Several months later Lindstrom discussed the results in a *New York Times* op-ed titled "You Love Your iPhone. Literally."

I got stuck on the larger picture.

Response is the crudest and yet the most profound external measurement of consciousness. I know that you are not just alive but conscious because you respond when I look at, speak to, or touch you; you know the same about me. Together we form the network of mutually reinforcing subjectivities we call human existence. We respond, therefore we are. Underlying Carlsen's belief in what he described as fMRI's ability "to make the subjective objective" is a coolly tautological redefinition of consciousness: you respond, therefore you respond.

The most obvious illustration of that statement's ontological bulk involves the seemingly vegetative patients revealed, through fMRI testing, to be suffering from "locked in" syndrome. Dr. Adrian Owen, the British neuroscientist whom Carlsen calls "the Michael Jordan of fMRI," is at the forefront of this research, having already proven brain response in at least one vegetative patient. The first step was finding a substitute for what "yes" looks like in the brain, so they could try to communicate with simple questions. The trick was developing a kind of neurological key, a pattern of response robust enough that it could serve as a marker. The motor receptors that control our movements seemed like plausible candidates—they are known to activate, for instance, whether we imagine throwing a ball or actually throw it. As hoped, certain patients showed the appropriate activation when they were asked to imagine swinging a racket, or booting a soccer ball. One of Dr. Owen's patients, a twenty-nine-year-old car-accident victim who had lain unresponsive for five years, was instructed to pretend he was hitting a forearm winner if he wanted to answer a question in the affirmative. Knowing the answer, Dr. Owen then asked the young man if he had any brothers. *Yes*, the subject's brain said, glowing at the top of his skull like a porch light. *As a matter of fact I do.*

Yet there is no way of knowing whether the young man had a subjective experience of that response, since scans have also shown that the unconscious brain is capable of responding to stimuli even when what we think of as the conscious mind registers nothing. One term for this phenomenon is *blindsight*. If patients who have sustained ocular trauma say they cannot see the photo of the smiling face being held in front of them but their unconscious brains say they can, are both responses true?

The legal and ethical debates over such questions will shape a larger discourse. In the future of consciousness, it would seem, subjectivity is somehow both paramount and beside the point. The protection of human life is ostensibly behind all medical advances, yet with neuroscience in particular the terms of what it means to be human are blurred. The question of quality comes into play more urgently in discussions of what it means to be alive, or to be capable of living the kind of life we think of as "good." Again, the concept of "bad" is defined by a kind of default. Only the scientific path is clear: it is always better to know more, to pursue the science to its ends and then treat the human conundrums that result as inevitable.

It's no wonder we have started pair-bonding with our iPhones. In device attachment resides the old struggle between the possessor and the possessed, the shifting sands of desire and consent. What we respond to is not the gadget itself but its promise of some personal and highly specific gratification. Yet love must find its object. The image of a phone shivering alone on a table is no more or less loaded than a pinup of Brigitte Bardot. The image of a human being strapped into a three-ton magnet to watch a vignette of a smart phone shivering alone on a table, however, is a dystopian icon of heartbreak.

MindSign studies offer clients something that eludes even the most elaborate analog focus group: reliability. It's pitifully easy, however, to outperform a system based on consulting college kids—"drunks and stoners," in Carlsen's words—for their thoughts on a $250 million movie. Carlsen cites his own time making the focus-group rounds while he was a film student as proof of their uselessness. After watching an early cut of a 2004 Dennis Quaid film called *Flight of the Phoenix*, Carlsen expedited the questionnaire like a man with better ways to waste his time.

"I literally was like 'Good, good, good, good, good, good,

good, good, good, good, good,'" he said. "I want my ten bucks, I'm done." Other data-occluders include our ovine tendency to defer to the loudest person in the room, and the inclination to tell a sympathetic or otherwise great-looking questioner what he wants to hear. As well as doing away with the obstructive veils of subjectivity, MindSign cuts the average focus group down from between fifty and one hundred subjects to the magic number of sixteen. "That's the number for statistics, as far as fMRI science goes," Carlsen said. "Sixteen is enough to speak for the population in a specific demographic."

Calming investors is a major selling point of this kind of science; calming investors has probably always been a kind of science. But when I point out that creating a better focus group bypasses the question of why the film industry began outsourcing their creative autonomy to average civilians in the first place, Carlsen is sanguine. He's seen too much to worry about furthering a process that began shortly after he was born.

"I just came from Hollywood," he said, in response to a question about the protests of writers and directors against his line of work. "You think those guys have any power? I worked for four producers [including Quentin Tarantino's longtime producer, Lawrence Bender]. I never wanted to be a producer, I just did it because I didn't have any money and I needed a job." Carlsen sat in on the meetings we all now know from the meta-genre of "backstage" movies and TV shows, where talent is massaged in the room and spit on the second it leaves, major decisions hinge on a coked-out executive's fuckability call, and assistants spend their days making twenty copies of the latest piece of shit movie because it tested well and the boss is excited about it again. "It's like that everywhere," Carlsen said. "It's just how it is. But great art will demand—" He paused. "Great art is *always* going to come through."

This, certainly, is the hope. The studio system, for its flaws and foibles, was a closed house, the proverbial dream factory from which all Hollywood movies flowed. The independent renaissance of the 1970s privileged individual directors over a tightly run system. Film was ordained as an art form and filmmakers as artists, complete with their infernal talk of *vision*. Then, as film journalist Mark Harris has suggested, the monster success of *Top Gun* in 1986 solidified a producer- and marketing-driven generation of "high concept" block-busters, "pure product" films interested chiefly in "the transient heightening of sensation." The 1990s hosted a resurgence in independent filmmaking, a flare of innovation whose ashes were sifted through for the next decade, mostly by studio boutiques hoping the residue of "quality" might rub off. What prevailed in the mainstream were tent-pole pictures based on established brands, endless sequels to fluky original hits, and children's movies.

Developing a movie the way you would a brand seems like the safest option in a time when audiences are fragmenting and piracy is making it harder with every passing evening to get people out of their living rooms. Even the toughest-minded forecasts from previous decades—all that high/low hand-wringing—read a little quaint today. Think of Pauline Kael forewarning of a future in which the good old popcorn movie disappears up Antonioni's backside in an anomic ten-minute shot. Or Joan Didion arching precisely 3.5 millimeters of her brow over the empire that produced John Wayne giving way to an age of masturbatory passion projects. And that was the *sixties*. As a mass, middlebrow culture loomed, critics were preoccupied with segregating taste levels to their respective cultural water fountains. Eventually a policy of separate but equal arrived, and soon after that miscegenation ruled. In recent years the folding chair of creative power—having been passed from the studios to the independent auteur to the superproducer—ascended into the response-card cloud. Exit interviews, test screenings, and now brain-imaging scans help shape a film. It would seem that the audience has never been more powerful: united we stand, loving *Bridesmaids* one night and Nuri Bilge Ceylan the next.

The phrase *lowest common denominator*, often applied to questions of taste, is actually a matter of biology. Our most basic human responses are basic because they are shared: hunger, sex, sleep, fight or flight, pain—the pain response is so old it's vertebraic. If you gather enough people together and question them along a broad enough line, their responses will boil down to the consistency of a thick, primordial ooze. No one is above an ooze-based movie; it's *designed* to stimulate everyone with a working spinal cord. But what's being stimulated is a body, not a mind or spirit or even a brain. The latter is required for the punching of sensory buttons, but the human housing those responses is not. Denuding those senses—through deprivation or overstimulation—is a quick way to dehumanize. As our digestive tracts learn to break down frequently eaten foods more efficiently and develop resistance to foods we avoid, the psychologist Jonathan Schooler has suggested that the threshold for sensory stimulation adapts by a process called cosmic habituation. Where that threshold might top out, nobody knows. But it might be worth a guess.

Anyone standing downriver of the mainstream cannot escape this stuff. After several years of being expelled into the evening with the stink of a bad movie on me, a hierarchy of badness emerged. The bottom two-thirds of shit mountain is just the law of averages in digestive action, the same crap there has always been and ever will be. Only from the pinnacle does the horizon's bleakness come into view.

I remember my first glimpse from the top of Shit Mountain well. It was 2007, and I was watching the third installment of *The Pirates of the Caribbean*, the three-billion-dollar Disney franchise based on an amusement-park ride. It is the first time I can remember feeling that a movie was providing a direct and seriously unflattering reflection of what its makers thought of me. Savvy advertising is always trying to tell you something about yourself; it traffics only in different, better, more fulfilled versions of you. That's why it's so miserably effective: an ad can adopt the stance of leading you toward your own best interests. But a brand-centric movie is stuck pretending its purpose is to entertain, even if its job was done the moment it got you through the door, $13.50 lighter. And that's where movies like *Pirates* get caught out—it's the ad *and* the product, a long commercial for itself with nothing to actually sell.

In my review I used a word that critics have adopted as shorthand for the sins of the modern theme movie: *cynical*. More than pandering or mercenary laziness, these often wildly profitable films give off the chill of the inhuman. Things we associate with a story line occasionally occur, yet no story takes shape. Action set pieces prime us for a climax, yet we stagger out feeling gypped. Actors who resemble human beings speak in understandable sentences, yet nothing they say sinks in. Actually, my visit to MindSign made more sense of films like *Cowboys & Aliens* and *I Am Number Four*—the latter a non sequitur genre amalgam with high activation potential and low everything else—than a third or fourth viewing could have. Here was an explanation for the persistent, peculiar feeling that much of what I watch has issued not from flesh and blood but a floating, flashing brain.

I tried to talk to Carlsen about how bad it is out there, as if he didn't know. He assured me that science can help. He foresees neurocinema decamping from the fear- and threat-assessment responses of the amygdala to resettle its interests around Brodmann Area 25, the section of the ventromedial prefrontal cortex thought to mediate between the external world and the working memory to produce a sense of self. It's the spot they see lighting up most often during what Carlsen calls "heartfelt" scenes. "In our opinion," he said, "that's the coolest area right now."

I mean, it sounds cool. But I'm not sure it can stop what has been started or outperform the lambent gold mine of the twelve- to twenty-five-year-old male amygdala. We are now weaning a generation that has assimilated activation as entertainment, to the dismay of at least one subway-riding dad recently overheard complaining to a colleague about the way that the Nickelodeon network's signature rapid cutting and jarring sounds and colors transform his seven-year-old daughter into one of those new breeds of zombie who can book it like a black bear. This is, of course, a very circular concern:

our parents told us television would rot our brains, but the age of *iCarly* and *Hannah Montana* makes *Sesame Street* look like *The Mark Twain Children's Hour*.

"I think that's why kids are kind of . . . *awful* today," said Carlsen, who wound up in the children's television arm at DreamWorks. "You know? They don't have good TV."

Evaluating the classics against this new metric produces scattered results. A 2008 study conducted by Israeli neurobiologists Uri Hasson and Rafi Malach found that an episode of *Alfred Hitchcock Presents* produced nearly identical patterns of brain response across a group of viewers, results that could only please a director who conceived of audience response as a form of reflexology. But Hitchcock was also profoundly interested in representing subjectivity; few directors made as plain the idea that we go to the movies to literally *see* how things *feel*. There may be no better statement on subjectivity vis-à-vis the movies than the one presented in *Rear Window*. The attempt to grab each viewer individually gives art to what would otherwise be an exercise in collective muscle control, something achievable by a lone tripod trained on a Wimbledon match.

Hasson and Malach's studies helped spark Carlsen and Hubbard's interest in neurocinema. They conducted a study of their own involving the original, 1968 version of *Night of the Living Dead*.

"Boooring," Carlsen said. "Unfortunately. It was very non-activating. And, like, that movie—it scares the hell out of me." I wondered how he felt about helping create a standard that contradicts his own experience of what makes something good or sweet or scary. "Culture is different now," Carlsen shrugged. "Often the people we scan are young college kids, and one could argue—I don't know if this is actual fact—but one could argue that it's just a different culture. They're attracted by colorful things, pretty things, not as . . . *old*." A movie like *The Kids Are All Right*, which Carlsen cited as an example of a recent film he loved—"it had me just as engaged as any *Harry Potter* movie or anything else"—will never activate the way a brain-pummeler like *Battle: Los Angeles* does.

I mentioned *Battle: Los Angeles*—concept: aliens versus marines—to Carlsen because it had recently jackhammered a spot in the forefront of my memory of violently unpleasant viewing experiences. It's the only film whose equilibrium-scrambling combination of epileptic camerawork and dysphasic, microsecond shots has actually made me sick. I was still nauseous almost forty-eight hours later, when I had to file my review. The judgment seemed obvious; the real challenge of the new generation of concept-driven, high-activation films is figuring out enough of what you just saw to write an opinion. The tighter the elevator pitch, the more elusive the explanation of the resulting film.

Renata Adler famously put a four-year warranty on the sensibility of any practicing critic; I think lingerie models have longer careers. I had been reviewing films for four and a half years the night I staggered back into the neon hippodrome of Times Square, my mood as black and bottomless as the divot in Aaron Eckhart's chin. For me steady reviewing was something of a fluke—a way to earn a living on the way to wherever I was going. It felt like a miracle then; for the most part it still does. But in addition to experiencing the habituation that can turn even a great job into a bit of a drag, I have come to suspect that writing for a living is one of the trickiest things a writer can do. With all due relativity noted, it is *tough* out there for a second-string reviewer; you can go to some *dark places* watching *Hoodwinked Too!* or blowing another evening on a movie based on a comic book that was invented for the sole purpose of spawning a movie that could then make the illustrious claim of having been based on a comic book.

And trust me, no one looks to the culture or nobility of the profession for sustenance: when the Internet is not whizzing on your reviews and calling for your commitment to a cultural reeducation camp, your own colleagues are pretending not to notice each other on the screening-room circuit, each time behaving as though they've arrived at a 6:00 p.m. showing of *Battlefield Girth* and are desperate for the lights to go down. Perhaps the only thing worse is when people start talking. The urge to concuss myself with a seat rest when I hear the adenoidal stringers behind me wondering if it's "reductive" to hate a film they've only heard about—maybe that's an overreaction. Or wanting to clink the tilted heads of the bald white men seated in front of me together as they segue from an appreciation of the timeliness of *The Help* to seditious whispers about that bald-white-man-disappointer President Obama ("I remember weeping with joy," said the one bitterly. "*Literally weeping*")—perhaps that is a disproportionate response.

Where criticism first seemed a natural and happy extension of my love of movies and writing, lately I have started to feel that there's something unnatural about habituating to—that is making a career of—a certain level of stimuli. I don't mean just at the movies but at the movies especially, where studios seem less interested in engaging individuals than equalizing audience response. That I am almost shy to admit fearing for my senses suggests how loath we are of being dismissed ourselves, aware on some level that to resist the culture's unchecked velocity is to fail.

"Neurological data is just another thing," Carlsen said, in response to a question about the impact neuromarketing will have on the creative gene pool. "It's not changing movies. It's just making better products for the consumer. And that could be anything—it could be a better movie trailer, a better movie, a better Oreo-cookie package." I asked what he meant by "better," wondering out loud about the nefarious possibilities of this kind of research, its capacity to exploit the parts of our viewing, wanting, buying selves that we are not aware of. MindSign's goal is to get the suits comfortable with scanning everything back to the pitch—to determine, say, if simply hearing the words *aliens versus marines* activates well.

"I don't know if Hollywood's ready to bite onto that yet," Carlsen admitted. "Somebody will, soon enough. That's kind of the thing with Hollywood, and America: somebody's gonna do it eventually."

The machine was free until one, and Carlsen offered to scan me while I watched a couple of movie trailers. A new *Pirates* movie was on deck—number four or five, neither of us could remember—and Carlsen had cited it several times as the exact kind of film that could use their help. The trailers on hand were a little older, one for *Red Riding Hood*—a gothy teen "reimagining" of the children's fairy tale designed to catch some tailwind action from the *Twilight* franchise's flapping druid robes—and one for the aforementioned *Battle: Los Angeles*.

I changed into a pair of the hospital scrubs stacked in the MindSign bathroom and stepped back into the hallway with bare feet, where a tech was waiting with a few questions about the status of my bra. Having failed the underwire test, I stepped back into the stall to remove it, and a barrette too.

A disclosure form designed to flag pacemakers, piercings, or bionic parts furthers the vetting process. I was clear until the question about claustrophobia, where I somehow circled *yes* when I meant to circle *no*. After a solemn promise not to hyperventilate, I was led onto the cool tiles of the machine's chamber; they keep blankets on hand for the easily chilled. I hopped onto the machine's sliding gurney and was fitted with a pair of earphones. Once she is laid out on her back, the subject's head is guided between two padded clamps, and a slotted contraption is fastened over her face. Inside the headgear, all the subject can see is herself: a mirror redirects images projected in from behind, but until then the show is her own two eyes.

In trying to ease my passage into this tunneled creep show, the tech demonstrated his awareness of the effect of the word *tiny* on a woman. We had just acknowledged my height and weight on the record, yet I'm sure every floret of my traitor brain lit up like the Rockefeller tree.

The tech slipped a squeezy panic button into my palm before retiring to the monitor bay. Then I was swallowed from the knees up. The sound piped in through the headphones competes with the machine's anabolic white noise, and not very well. The screen went black except for a small white crosshair in the center. Trailers run twice for a proper reading, and the crosshair returns for exactly sixteen seconds between showings—long enough to return your brain to its baseline. The tech cut in with a few last words of advice: the most important thing is to keep as still as possible. I concentrated on this until I shook from concentration, like a husband with something to hide. If it was possible to ace such a thing, bias probably didn't help, so I focused on clearing *Red Riding Hood*'s bad buzz from my mind, until all I could think about was not thinking about how every person in the entire world knows that *Red Riding Hood* bites, with a subfocus on what terminal self-consciousness might look like from the inside—a rainbow-colored question mark? Emergency broadcast stripes? Psychedelic hamster wheel? The second time through I tried to simply see what I was seeing, which went something like this: *Man, Amanda Seyfried is one odd-looking duck. Wow, the cape and basket and everything, huh. That is some extreme robe-flapping—gotta be CGI.* And: *Gary Oldman? Really?*

With the cruel *Battle: Los Angeles* redux, both times I just tried not to cry.

After refastening my bra and barrette I ran into MindSign's one o'clock in the hall. I knew the fragile, middle-aged woman perched on a red indoor scooter hadn't come to watch movie trailers or pine for her iPhone. In recent months, Carlsen had told me earlier, the company had redistributed its resources to accommodate a potential breakthrough in multiple sclerosis research. Their subjects are now split more or less evenly between focus-group volunteers and MS patients hoping for a miracle.

It happened like this: After receiving an MS diagnosis in the midnineties, thirty-seven-year-old Elena Zamboni's health deteriorated swiftly. Horrified by her suffering, Elena's husband, Paolo, a vascular surgeon in Ferrara, Italy, devoted himself to vanquishing her disease. A century of MS research had yielded a set of symptoms but no clear cause. Dr. Zamboni began with one of them: MS blood is typically iron heavy. Over a decade later, in 2009, he revealed his theory that MS is not an autoimmune disorder, as is widely believed, but a vascular one. Dr. Zamboni had discovered that the neck arteries of a majority of MS patients are either blocked or malformed, and improper blood drainage, not an autoimmune malfunction, leads to the excess of iron, which can lead to neural pathology—specifically the brain lesions associated with MS. In 2006, Elena was among the first to undergo the experimental stent and balloon angioplasty procedures of the "liberation treatment" and has since made a complete recovery. Evangelical-type stories of patients suddenly rising from their wheelchairs and regaining movement in their extremities soon emerged from Ferrara. The media were alerted and the entrenched interests of the neurology community prepared for attack. If Dr. Zamboni was right, it was both a watershed breakthrough and a huge embarrassment for a field approaching a basic plumbing issue as if it were curing cancer.

Shortly after Dr. Zamboni's discovery was made public, Devin Hubbard was diagnosed with multiple sclerosis. Dispirited by the stalemate in MS research and inspired by Dr. Zamboni's findings, Dr. Hubbard scanned Devin at MindSign, found the suspected blockages, and convinced a local surgeon to clear them. Some countries have already banned the liberation treatment, citing insufficient research. All the Hubbards know is that Devin has been symptom-free for over a year. Dr. Hubbard has unofficially emerged from retirement to advocate for the study of what has been re-branded chronic cerebrospinal venous insufficiency (CCSVI); his daughter Alexandra now heads a family foundation to find and help sufferers; and MindSign has overseen the overwhelmingly successful treatment of more than four hundred MS patients.

Among other things, the deeply personal motivation behind what could be one of the first major medical developments of the new century is also a clear affirmation of the enigma of subjective response, and the immensurate value of a single emotional investment.

"We do the neuromarketing because it's fun, it's kind of hip," Carlsen told me. "And then the MS just . . . makes us feel like decent people." He laughed. "We could use the karma." I asked him to explain, but Carlsen was still smiling to himself: "Well, Devin and I were college roommates . . ."

They'd need two weeks to analyze my scans, which were clear at least. For a moment the familiar dread that one will be unveiled as a fraud—in this case a brain-dead or possibly tumor-eaten one—returned. Heading for MindSign's exit I saw my tech leaning over the red scooter and decorously inquiring about his next subject's bra.

I felt like walking after my time in the Tesla bore and wound up on Pomerado Road, a thoroughfare lined high with eucalyptus on either side. A sign posted near Thurgood Marshall Middle School warns against drinking the recycled irrigation water, though I didn't see any around. The sun rode high and crisp in a Microsoft-blue sky; its consistent show of purpose is the pride of San Diego. When it rains the next day, lightly and briefly, strangers offer the kind of mortified, self-doubting apology usually reserved for the accidental injury of a small child.

The E. W. Scripps Company, headquartered in Ohio, runs fifteen remaining papers, including the *Abilene Reporter-News*, *The Henderson Gleaner*, the *Kitsap Sun*, the *Naples Daily News*, and the *Corpus Christi Caller-Times*. A few years ago, the company divided in two, separating new cable and interactive properties like the Food Network and Shopzilla.com from the dead weight of "slow growth" print operations. The company's hometown pride, *The Cincinnati Post*, was closed in 2007.

Stomach purling, I humped a mile or so down Interstate 15, toward what turned out to be a Carl's Jr. I've seen the commercials for years but never had the pleasure. I saw another Carl's Jr. commercial inside Carl's Jr., on the television mounted right above my table. The screen was fractured into five miniscreens, so that ads for Carl's Jr. competed with ads for the American Heart Association, and vignettes about Hurricane Katrina relief alternated with footage from a press junket for *The Hangover: Part II*. Carl's Jr.'s cable package has only one channel—Indoor Direct, a "restaurant entertainment network" self-billed as the country's fastest-growing "place-based" media. Slogan: "We entertain Americans while they eat."

In the time it took me to get to Carl's Jr., Philip Carlsen had found and followed my Twitter account. I liked the idea of having been googled among the eucalypti, of wandering the freeway insensible to e-transactions made in my name. I'm sure someday we'll know such things—we'll develop data-collecting, clip-on senses to remove all doubt from the inkling that one is being thought of, vetted, conspired a Some-day soon, it only gets sooner. We will think w and kiss with our brains. For a moment the n augur was overtaken by the news that I was judged not to be a total doof. Ping! I followed back. I wondered which me he'd found out there, and what she might have to do with the one over here.

After wedging my salad's enormous clamshell container through the flap of a Carl's Jr. trash can, I flagged a cab at the nearest intersection, in front of one of the car dealerships clustered at the corners. We headed southwest to San Diego proper, bisecting the military twins of the old naval air station on the left and the operational marines base to the right. Much of *Top Gun* was shot in San Diego, then home to the elite naval program that inspired the film. Top Gun was moved to Nevada in 1996, though the navy's amphibious base remains on Coronado Island, off San Diego's downtown coast, where every few minutes a fighter jet eases down over the water like a tired woman into a tub.

There's a statistic, often quoted, that *Top Gun* boosted naval aviator enlistment by 500 percent. The Pentagon declined the studio's offer to add a recruiting video to the VHS release. Sounds kind of redundant, they said. They had cooperated extensively with the film's production, lending planes and airspace and expertise to inscribe the much-desired mark of the real, and everyone agreed it worked out pretty well.

Although the film is dedicated to him, the fate of stunt pilot Art Scholl is lesser known. He was sent up to shoot subjective, point-of-view stuff for a dogfight scene, extreme footage designed to show us how it feels to enter an inverted flat spin, what a death spiral looks like from the cockpit. The only theory to emerge about what happened next is that the cameras threw off the plane's balance, sending Scholl into a centrifugal dive. Scholl took pains, in his last transmission, to make a certain distinction. "I have a problem," he said. "I have a *real problem*." Neither the plane nor Scholl were recovered; both were last seen spiraling into the Pacific, just off the Carlsbad coast.

Over the following weeks and months I would elicit and re-elicit Carlsen's word to send on the scan results. He'd always say they were coming, and I'd always believe him. I needed an ending, something to make sense of it all, something revealed. How footage of my brain in action might accomplish that was unclear, but still I waited. What could it tell me that I didn't already know? What couldn't it? Surely there was something beyond the facts: that I left some garbage and part of my mind in San Diego, neither to be seen again. Anyway I waited. I watched more bad movies and wrote more exasperated reviews. Eventually Carlsen stopped replying to my e-mails, though our Twitter bond remained intact.

Nine months later it seems clear the images will not arrive. I suppose some part of me will continue waiting. Part of me knows it's coming. In what I've come to think of as the meantime, there is little to be done. For now the future is a foreign country, and I really feel okay about that.

Ways of Escape

Only one receives the prize
So run, that ye may obtain.
—Paul, 1 Corinthians 9:24

Two years in, slouched at the kitchen table with bloody feet and aching shoulders, I told my father that it sometimes felt like God was punishing me. There was a brief, exasperated pause before his reply: *For what?*

I didn't answer because I didn't know, except that it was obvious.

The basic problem was that I could not seem to stop running. Specific to the basic problem was the extreme seasonal battery involved in daily, outdoor, three-hour expeditions. The Ontario winters were thick with snow hazards and ablative winds; in the edible smog of summer I ended twenty-mile runs dizzy and crusted with salt; all-year-round, sudden, Sisyphean storms washed the buds from my ears and the shoes from my feet. For seven years I showed the elements the top of my skull, giving no ground. Some days, though, it's true that I was mortified by the January headwinds that seemed to pivot their direction with mine, or the stray plastic binding that caught my feet up and sent me flying, or the horizontal rain that pounded at peak force for two full hours, daring me to forfeit. It's true that at these moments I fancied myself God's lonely runner.

When I try to think what started me running, I remember first the urge to swallow time. There seemed to be, as I recall, too much of it in a given day. I first set out in the months before university, after returning from a stint out West distantly apprehensive about beginning my life and sluggish from a diet of beer and machine-vended meals. Historically I had considered running an aberrant form of activity. After a particularly gruesome wipeout during a fourth-grade cross-country practice, I thought it better suited to genetic freaks and the generally insensible. The truth is I tended to resent things I found difficult, and few things felt as unconscionably *hard* as long-distance running.

It started slowly. I'd canter around the block after my shift line-cooking at a downtown lunch counter. Just to see if I could. The thing to remember, perhaps, is that I was easy in the summer before I left for school. If most of what we experience as happiness amounts to invention, I can only explain the bliss of those months of flipping eggs for office drones, bird-dogging dudes, and careless nights with friends as some of my best work. After failing to prevent the dissolution of my first, I had built a second family—one that felt more controllable, or in any case the source of more consistent rewards. Part of the corrosive disappointment of the years that followed was discovering how fragile that feeling is—that each day I was exactly where and as I should be—and mistaking fragility for fraudulence. What I can say more certainly is that time was in its proper place and proportion, and this brought me immense comfort.

The other thing to know is that a creature of discipline lurks inside me, an inconstant companion who acts as often out of solidarity as self-interest, rarely missing the chance to seize full dominion of a fundamentally dreamy soul. Though I am not the creature, the creature, for better and worse, has been me. As a kid, cycling through the day's intake of knowledge and assessing my grasp of tomorrow's rigors was my idea of a soothing bedtime ritual. Intense determination wasn't stressful; exerting control over my abilities had an almost opiate satisfaction. Discipline made the world feel more constant and carved a spot for me in it.

I cleaved to the scholastic model of success until my heart went out of it—which is to say until high school, where I swapped out métiers to play one long game of social chess. It was a new system to master. Even in latency, discipline anchored me through some pretty sloppy years. At times I resented my own sense of self-preservation; it was obviously more romantic not to care, to let go of your life, cross that one bridge further, take that second hit, get that ridiculous tattoo, move to that subtropical country with that silly guy. The risks I took were all on my own terms, and after pushing those terms as far as they would go, I was left with the fact of a divided nature, one that sought both total freedom and a reliable rhythm to the days.

Until some more stable sense of self could be the source of that reliability, I looked to discipline. Unsure of what lay ahead, I imposed a small measure of order on the day. Running—a little more all the time—set down a preemptive cornerstone, something to build around. When school began,

I was out every morning, thirty or so minutes looping around Queen's Park in downtown Toronto.

A few classes into a film intro course, I knew I would double my major to pair cinema studies with the default choice of English. So little thought had gone into my accession to the University of Toronto—where my parents had met as students in the 1960s—that I was only vaguely aware of my guidance counselor's having placed me in the school's Catholic college, St. Michael's, and an all-girls dorm run by the Sisters of Loretto. That men were not allowed past the lobby was a complete surprise; by November my out-of-town boyfriend was out of the picture. In the mornings I ran; in the afternoons I watched scratched-up prints of *Citizen Kane*, *The 400 Blows*, and *8½*; at night I read Brontë, Fielding, and Plath; and on weekends I drove my mother's old '84 Celica down the 401, back to my father's house in London.

I had refused all of the school's orientation activities and never once—it became a point of pride—partook of the meal plan. Though my poor roommate pressed on, I went to terrific lengths to make sure no one got a piece of me. I maintained an attitude that was new to me then but proved tough to shake: that I was only passing through and needed to stay light on my feet. I wasn't interested in the university "experience" and resented the idea of social groups arranged by random administrative selection; I had spent years cultivating my clan and took new attempts at friendship as an affront to them. I developed a morbid sensitivity to fakery and enforced revelry, which felt like unfortunate timing even then. I wouldn't decorate my side of the room, which was bare except for a single, magazine-torn image of Kurt Cobain, his exquisite left hand poised over the strings of an acoustic guitar. As though in the grip of a nerd reawakening, I hit my Charlie Brown–sheeted bed early and had my papers triple-drafted and typed up weeks in advance. In short I was unbearable. Returning to the dorm on a midautumn Sunday evening, I found my entire wall artfully plastered with litter—ads, balloons, pinups, pie plates, the odd condom wrapper.

I have two strong memories of that fall. One is an unhurried walk to class on Halloween, the first in my life to pass without a plan for candy, costumes, or mischief. The evening had a mulch-scented coolness, and the campus, with its orange-tinted floodlights and Victoria-bred, limestone-bricked buildings, seemed to sigh in the peak of its campus-ness. As the moment rose into something more, I tried to calibrate the feeling—a combination of lush melancholy and pleasant but lonely purpose—as it rushed past. I'd hoped it meant I would be all right, though I felt foremost the certainty that there was no way to know.

Shortly after that night I attended my film class's evening screening of *Tokyo Story*, Yasujiro Ozu's 1953 Shinto disappointment piece. As those long, pellucid scenes of familial drift wore on, I felt myself lifting out of the room, passing through and then outside of time. I had never seen a film that felt so long ago and far away, yet so present; my response to its lunar rhythm was itself a revelation. As cinema reached its centenary, and one could watch midcentury masterworks with the awareness that not a single person involved in their making still walked the earth, its resurrections came into a new fullness. By the end I was so moved I found it hard to actually move. Cutting through Queen's Park in the darkness, I was overwhelmed by grief and the strange succor of its delivery, the promise of human precedence. I wept all the way, punctured in some hidden place by the feeling that I would not be all right. Not at all.

Whether time got away from me or caught up is hard to say; the shape of its shadow is the same. Returning home for the summer after my first year, both the city and I seemed much changed. My beloved friends had scattered, my parents were freshly divorced, and for weeks I looked for work without luck—all factors I am loath to cite as more than incidental to the ticking void that opened before me, and the haste with which I turned and hit the bricks.

I have felt extreme aversion, over the years, to figuring out what happened that summer. When asked how I came to spend my early and midtwenties running up to twenty miles a day (and does that convergence harbor meaning?), I realize that I'm still not sure. Certainly I've thought about it—what I have resisted is shaping a story, which, once set down, will become *the* story, when after all I am not certain there is one story, or one I am capable of telling, or one telling more truthful than any other. In trying to get at the *most* true version, all of the glaring facts of circumstance shrink behind the ropes, leaving the fixed limits of time—fight name: *Il Morte*—leaning coolly in one corner and the enigmatic, many-footed creature of discipline huffing and glowering in the other.

It's a word with as complicated a history as the most road-battered feet. Derived in English circa the thirteenth century as a term of penitential punishment, *discipline* comes from the Old French *descepline*, meaning variously physical punishment, teaching, suffering, and martyrdom. The Old French derivation's direct Latin root, *disciplina* (instruction given, teaching, learning, knowledge), is itself the heir of what we know more directly from the Bible as *discipulus*, or "disciple"—the object of instruction; pupil, student, follower—which is in turn derived from the compound *discipere*, meaning to analyze thoroughly, to grasp intellectually. Where things really go pear-shaped is the breakdown of *discipere* into *dis*, meaning "apart" and *capere*, "to take, to take hold of," also the root verb of *capable*. Logically the infinitive suggests the intellectual analogy of taking a thing apart, figuring it out; literally it conjoins possession and separation into a divine conundrum.

That dumb, seething summer there seemed a prohibitive number of hours ahead, and a baseline of dread that extended further still. In the mornings I set out as usual around eight thirty, just as the sun was settling its warmth into the sky, coming fully awake through the second mile. By the third, when I would normally turn for home, the day's blankness bloomed with invitation: with nowhere to be I might go anywhere—or anywhere my body would take me. The farther I ran, the greater the sense of progression I needed to earn the day, and the less of that day I had to spend at excruciating rest. If discipline appeared to be the last of my old friends that summer, I soon gained a new understanding of its many applications. Having relied on it as a kid to instill narrative consistency at life's sentence level—to maintain a sense of both myself and the world—I began to explore its limits as a means to both separateness and self-possession.

I wore a Walkman, always. Although my mind worried and argued and drifted as well, at cruising speed it turned primarily to the present, ecstatic moment, the collision of music and consciousness with motion. I've directed hundreds of videos on foot, reorchestrated thousands of movie scenes, blocked a million heart-stopping shots. If, early on, I played with the theme of punishment, say, in pushing through the last few miles, it was only in the sense that I occasionally imagined being chased by Tauntauns, or making an end run for first place while a row of dazed ex-boyfriends looked on. On well-defined terms I felt free to get lost within myself, territory that otherwise felt increasingly foreign and un-friendly. I even enjoyed getting lost in the streets, sometimes pitching myself deep into unknown trails and suburbs just so I could find my way out.

In this way I threaded through otherwise unpatterned hours, stitching their surface with a design that described time without being *of* it. The afternoons had no such scheme, so that the clock and I slipped, each day, into dull antagonism. When we talk about *killing* time, we refer to the banal death of disappearance; to kill time successfully is to have no mem-ory of its passing. I labored through the ear-ringing boredom of the siesta hours with tools that included the entire Jane Austen canon, the endless O. J. Simpson trial, the garage's gardening arsenal, and dozens upon dozens of hollowed-out eggs, which I decorated—bent over murderously tiny scis-sors, glue and glaze pots, and decaled origami paper—in the Japanese style. The evening's soreness, when it came in, felt like purpose, the next day's route like plot.

I had never spent so much time alone, at such a stretch. Initially, at least, the novelty of extreme solitude suited me. If nothing else it was the endgame of what appeared to be my goal: a life free from not just conformity but the whole concept of choice. What a drag, this having to *choose* and then forever do/love/be that chosen thing. What a fiasco. The thought of committing to any one of the selves racked up before me like labeled garment bags—aspirant, striver, student, daughter, desired thing, *woman*, wife, mother, Catholic, Canadian, girlfriend, *girl*, straight, white, mammal, material, extant—filled me with dismay, so that even my clear choices were executed as halfsies. With no clear way forward I invested heavily in a personal hedge fund, opting for solitude whenever grazed by expectation and drifting, for all my will and granitic intent on the road, into a greater passivity. That being a social refusenik was not my nature only enhanced the challenge and the bitter purity of its reward. I started turning down invitations and stopped taking calls out of spite for the silence surrounding them: if loneliness is life's abiding, unifying certainty, then make me an expert of loneliness; make me the loneliest person in the world.

From those first outings in May, my route doubled every couple of weeks, an exponential loop that eventually traced London's outer limits. Having never seen my city from its distant sidewalks and soft shoulders, I mapped it out to the corners with a prospector's constancy. By July's height I was out for three hours at a stretch, sometimes more. Out there too, life's options shrank to a vicious few: the experience of running through to the far side of pain was an ecstatically private triumph; fatigue, boredom, illness, compact-size blisters—I braked for nothing. Each day's effort fueled a self-drama of exertion, of consuming endless swaths of pavement, the hours dissolved through my skin and dried to a saline dust on its surface. Here were the raw expressions of discipline: blood and sweat, of me and yet outside me. I ran and I ran, taking godly comfort in the endurance shoring my bones and in knowing that no matter how far I went, I had the strength to carry myself home.

Though I began to bristle when pule-ish terms like *jog, jogging,* or *jogger* were applied to my travels, I refused to be wholly a *runner* as well. The notoriously scant basics of the sport eluded me; I ran as though a gunshot sent me flying out the front door each morning with whatever I had on my back. In the time it took to look into things like a proper sports bra, bulletproof sunscreen, balanced nutrition, and well-engineered footwear, permanent damage was done in the form of scarring, freckling, anemia, and a couple of extra bones.

It wasn't intentional in that it was not really conscious: even as metal fixtures rubbed wounds into my chest and back each day, it never fully occurred to me to address the matter. It never occurred to me that discipline could be a fickle companion, chimerical in form and purpose, loyal chiefly to its own insinuation. I thought I was writing a story of grit and perseverance, but for all of my exploring, my seeming kinetic engagement, rather than striking a balance with the world beyond my body and its powers, I had hit upon a way—even from moment to moment—to disappear.

In August I began to talk of feeling bad for my body, as though it were a neighbor who had just lost his job adjusting insurance. Fellow runners inquired of me in the presumed common language of distance and time—the metrics of control—frowning when I told them I didn't enter races and always ran alone; the lack of a finish line and the avoidance of crowds were kind of the point. I pitied them, I really did. *You don't run like I run,* I thought. *We're not the same.*

An extended-family member and frequenter of 10K charity runs became fixed on my refusal to bring a water bottle on my treks. I had to wonder that it wasn't perfectly obvious: I don't carry water, even for myself.

Late that summer I made my course selections for the coming year, organizing a schedule around the occupied zone that was now the morning hours. Because I was couch surfing, three to four days a week, off campus in my mother's midtown Toronto apartment, consolidating to limit commutes was priority number two. If a class met those conditions, I might consider enrolling.

Of greatest interest to me that year was a course on auteur theory—a study of four directors over two semesters: Howard Hawks, François Truffaut, Michelangelo Antonioni, and Martin Scorsese. Rumor had it that the professor hailed from New Jersey, had a terrifying background in semiotics, and was tougher than buffalo jerky. At the time cinema studies still suffered from its avian reputation, and every film professor I had—including this one—introduced the class with a bad Lee Ermey impression, urging those students who had signed on for a semester's nesting to watch their asses on the way out. I always thought a little less of them after that.

The auteurism class, held in the clammy auditorium at Innis College, the cinema studies department's home base, met twice a week—screening on Monday, lecture on Tuesday. During the break in the second week's talk, a boy seated behind me spied the *Sassy* sticker affixed to my binder's inside margin. The sticker referred to a progressive young women's magazine—often secretly read by intrepid young men—that had folded the previous year. It was my first subscription, and the mourning was heavy. Some part of the magazine's appeal, which I read throughout high school, was that no one else knew it existed.

"I like your *Sassy* logo," he said, leaning forward. His voice was vintage So-Cal skate park: reedy but amiable, super-enthused. "Were you a fan?" After my happily indefatigable former roommate, the tall, tea-green-eyed, endlessly solicitous senior attached to that voice became the second of the two people, total, that I came to know over four years of university.

The auteur theory is an ungainly animal, and our instructor took the ten-foot-pole approach, presenting the notion of the director as a film's sole author as ours to "unpack"—a term I hadn't heard before university and didn't hear again until I enrolled in graduate school. Part of the year's work was deciding whether to emigrate to the floating, pseudo-exceptionalist kingdom of auteurism or whittle the spears that would send it caroming like a flatulent French *ballon* back to earth. Somewhat at odds with this was our plotting of each of the four directors on a map that was never firmly pinned to the table; one corner was always peeling up. The famously pan-genre work of Howard Hawks put up a terrific fight: certain of his films would inevitably scramble the meticulously cracked codes of the others. The rule there seemed to be that when faced with, say, Joan Collins's canine performance as a Cypriot princess in Hawks's only historical epic, *Land of the Pharaohs*, one should avert one's eyes or formulate an exception that proved the rule. Auteurism's sketchy diagnostics put it always on the brink of submitting to the interpretive sooth-saying of ascribed intent. Because of this, its study served as a spot test for budding academics: either you took joy in the premise of unlimited speculation or it filled you with horror. If horror struck because yours was the obviously and only correct speculation, you became a critic.

Auteurism, unlike *Land of the Pharaohs*, is much easier to

grasp in context. A product of the French cohort of critics behind *Cahiers du Cinéma* in the 1950s, it reflected the move to raise cinema to the level of literature—painting, music, theater—as a storytelling art. Still a coltish medium, film's champions—several of whom, including Truffaut, Jacques Rivette, Jean-Luc Godard, Éric Rohmer, and Claude Chabrol went on to become directors themselves—were compelled to define it against the traditional artistic rubric of individualism.

Like the film professors who framed the mortal rigor of their coursework as half a notch below that of a winter term in the gulag, the study of film in its second fifty years was plagued by the perspirant whiff of overcompensation. To force all credit onto one artist and cohesion across a broad, inevitably business-inflected body of work is to escape the question of cinema's unique nature. All films, like all lives, are collaborative efforts with varying levels of leadership, vision, and exertions of style. No art is as lifelike, and as like life—never more so than in its surly coming of age, when fronting as a solo act seemed like the path to self-definition.

Heading into the auditorium the next Monday, I found Rafe, my *Sassy* co-fan, seated in my usual front-row spot, smiling. We were watching *Jules et Jim*, Truffaut's fiercely romantic World War I–era love triangle, and the experience of absorbing it in combination with the near-radiant designs of the body beside mine made a larger predicament plain: I had managed to trap myself between a girl's interest in the novelty of her own desirousness and the suspicion that there was something fundamentally embarrassing about being a young woman.

It came at you two ways, but primarily as a problem of archetype, of being perceived first and foremost as young and a woman. If an abundance of options is oppressive, feeling cornered by one in particular produces a slow-burning discomfiture. It was also the embarrassment of wanting to be more assured, more substantive, more whole, of moving to tap resources that simply weren't there. The limits were absolute and the expectations implied but definitive; you couldn't escape them because you couldn't escape the conditions of time.

Because they defied my usual tricks on that score, more and more I held myself apart from the unruly collaborations of the everyday world, where I was first and foremost a young woman. They presented as the enemy of discipline—my wife, as a family friend used to say of his, and former sweetheart. Rafe, his shy smile, and hopeful, high-beam gaze formed a kind of isosceles threat.

After the film ended, Jeanne Moreau having driven herself and her long-suffering lover off a bridge as her Austrian husband looked on, Rafe and I stepped through shallow ponds of lamplight on the way to the St. George subway, stunned and mostly silent. For us there was still revelation when unknown films from what felt like the distant past turned out not to be musty historical objects but vital in unimagined and frankly devastating ways. To analyze and perhaps admire was the hope; to be ravished on a coronary level was completely unexpected. We both knew the story, or versions of it, but Truffaut's telling put a fresh edge on the blade: it appeared the damage we could do to each other was incalculable when it wasn't total.

During the gap between my afternoon and evening classes I headed over to Yonge and Bloor, where a cluster of movie theaters offered refuge in the form of a single ticket spread two or three ways. The field of independent filmmaking had undergone heavy mulching in recent years, and 1995 was a season of high harvest. I've never been an omnivore at the cineplex—I don't have the nerves for horror or the chromosomes for science fiction—but even at that, there always seemed to be a respectable way to fill the afternoon. In high school, the lingering effects of a preteen fixation on River Phoenix had moved me to rent (abetted by my bemused father) and furtively watch what turned out to be my first art film, Gus Van Sant's *My Own Private Idaho*. (Unless you count *9½ Weeks*, a film my best friend and I spent entire evenings plotting to extract from the local Videoflicks with the aid of her mother's car phone and a pince-nez impression of an adult.) A few years later we were all in the theater for *Pulp Fiction*; dying of Kevin Costner fatigue, a generation of viewers was radicalized by ersatz sixties dancing and the déjà-vibe of surf guitar.

Devoted to Van Sant ever since *Idaho*, his *To Die For*, David Fincher's *Se7en*, and Bryan Singer's *Usual Suspects* required watching that fall. I reported for action most days, preferring, as with running, to fly solo. The previous winter I had made my first sortie to the box office on my own, determined to see Richard Linklater's *Before Sunrise* on the big screen. The girls at the dorm would have laughed if they'd known: movies were supposed to be social, like every other part of life. I used to think so too.

As a wee parochial tot, a lonesome fascination gripped me whenever the older women who crashed our school masses sat among us in the pews. In grade four I joined the funeral choir—an elite, macabre little group, we were excused from class to sing mourning hymns at parish funerals—and was piqued to find that the women audited those services too. One in particular stood out. She wore a dove-gray trench coat through every season, had an impeccable, mesmerizingly passé pageboy bob, and made what I thought to be the flamboyant and—given her age and proclivity for skirts—potentially disastrous gesture of dropping to her knees before the monsignor whenever she took Communion. Even more boggling than the question of who went to mass when they didn't have to: Who went alone?

The year I spent in the funeral choir was also the one dedicated, in our school, to the sacrament of penance. We learned about what it meant to sin—which, as it turned out, was what it meant to be alive—and spent most of the preparatory classes memorizing the preamble and combing God's forgiveness policy for loopholes. When it came time to log our first confessions, we coated up, formed a solemn double line, and marched the couple hundred feet across the schoolyard to the church. As we filed into the back rows, close to the confession booths, I saw the hunched form of the gray lady up front, kneeling alone at the end of the second pew. *Jesus Mulvaney*, I thought. *How bad can one person be?* Aware of sinning right there under the twelfth station of the cross, I returned to the litany I had been rehearsing, which had mainly to do with my brother and my bottomless loathing for him.

Of all the sacraments in my repertoire, penance is second only to Communion in conceptual flair. I had known few performative terrors like that of stepping into a darkened closet to speak through a perforated screen to the invisible man installed next door. Even so, in its total the act was a whopping letdown. The first time out, we virgins felt a little scandalized that our notes compared so blandly. With a few more monthly purges under our elastic rainbow belts, it became clear that no matter what was confessed—from foul brotherly thoughts to lunch-box theft—the penance amounted to a handful of the prayers we said every day anyway. Though the intrigue of praying alone lingered on—for fourth graders the idea of gaining a sacred privacy was key to the sacrament's allure—we had expected something, somehow, *more*. And if the gray lady in the second pew wasn't saying the world's longest penance, what in Krishna's name was she doing there?

Our local Catholic school board's motto—"The spirit is alive"—invokes the one thing a religious education cannot instill in a child. The rituals, culture, and doctrine of faith combine in a child's experience to form a burden—if she is pious, as I was, a glorious burden. What it is not is a quest—which is to say a choice—though we might strive to make it so. That part tends to come of its own necessity, and is attended by the hunger—if not the dogmatic zeal—of the convert.

While preparing for my First Communion at age seven, I became a student of the suffering of Jesus on the cross. Along with the rest of the day's assignments, at night I went over the story in my head, transfixed by its barbarism and especially stuck on quantifying the pain of such a death, making it comprehensible. I vowed to work, over time, to claim that suffering, beginning with the self-administering of a long, ruthless pinch under the covers each night—my idea of the hurt of a single thorn. I continued for some time, in this private, piecemeal fashion, to offer myself as His disciple, to trade His suffering for mine. Eventually, maybe half a crown in, the pinching stopped—without a clear equivalent for crucifixion, it just seemed like bad math—though two years later

I recalled it proudly as a better run at penance than rifling through a few rosary beads.

One fourth-grade night, after being tucked in by my father and told to say my prayers, I called out mildly as he left the room, "But why?" The reaction was instant: "Don't you ask me that," he hissed, wheeling around at the door. "You just *do it*." I was startled, angry maybe, but not scared. What scared me were the Sundays when we returned to our pew after Communion, and I watched my dad praying with his head in his hands, not moving his lips or anything.

I abandoned confession after elementary school, when it was no longer mandatory. Though my guilt about that had largely abated by the time I entered university, even as I eluded Loretto's nuns and other sisterly comforts, I found myself visited by the memory of the gray lady, ever kneeling. Along with her hypnotic coif and majestic genuflections, I recalled the confidence of her belonging in that church and the calm of her attention—the outward aspect, perhaps, of what Kierkegaard called "passionate inwardness," a faith that was no burden but a choice that marked "the highest point of individual freedom." I was acing philosophy, to the incredulity of my TA, who capped a private interrogation about my inaugural paper with a feeble pass, ending my short career in the field.

And then, on a February evening a few months later, a disciple lacking a deity sat alone in her church for the first time, watching the ripe faces of Ethan Hawke and Julie Delpy tender their youthful promises, waiting to disappear long enough that she might be filled by something holy.

Having acquired the idea that this new, Radiohead-loving, hothouse breed of boys were as apt to expire as laugh if a girl worked a little blue, I began telling Rafe the most vulgar jokes I could think of on our postclass walks, watching for signs of wilt.

As romantic disincentives go, the one about the Newfie, the dildo salesman, and the mistaken thermos seemed like a solid choice. But Rafe was grinning by the door the next week, just the same. He later told me that after we parted on those days, he would add some new embellishment to a deeply architected fantasy of my life. He had me heading straight to my boyfriend's place—my virile, varsity boyfriend, who lived among the bohemian swells in Toronto's deciduous Annex neighborhood—where we snickered over my poor, smitten classmate as I heated up Bagel Bites in the kitchen of his exquisitely distressed Victorian town house. He could see us watching television, washing dishes, heading out to the bar—laughing all the way. It seemed incredible to me that anyone could even gin up such a scenario; it seemed evidence of how completely we can be deceived, if we are willing.

After our final class we faced each other in the same spot on the same corner and exchanged vows to see *Flirting with Disaster*. Rafe asked for my address and said he'd write; if all went as planned, he would wind up in London for teachers college. We wished each other luck on our final papers and turned to our respective directions for the last time.

I had written about *Mean Streets*, *unpacking* Scorsese's use of point of view with a terminally psychoanalytic reading of the film and its lead character, Charlie, played by Harvey Keitel in his satyr youth. Reading it today, I'm struck by the baldness of my feints: finding conflicted-Catholic Charlie's idea of penance to be "wishy-washy," I taunt him for being "cowardly" and "weak" on every other page, accuse him of "continually feeding his reality through a movie projector in an attempt to stave off his problems," and cite Charlie's belief that "nothing is private" as an excuse for using the world and the people in it as vessels for the spiritual crisis he's too chickenshit to face on his own.

The previous semester I had turned in a similarly aggressive paper, titled "Comedy of Errors or Tragic Surrender? The Dichotomy of the Hawksian Couple in *Bringing Up Baby* and *Monkey Business*." Still feeling around inside the liberties of auteur theory, I felt no compunction about challenging the likes of Stanley Cavell and his *Pursuits of Happiness*, a book that examined the "comedy of remarriage" and the cinematic construction of a curiously autonomous "new woman" via several classic Hollywood films, including *Baby*. Cavell, whose background ran to philosophy and classical studies, applies a Shakespearean trope—that of young lovers retreating into the wild, then returning, clarified, to regenerate society—to several of the films, with varying success. The romance between starchy scientist David (Cary Grant) and brazen, regressive Susan (Katharine Hepburn) in *Bringing Up Baby* fits both more obviously and less strictly into the mold.

Cavell admits as much, but I saw something much darker in the couple's final, dangling embrace. In the Hawks universe, I thought, love could result in a fate worse than death: *having no fun.* "Love exacts one's security and individuality" was my take on the ending, "no comfort is taken in it." In the youth-serum caper *Monkey Business*, Cary Grant and Ginger Rogers play a married couple so comfortable they're comatose. Romance—the "adult affliction"—ultimately ruins fun, unless it's child's play, in which case one can't call it romance at all, can one? I wrapped up by invoking a different Shakespearean cycle, where every comedy is sown with the elements of the tragedy that will succeed it. "Hawks is deftly, if a little sadly, aware" went the last line, "that once one has come full circle, there is nowhere to go but around again."

This is all to say that I peaked early in my academic career. I remember feeling proud of the first essay but a little purged by the second, as though I'd pushed my interpretative flexor farther back than it was willing to go, and I'd never walk quite the same way again. I was back to grades I hadn't seen since the penance years—school had resurged as a life-structuring force—and though I left Authorship in Cinema 224Y a practicing agnostic, in arguing Hawks's sly antiromanticism I had struck upon something I actually believed. The nebulousness of the auteur theory had cleared a space for a form of passionate inwardness, where the willing might commit themselves to a leap of faith. Yet the result of that kind of commitment is so personal it's almost painful to see, more so when private belief is reified on academic terms. It felt crafty at best and dead dishonest at worst: Can a faith and its Church be separated? Didn't I just do this?

My father, an English professor, had been recruited into his school's makeshift film department that year. Our reading lists were compared for degrees of difficulty, and raids of his essay piles yielded a depressing sense of the mean. Cinema studies was desperate for scholars, he often hinted, and would be only more so in a decade, when his cohort retired. The professor's life is a good one, he'd say, coming as close as he ever would to persuading me to do anything.

And I'd think: *Run.*

The road was home that summer. Something had to be. The in-betweenness of student living—generally little more than a sleeping arrangement—and the displacement of childhood bedrooms had sent the concept of home into its scheduled state of flux. Not expecting to have a job helped offset the heartache of not finding one: more time for the pavement. Every morning I ran by my old school and the adjacent church, cutting into the local park across the street and passing the deer and goats pacing their petting-zoo enclosures. A single, rogue peacock ever stalked the grounds, scaring children and uninitiated runners with his appalling, woman-in-peril call. In Springbank Park I'd find the Thames and its slacker patrols of Canada geese, following it downtown through to the north end, past the university. From there I turned east or west, depending on my mood, and took the big roads back.

My toenails were blackening and falling off as quickly as they grew in, and my period had stopped completely. As a way of escape, distance running is the sensory negative of sexual oblivion, the cosmic hiccup of swallowing and being swallowed at once. Ruled by a kind of bodily intuition, runners develop an animal awareness of their surroundings, twice a second deciding where the foot falls, trusting churning legs over uneven terrain, gauging the relative traction of four hundred kinds of ice, predicting the paths of three dozen moving bodies, sensing whether the inevitable car sneaking up behind will yield or try to force itself past at the moment of convergence. Only when I lost track of the passing minutes would time show itself every moment. On returning home I would stand in the kitchen where I used to bang pots on the floor, sweating and staring at the clock in disbelief.

The city was an open question I attempted to answer each day. Looking back, looking from above, all that running appears as a radically, almost pathetically physical solution to a metaphysical problem of homesickness, a search for the portal or spatial alignment that would release me back into the world, even as I pounded into my bones the idea that to get anywhere a person had to be alone.

At the time it felt more like obeying a survival instinct, that what kept me running was the future's scorch at my heels, the threat of engulfment from all sides. The present, with its finger puzzle of feminine identity, was only more untenable. Better to be nobody, maybe, just a streak on the road. Better to hide than to show the world your halfness.

In the safety of that suspension I could wait things out as a pure observer. Not that there was so much to take in, on the surface, anyway. My news of any given day shrank to civic esoterica: a roving micro-reporter on the morbid tip, I collected accidents, roadkill sightings, insect conflagrations, and sad tableaux, like that of a smattering of cars parked outside the liquor store at eight forty-five in the morning, their drivers counting down to the day's re-up. I'd devote weeks to exploring newly discovered cemeteries, collecting archaic or punny names, felicities of phrasing, a particularly staggered stone angel.

The sound track to this ecumenical smallness had a new supplier: a few weeks after our goodbye in Toronto, the first letter from Rafe arrived, and soon after that a cassette tape. Other than the polar force of his interest and a few fragments from our walks, my impression of Rafe from the previous year was smudgy: I had grown unused to regarding things—that is to say humans—in situations where they might regard me back. I tended to be surprised when people noticed or spoke to me—even a little disappointed—and narrowed focus until the moment passed. But letters, those folded emissaries of personality, could be pored over outside such pressures. They could be created, in other words, and create their readerly ideal. The tapes, with handcrafted covers and calligraphed track lists, were a blend of Wilco, Weezer, and Pavement, obscure neo-punk like the Queers, the Donnas, and the Muffs mixed in with their antecessors. Stuck between CDs and preteen tapes, I had been surviving on a diet of the Police and old Tom Petty from my brother's abandoned cassette collection; anything outside of nasal, blond eighties rock was a gift.

Rafe, who displayed a seismographic exuberance on the page, was still doing all the things I used to do: going to shows, goofing off with friends, pining after the unavailable. We felt far apart indeed, and so I did what any girl would to bridge the gap: I wrote to him. I answered every letter and eventually made tapes of my own, and in this way we passed the months, ferrying various selves back and forth, submitting ideals for approval and carrying home the blueprint for what the other preferred us to be. Which is to say we amused each other, greatly, and grew attached to our amusement. Over the following four years of correspondence I became the more attached by far, an attachment that manifested in the physical world, naturally, as near-total evasion.

At some point in my third year of university I sent my first e-mail—in reply to my first receipt of an e-mail, from Rafe.

The keystroke-by-keystroke creation of an entire medium suited those just then pioneering their voices very well in that it concentrated mutual, epistolary invention into a full-blown phenomenon. Much advertised for its connective properties, e-mail was a godsend to a budding isolationist because it created the illusion of remaining in touch.

By then Rafe and I were also sessioning into the night on the telephone. We talked about old movies, new bands, our eccentric, ordinary families, and, after a late-summer confession about the extent of my habit, the status of my feet. A sometime runner himself, instead of raising an eyebrow over my running the better part of a marathon every day, Rafe extolled my discipline. I had given myself away, he said, by showing up to class one day in a pair of Sauconys—the sneaker of the serious. In fact I only wore Nike, and never to school. Even at the time, I noted the greater misapprehension—coming from the most curious, observant person I'd ever met—with a mixture of relief and disappointment. Another second hand was added to the master clock: How long before he finds me out, and this whole thing implodes?

So much of falling in love is a biographical project; we turn our stories over and hope for the best. Should you inspire the full-dress treatment, you will find yourself loved but also much altered. Rafe could have sent Boswell to his cups: if I let slip some uncomfortable family angst, he would clamor for more; if I mentioned the constant and repulsive shedding of my toenails, he'd leave a packet of customized press-ons at my doorstep; if I acted like a jackass he—and this really beat all—was quick to forgive. Especially if you haven't yet pieced together a workable self, to find yourself fully formed in someone else's imagination is irresistible the way Kryptonite is irresistible. When inhabiting her felt like cheating, I'd try to undermine this other me, but nothing—no weirdness, no open disabuse, not all the tasteless dildo jokes in the world—seemed to shake her hold. I'd never seen anything like it and worried, in lieu of precedent, that this kind of fascination amounted to a form of idolatry, or at least a profound self-distraction. It took years for the shadow my interlocutor was dodging—the sometime girlfriend he rarely mentioned, and then as a casual acquaintance—to emerge, and in the early months it hardly seemed to matter: we were pen pals, mostly; phone buddies, at best; e-mail—what? What even was e-mail?

Rafe was a kind of savant of the form; no one had told him it was too cold and impersonal for tone and feeling. His dispatches brimmed over with his personality, his wit and humor, his maximal syntax. Where I plodded along worried about spelling and spacing, seeking a reflection of the familiar, e-mail was just another way in which everything Rafe touched became a natural extension of him. I'm not sure I ever learned more from another writer. For him our daily correspondence comprised the vivid description of a life in progress, where I was trying to write myself into the world.

Both of Rafe's parents were high school teachers. This was his plan as well, and no postgraduate detours kept him from it. He headed straight into teachers college—in London, as expected, where I stood him up one evening that fall out of pure, nervous stupidity and he temporarily lost my number—and then to a placement in a Toronto high school. Among many other traits, I envied his certainty, the easiness he exuded toward all things except, increasingly, me. The relationship we had built from longing and fiber-optic lines was bulging in unsightly places. I pretended not to notice. Wasn't this the fun part, anyway? Wouldn't the dreary confines of adult romance put an end to playing around in our pretend world? Did we learn nothing from Master Hawks? Although constant, enigmatic communication suited the wearier half of us just fine, for Rafe the question of our future evolved into the crisis of discipline already familiar to me: Can a pursuit have meaning if it extends beyond choice? Is it devotion or just masochism to go on uncertainly?

I took a full-time job at a public-broadcasting network two months before graduation, vowing to maintain the running, to just peel back the days at the top and keep going. I began waking up before five, exploring the local parks, cemeteries, and reservoirs in the dark. To miss a day was to admit weakness, a system failure with ominously undefined ends. The appearance of supreme self-control belied the fact that I no longer had much say in the matter of what made me good or bad; there was only running or not running. As much joy as I still took in those long, lapidary, arch-ruining runs, my reliance on them was unsustainable: in fact I had lost control of my life, and I'd done it my way. The world was revealing a complexity that would not be mastered by discipline alone, and the thought of having to battle my way back into it every single morning of my life basically made me want to die.

The previous winter I had published my first piece of writing, nine hundred words on my relationship with running. I had thought it was about toughness and solitude; the editor titled it "An Addict Confesses."

If you were searching for clues about how to tell a story in 1998, that noun/verb axis was the first and biggest to be found.

The way to tell a story was to reveal the weird or painful thing that made you special. Your liberation would liberate the reader, and together you could bask in a kind of empathic synergy. Confession was a narrative form whose only sin was holding any part of yourself back; it developed its own house style and sense of what it meant to be good (relatable), to be moving (vulnerable), to tell the truth (to tell all). But like penance, with its standard opening—*Bless me, Father, for I have sinned*—and carefully whittled laundry lists, all such confessions are calculated, perhaps most when they hope to erase the signs of calculation. I felt uneasy about the publication of the essay, whose contents surprised Rafe; it was so unlike the girl who confided little and admitted nothing. But I had wanted to tell a story, and that seemed to be the only one I had. If I hadn't quite admitted to myself that I was making a confession, in addition to danger and distaste the whole thing had something satisfyingly punitive to it. Something familiar. I liked it and I didn't like it.

The part I didn't like was how permeable the formula seemed to be. I adored *The Crack-Up*, *Drinking: A Love Story*, and anything Mary Karr had so much as cursed at, but more often you got raw self-exposure, conformed to a predetermined idea of what will inspire—or worse, trigger—the coveted empathetic response. All the better if the author is mixed up in the difficulty and discomfort of being a girl. Disconcerted by my own predictability, I retreated to my notebook and the fledgling art of e-mail, where I set the limits and decided how I might work within them.

Along with discomfort, that headline delivered an etymological redundancy: *addiction*, drawn back to its Latin root, *addicere*, suggests a form confession: *ad*, "to," and *dicere*, "say, declare." In its earliest, compound form, the declarative sense of the verb had weaselly connotations, meaning, variously, "to sacrifice, to sell out, to betray," but also "to devote, consecrate; to adjudge, allot; to deliver, award; to yield, give assent; to make over, sell." Our modern refurbishing of the word—begun in the early twentieth century, when the seemingly helpless state of opium and morphine stoners begged description—has given it a more passive meaning and therefore an ever-widening application. Addictions are still statements, of a sort—clinically they are often cited as symptoms of some larger issue—and in that sense generally involve a substance. But in becoming medical and then submitting to vernacular indignities, the concept of addiction has turned inward, and in that corollary realm its original meanings are more or less intact. Rather than engaging, betraying, devoting, awarding, assenting, or adjudging in relation to the world, we become the world—its innocent and all-knowing, the pure and the deceitful—and make those same statements unto ourselves.

I felt myself falling behind that spring, as though a train were leaving the station and a whole season was passed trying to run it down. I graduated on a bright, cool June afternoon, with a decent job and a boss promising to make me the youngest producer in the building. Rafe had made a confession of his own, bringing our meticulously unspoken feelings into the open for discussion, for decision. Soon after that we met: a drink, a show, a long talk in a cemetery. A blissful night. The next week I started up a fling with an intern who spoke only spotty English, then another colleague after that. Rafe was full of living plans and promises: he would tie my laces before dawn each morning and send me out the door in the stipulated pre-run silence; he had our children named and a dog picked out. I had no fantasies about our life together because beyond a nebulous dream involving New York, I couldn't imagine my own future at all. Unable to commit but unwilling to let him go, I made it my essential purpose to catch up. And learned, over the next two years and best as I ever have, what it is to fail.

In his 1965 novel *Stoner*, which details the life of an unexceptional Midwestern English professor with the close emotional scrutiny and epic compassion of the Victorian masters, author John Williams describes a distance no amount of miles can cover. In his extreme youth, Williams writes, William Stoner "thought of love as an absolute state of being to which, if one were lucky, one might find access." On reaching maturity he decided that in fact love was "the heaven of a false religion, toward which one ought to gaze with an amused disbelief, a gently familiar contempt, and an embarrassed nostalgia." Then, in middle age, "he began to know that it was neither a state of grace nor an illusion; he saw it as a human act of becoming, a condition that was invented and modified moment by moment and day by day, by the will and the intelligence and the heart."

I felt positively wizened at twenty-three and affected a tragic knowledge about Rafe's attachment to me, the irony of that knowledge being that his feelings amounted to a terminal infatuation, perhaps even a drive toward my deficiencies, while mine had the fixings for a whole enchilada, if only I could get my human act together and become it. I couldn't say what was more frightening: his love for me, which threatened total, heat-seeking consumption, or my love for him, which was wild and untrained and a danger to itself. Competing with an idealized entity based on you is a dilemma with two potential outcomes, neither of which I was prepared to face. Beating an untenably romantic nature out of yourself by force of will is a job with no real dividends, being a highly, untenably romantic thing to do. Keeping both predicaments in their balance until I could resolve them seemed the only option, but it required time. Of all my failures to offset the mortification of wanting, expecting, or caring too much, the most humiliating was having no real answer for the love of a good man. It humbled me.

I made a scrupulous accident of my entry into the working world, having accepted a job because it seemed the sensible thing to do. The network was in the midst of a push toward all things *interactive*, *online*, and *virtual*, and we impressed ourselves with big ideas that fizzled in execution or launched to an indifferent public. The bursting of the dot-com bubble coincided with a wave of layoffs that swept twenty-five-year veterans out to sea along with most of my colleagues, every day a new one gone. I jumped departments and stopped thinking in terms of job security.

Slowly, ever so, I weaned myself down to two hours of running a day. By the summer of 1999 it was ninety minutes on workdays, as long as I wished on the weekend. I even took days off now and then. My first real injury, a groin pull, forced a two-week hiatus, longer than I had been off my feet in years. And, lo, the world did not end. I just walked it with a slight hitch.

I moved into my own apartment. I made my first trip

overseas, alone, taking a call from Rafe moments before I was to leave for the airport. As we spoke, I watched a sketch he had given me that I had framed and hung on the wall, a simple line drawing of a boy stretched out supine, his head in the lap of a hollow-eyed girl. The boy's eyes are closed as she sews his sweet, untroubled smile shut.

We had been having a dreary old time, him protesting my well-maintained distance, me pleading for more of his patience. Rafe said I was selfish—that I had a responsibility to give more of myself. I said exchanging accusations of selfishness is a sucker's game. Though the eleventh-hour call—a multitiered goodbye—was awful, our most painful conversation, perhaps the most painful of my life, had already taken place. Again Rafe had pressed for an explanation of what it was I thought I was looking for, how I could justify what I was putting us through. The anguish in his voice was crushing, and I was startled to hear it refracted in mine. "I want to be *good*," I had blurted. "I want to be *better than I am*."

After a long, silent summer we tried again. At last and all of a sudden, it was the end of the century, and the world was counting down to Y2K. Media memos about a global infrastructure seizure befogged the air. Digital chaos threatened the perfect blight to an age of tech worship: sending us back in time. Ironically and otherwise, we began to prepare for the "apocalypse," buying canned goods and water in bulk, daydreaming of barricaded homesteads run on personal generators.

Rafe and I spent more time together, not all of it tortured. More often we e-mailed and traded other loaded placeholders. Poems, mostly. Rafe was a "Fern Hill" kind of fellow, where I was deep into Donne. Over Thanksgiving, he snuck into London and hid a note in the phone booth outside the local Chinese dive where I had stretched cups of leafy tea across many teenaged afternoons. He had written a passage from my favorite holy sonnet ("Batter my heart, three person'd God . . .") and another from "The Apparition":

> *When by thy scorn, O murd'ress, I am dead,*
> *And that thou think'st thee free*
> *From all solicitation from me,*
> *Then shall my ghost come to thy bed,*
> *And thee, feign'd vestal, in worse arms shall see*

I ran all the way there, on telephoned instruction. Then limped the folded slip of paper home like I was pulling a plow.

By early December we were both reading *The End of the Affair*, in preparation for the release of the film. Time was within earshot now—ever-present, undead, telltale earshot. Little, glowing, red, insect-limbed numbers are fine and functional keepers, but that mother's just a vague idea until you hear it coming. I don't remember much about that night—having just discovered my favorite book, the movie was a minor, almost inevitable disappointment—and less about the weeks that followed. I only know I never saw Rafe again, though his ghost arrived as promised, and without much delay.

The next thing that comes to mind with any clarity is New Year's Eve, which I spent alone, back at the movies. *Magnolia* and *Girl, Interrupted*, a double-bill bummer royale. I remember too that I made my way home in a light-smeared daze, in time for the turning of the clock. I turned off my television as the minutes drained down to the hour, but the walls kept dancing: great blooms of colored fire overtook each other, painting the sky with bravas beyond my balcony. And for the first time in a decade I knelt down at the side of my bed, closed my hands against my forehead, and began to pray.

In his "Reflections on Gandhi," George Orwell wrote, "The essence of being human is that one does not seek perfection, that one *is* sometimes willing to commit sins for the sake of loyalty, that one does not push asceticism to the point where it makes friendly intercourse impossible, and that one is prepared in the end to be defeated and broken up by life, which is the inevitable price of fastening one's love upon other human individuals."

At the time of writing, Gandhi was a year gone and already discussed in terms of sainthood. Orwell didn't believe Gandhi was a saint because he didn't fathom saints, or seekers of goodness for whom "there must be no close friendships and no exclusive loves whatever." He saw in them a degree of nonattachment that "makes sense only on the assumption that God exists and the world is an illusion to be escaped from." As far gone as Gandhi's means may seem to most of us, his end is more commonly and perhaps more successfully sought in the age of secular connectivity than it has ever been.

Orwell's argument is *Stoner*'s argument: a case for the world of human action over spiritual absolutes or killjoy cries of illusion. A case, after all, for love, though it is well applied to the concept of solitude: in extremity, aloneness is not grace but isolation, acknowledged by those who know about such things as the most inhuman form of punishment.

I still run. I ran this morning. I run like the average person does—if anything, the average has surpassed me, the habit has grown so commonplace—and am still and often questioned about the integral details. Though I no longer lament those old, heroic numbers, I don't much care to talk about it, or compare, or compete. It still feels sacred. I don't care to discuss it too because so often such interviews end strangely, with a wistful benediction: "You're so *good*," they say. *"You're so good."*

I still see movies too, often alone and, oddly, for pay. If anything, those early feelings of blissful concord formed a standard as well as a sensibility. I wouldn't take those sprawling afternoons back: a sort of escape from escape and discipline free of discipline, they were the only thing connecting me to the world and its less arduous pleasures. It is perhaps of interest to note that what I don't do is e-mail. Not in the same, boundless way, anyway, or with the same appetite for invention.

But I'm no saint, hell. A few years ago I ran almost straight through a case of pneumonia, making myself approximately 12.5 times sicker than I might have been. I still prefer to watch some of my favorite movies alone, greedily, piously. And were you to send me a charming e-mail tonight, I would confront and perhaps succumb to the impulse to engage you on over-hopeful terms, generating a new distraction with only the rarest odds of proving more than that.

What I can say is that, having known isolation in all its trickster forms, I see it where and for what it is. I see that we are all running now. And I'll see you out there.

Acknowledgments

Many and prostrate thanks to Sean McDonald and Emily Bell for giving me this opportunity and helping me see it through, and to everyone at FSG for their attention and care. Thanks also to Melissa Flashman for her invaluable support.

Stephen Elliott, Evan Hughes and Adelle Waldman, Meline Toumani, Carlin Flora and Giovanni Escalera, Gary Sernovitz, John MacFarlane, Pamela Kerpius, Kristin McGonigle, David Haglund and Maissa Boulos, Jeremy Keehn, Sarah Fan, Megan Hustad, Erin Craig, Kara Kaczmarek, Elise Tremblay, Pasha Malla, Dimme van der Hout, Jeremy Rodgers, Meredith Martin, Greg Marshall, Trevor Ross, Helen Coltrinari, and Ted Brunt are treasured and endlessly supportive friends.

Thank you to the exceptional editors I have been lucky to work (and occasionally play) with these last few years, especially Stu VanAirsdale, Stephanie Zacharek, Allison Benedikt, Elizabeth Ellen and Aaron Burch, Eli Horowitz, Lorne Manly, Ted Genoways, and Miriam Markowitz. A special thank-you to Gary Greenberg for his generously given time and advice.

I am indebted, with fond gratitude, to many of my teachers and professors, notably Charlie Keil, Bart Testa, Cameron Tolton, Jim Hoberman, and the late Pat Proulx.

Here I can only offer sincere but insufficient thanks to my family—to John Orange and Jackie Orange especially, and to Frank Clayton, Dana Orange and Matthew Tierney, Jeannette McGlone, and the late Rita Boyle.

If you are in my life you are in this book; the inverse also seems true. So thank you finally, and hello, to those readers I hardly knew.